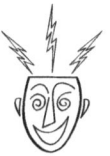

COMICS CREATOR PREP

*A Comics Course for
Writers and Artists*

LEE NORDLING

ABOUT COMICS

CAMARILLO, CALIFORNIA • 2016

AN ABOUT COMICS BOOK
This is an original publication of About Comics.

COMICS CREATOR PREP. Copyright © 2016 by Lee Nordling.

Cover and interior designed by Lee Nordling and The Pack LLC.

Published June, 2016 by About Comics.

Library of Congress Catalogining-in-Publication Data

Nordling, Lee.
Comics Creator Prep: A Comics Course for Writers and Artists
p.   cm.
ISBN 978-1936404-58-2
1. Comics 2. Graphic novels. 3. Writing. 4. Vocational Guidance. 5. Hollywood.

Print-On-Demand and electronic versions published by About Comics.

File date: June 25, 2016

Contents

Part 2: Working With Others

FOREWORD

PREPPING
BY MARV WOLFMAN

A long time ago, in a galaxy far, far away, if you were a comic book fan with aspirations to become a comic book professional, you were pretty much out of luck. "Go home," they'd tell you. "We're not looking for new talent."

You see, the guys who founded the field back in the 1930s, were still toiling away through the 1950s and most of the 1960s, writing and drawing the comics that we, the Baby Boomers, were scooping up by the ton.

But these creators were the men (and maybe one or two women, max) who, if they were writers, actually intended to be novelists, or if they were artists, craved to become newspaper cartoonists.

Back then almost nobody wanted to work in comic books, which was considered by everyone to be a step down.

From everything.

After all, comic books didn't really exist before the 30s, so nobody grew up as a fan of that business, desperate to break in because they absolutely loved the medium. The writers and artists of the 30s grew up with books and comic strips. It should be no surprise that those were the fields they wanted to be in.

But then, in 1938, Superman leaped into the pages of *Action Comics*; the comic book business exploded. And, lets face it, that was where the work was. In a world slowly crawling its way out from the Great Depression, work was work. Writing comics was still writing, and drawing comics was still drawing. The first generation of comic book professionals would go on to create the business as they did it, and then, when they were good enough, they fully intended to move up and out.

But most of the people stayed in the field and grew with it. And along the way they created all the rules of comic book writing and art. They learned what worked and what didn't. They learned how to tell stories and they learned what to avoid because doing X or Y or Z simply didn't work in the deceptively confined space of 6-10 panels per page.

By the 1950s, when the Baby Boomers started to read comics, the original writers and artists were creating the very stuff that dreams were made of. At least for us. Their books fired up our imaginations. Their stories and art inspired us. The creators may not have originally intended to remain in the comic book field, but we, the readers, loved what they did and because of them fell in love with the medium of comics. We embraced their stories of spandex-clad heroes and heroines as well as their tales of talking mice and ducks and ghosts, both funny and scary.

The early comics were extremely crude. The art was loose and the stories often made no sense. But that didn't matter to the barely-out-of-childhood readers; they were witnessing the birth of something that simply hadn't existed before and they were thrilled by it all.

Working full time and being guided by editors who knew what they were doing, the Comics' Founding Fathers began to learn their craft. Their art got stronger. Their storytelling became sharper. They learned what to do and more importantly what not to do.

So, a decade or so later, by the time we Boomers started reading their comics the original guys had become masters of their craft, as good as the book writers and comic strip artists they originally aspired to become.

They had invented a form, they were at the top of their game, and we readers loved it all.

But by the late 1960s, many of the creators, reaching their sixties or older, started to retire. Also, their stories had become repetitious and the Baby Boomers, who were now watching TV as well, grew tired of the same o', same o'. We were getting older and though we still loved comics, the kinds of stories that appealed to us when were eight years old no longer appealed to the teenagers we had become.

Sales dwindled, companies collapsed and many of the original creators were leaving the field or being forced out. Suddenly, an industry that almost never needed to search for new talent now discovered they had to.

Fortunately, the new kids, who grew up loving comics, who went to the early comic book conventions and saw that their precious four-color magazines were actually produced by real human beings, now wanted into the industry. But the problem was they couldn't be only as good as the original guys were when they started. They had to be at least as good or better as the Founders had become. Without the decade or longer learning experience. They had to instantly be able to appeal to those who had been reading comics for years and were demanding a lot more than they were getting.

They had to have their act together right out of the gate.

And very, very few of us were that good that fast.

Fortunately there was a little bit of overlap as the originals retired and the newbies clawled their way in. So, if you were lucky enough to allowed to submit material to an editor you might have met at a convention, and were able to convince them you were the guy they needed, you found yourself starting small. Real small. Writing or drawing one or two page filler stories small. But in just a few panels we had to be able to construct a story with an intriguing although simple plot, maybe include a plot twist, and of course create immediately identifiable characters, with solid, emotional dialog. You had to do everything the old pros did over 8 to 10 pages, but in only 6 to 12 panels.

If the people in charge liked your work, maybe a year later they would ask you to do a 5 or 6-page story. You'd take what you learned on the short stories and expand them. That meant even stronger character writing and more involved plots and themes. Then another year would pass as you'd learn enough to take on even longer material. If the original creators had the luxury of time to learn, the new kids on the block had the benefit of working with editors who had also learned their craft over time, and were now imparting that information to us.

But here's the rub. In the "good ol'" days the newbies learned their craft by writing or drawing short stories, filler material that gave them time to improve. But comics with filler material no longer exist in the 21st century. There simply isn't a place where one can be bad (or just amateur) for several years as you learn their craft. Today, if you ever expect to get work at one of the major companies, you need to be as good as the very best. No. Actually better.

Right out of the gate.

If there's no place to slowly learn, how do you get better? Well, because it was expensive to hire editors and writers and artists and of course Manhattan office space (since pretty much all the publishers worked out of New York) and get distribution and so much more, there used to be only a few companies. But with the Internet and the ability to become a publisher anywhere in the world, there are now literally hundreds of small comic book companies out there.

But unless you're lucky enough to raise enough money to publish your own comics through Kickstarter or just upload it digitally to your own website or ComiXology—comics' main digital distributor—you still need to be really, really good at what you do.

But if there's no place that will hire you until you're as good as the best of their people, how will you learn?

This is where *Comics Creator Prep* comes in.

Many books have been published in the past decade or so on writing and drawing comics. But those are mostly about the theory of writing and storytelling, talking about process and how one should think.

Comic Creator Prep, on the other hand, gets right into the trenches and gets you working. As if you were submitting your work to a real editor. With *CCP* you gotta do the work and earn your keep. If you have the talent and put in the effort, the same kind of effort the original creators had to do to begin to learn the craft, you should get better.

CCP takes that ten-year learning curve and distills it to 292 print-pages.

What Lee Nordling has done is approach comic book creation in a unique way. He talks about writing and art, but also about the business. He talks about what you do before you create your comic; how you pitch your ideas and how to sell it. Beyond having the talent to actually do the work, learning how to sell it might be even more important.

Lee breaks down comics into all the practical little things one needs to know, then thoroughly explains them. But where the original creators learned them over a period of time, Lee helps you learn about them pretty much as fast as you can read. All roads to great storytelling have patches of quicksand ready to gobble you up then spit you out. *CCP* helps you learn how to avoid them.

As you read the book you will learn about theme and plot and what the differences are between them. This is something I talk about in detail when I do writing seminars at conventions. But where I talk to 300 people at a time, Lee can talk to everyone who reads this book at once.

And he talks about pretty much everything you'll need to understand how to master the field. Today's editors simply don't have the time to teach newbies who want to work with them. They want creators who have already proven themselves.

CCP can help get you there.

Comics is about sequential storytelling. Panel two may follow panel one, but it also precedes panel three. You have to learn about the continuance of action and how to manipulate time in a story. An entire story can be conveyed in the seemingly empty borders between each panel, and if you don't know how to make those spaces of time do what you need, you won't fully understand how comic book storytelling works. The way you write for comics is not the same as writing for books or movies. It's a unique art form with its own rules. To navigate the field you will need to understand them. Sound confusing? It is. But Lee breaks it down so even I understood what he meant. In just a few pages he's giving you a lesson that those of us in the business needed years to learn. This book is going to create real competition for us old....

Wait a second! Forget everything I said. Don't buy this book. Wait another second. If you're reading this you probably already did buy it. So, *umm*, just ignore everything you read here. We don't need the competition.

A personal aside: Something tells me nobody's going to listen. The horse has already left the barn. This book is going to create the talent that will take comics into the next generation. Damn!

So, *umm*, where was I? Oh. Right.

CCP not only talks about storytelling, but how to apply that to the business of storytelling, something most of those other books on comics never get to discuss, but is necessary to understand. Unless you learn how to get past business and editorial roadblocks, you will not be able to survive and thrive in the business for long.

But the real treasure here is after Lee carefully explains each facet of storytelling, he challenges you with tests.

You're not just passively reading this book; to take full advantage of what *CCP* provides, you have to prove you learned its lessons.

These are not silly, useless exercises. Take the tests. Then think about what Lee says as he goes over your possible answers and take each test again. Keep taking them until you fully learn its lessons. Then move onto the next. And the next. In very short order you will be getting much of the information your predecessors needed a decade or longer to fully understand.

Lee Nordling talks at length about writing with intention. Knowing what you're doing, but more importantly understanding *why* you're doing it. This is perhaps the most vital message this book can impart. Learning its lessons will take time, but trust me, that will be time well spent. Vital, even.

But you need to start somewhere and Lee Nordling has written the book to help you get there.

So, you still wanna break into comics?

Prove you're good enough!

Marv Wolfman
May 8, 2016

"Small dreams work this way:
figure out what's available, then choose your favorite.
Important dreams are based on what needs to be done,
and then...find your how.
It's always easier to order off the menu.
Is easier the goal?"
—Seth Godin

"Wax on...wax off. Wax on...wax off."
—Kesuke Miyagi
(played by Pat Morita in *The Karate Kid*)

*"And he looks like such a **nice** old man."*
—Andrew Foley
(after working with Lee Nordling for over a year,
via phone and email, then seeing him for the first time
at Comic-Con International in San Diego.)

INTRODUCTION

BABY STEPPING STONES

I n its many forms, success comes from being the right person at the right time at the right place. The trick, though, is preparing well enough in advance to take advantage of opportunities that present themselves, so let's expand the paradigm to being the right person at the right time at the right place with enough of the right skill set and requisite level of talent, inspiration, experience, resilience, and enthusiasm.

It makes you want to crawl into a hole and pull the dirt in over yourself, doesn't it?

That's because you're looking at your ultimate intended destination instead of simply the next available steps, the ones for which you're actually prepared.

Comics can be a solitary profession. We work mostly alone, chipping from raw granite every steppingstone on our professional pathway.

In late fall 2009, I began writing *Comics Pro Prep* as a weekly column for projectfanboy.com, always intending it to be the foundation of a book, this book.

Not all things come out the way we plan, and sometimes that's a good thing.

I'd intended *Comics Creator Prep* to be a series of chapters written solely by me, not unlike this introduction.

After the first columns, online readers (let's call them students) raised their hands, asked questions, needed clarification, or simply saw things differently.

I needed to discover where my intentions were not perceived as I intended, and explain myself further, deal with open rebellion for espousing some comics- or film-related heresy, or direct the conversation away from what students *wanted* to discuss and toward what we *needed* to discuss.

Comics Pro Prep became an interactive classroom.

I started assigning homework.

Yes, I was *that* professor, the one you wanted to flatten for his arrogant snarl, the one who made John Houseman in *The Paper Chase* seem like Mr. Rogers.

From writing the column and working with students who were willing to absorb each important point, do the homework, set egos aside, fail, fail, fail again, and stick with it until they succeeded, the following is what I learned that you will or won't glean from *Comics Creator Prep:* if you don't do the homework and practice, you'll only be able to apply some of what we discuss toward your work in comics, and will waste years figuring it out for yourself. Save yourself that unnecessary pain and frustration. Practice, do the homework, and practice again. This is the foundation of your craft, and it needs to be practiced, learned, ingrained, and adapted to your own talents, strengths, and weaknesses.

By doing the work, you're taking yourself to school, and none of this is about passing a test and getting an "A." It's about building a better wheel right now, not wasting years reinventing the ones that already exist.

This is about creating the best possible toolbox so you'll be prepared for every project you initiate or that comes your way.

While it's fair to say I am largely self-taught, the truth of it is that I had many teachers, dozens of them—family, friends, peers, *and* teachers (even if they weren't the kind of teachers I thought I needed)—who have been there for some portion of every steppingstone I chiseled from my available opportunities.

Our careers are a daisy chain—sometimes continuous, sometimes concurrent, and sometimes broken—of introductions, networks, and opportunities.

If this volume influences you (one way or the other), then my daisy chain connects to yours, and the people noted herein deserve your consideration.

* * *

To assist you on your journey, consider the following:

"A Comics Creator's Creed"

I have all the sequential art tools at my disposal,
and I will use them to ensure that the
finished version of my work
is perceived as I intend it to be perceived.

Part One

Working With Intention

Chapter 1

Your First Day

*"There is no such thing as a good or bad tool.
There is only the good or bad use of a tool."*
— smartass author of this book,
who's also been called a tool

Welcome to *Comics Creator Prep*.

"What's this 'prep' thing?" you ask. "You mean like *prep* school?"

"Exactly like that," I reply.

"And you're the teacher?" you ask.

"Think of me more like the guy directing the conversation. I've been around for a while, have picked up some stuff, and want to share it for others to consider when making choices about their own work and careers.

"In this volume, we'll explore the professional craft of comics, as well as the realities of being a comics creator in a multimedia world, and we'll do so through lectures and the occasional Socratic discussion."

"Yeah, words like 'Socratic,' sounds preppy already," you remark. "What are we supposed to learn that we don't already know?"

"We're going to be discussing everything related to the craft of creating comics, as well as some practical knowledge about the various publishing and entertainment industries that deal with sequential art."

"Hmmm...sequential art. Another preppy word."

"Two words, actually," I remark, beginning the discourse by borrowing from Aaron Sorkin and *The West Wing*.

"Smart guy, huh? Well, if this is prep school," you say, smirking, "what are the school uniforms?"

"Bathrobes with a CCP patch sewn on," I reply, smiling. "You supply the bathrobe, and I'll design the patch."

"Sounds pricy," you mumble, hands shoved deeply in your pockets, careful to not let a dime escape without your fair consideration.

"Just the price of a book or library card," I respond, smiling, "You'll make your real payment in blood, sweat, and tears."

"Cool," you say.

"Ninety-eight point six," I reply.

"So why the witty banter?" you ask.

Great question.

In the original online incarnation of *Comics Creator Prep*, readers sometimes missed the intended point or I failed to make it well enough, revealing a specific need for some points to be driven home like hammers on nails. Those hammers became the discussions, the questions and answers became the exploration and challenging of ideas. The interjected dialogue allowed us to emphasize points that were otherwise missed or not taken as seriously as they should have been. It allowed us to challenge precepts, test theories, and evaluate assignment results.

It worked.

The banter also helped keep the read entertaining. (Imagine the smiley face icon here.)

While we won't have the opportunity for me to help you with your assignment results, I will offer methodologies and checklists so you can do it yourself. The added gain is that, sooner or later, you're going to have to learn to do it yourself anyway.

So it's sooner.

Every professional comics creator needs to be able to evaluate whether they accomplished what they intended to accomplish, making sure the results will be perceived the right way by their collaborators, editors, and readers.

This is easier said than done, because we are often too close to our material to make this evaluation. Accomplishing it requires being able to distance yourself from your creation, to be as tough on it as you are on the work of others.

Remember what you had to say about *(INSERT TITLE OF THE BOOK YOU HATED SO MUCH YOU COMPLAINED ABOUT IT TO*

EVERYBODY YOU MET)? Try turning that same critical eye as mercilessly on your own work.

Sometimes this takes time; that's certainly the case with me. What I like one day, I despise the next, refashion it to fit my standards, let it sit another day, and repeat the process. Sometimes it takes more than a day, a week, or a month. On and off, this volume has taken years. But it's the end result that matters, for better and for worse.

Hopefully we learn to shorten the amount of time it takes to distance ourselves from what we create, but that's not certain, even with practice. Everybody's different in this regard, though one thing remains constant: if you learn to consistently apply your highest standards to the creation and evaluation of comics, your results will come closer to what you intend them to be.

*   *   *

At a glance, *Comics Creator Prep* may seem more oriented to comic writers than artists, but that's not the case. Without the ability to draw, writers need artists. Without the ability to write, artists need writers. They will have to collaborate, even if circumstances necessitate an editorial go-between, but writers and artists come from different disciplines with different focuses of interest, different types of training, and little of this training, besides experience, involves learning to work with each other. *Comics Creator Prep* simply creates common ground, a foundation of comics craft through which writers and artists can work well together.

It gives writers an opportunity to be clear about their intention, as well as providing artists a process with which to evaluate whether writers were in fact clear. If what they agree to isn't what they think they're agreeing to, the relationship is crippled from the start.

When artists ask, "What's it about?" a writer with the requisite level of craft can answer clearly, succinctly, and accurately.

When a script doesn't have a requisite level of craft, artists can elaborate on "I don't like it" or "it doesn't work for me." Artists will have the tools to get writers to clarify intention and explain in terms writers can understand why panels can't be drawn as written or intended.

Scripts with a high level of craft will sidestep the too common and frustrating issue of an artist drawing what was *actually* in the script, instead of what the writer *thought* was in the script, an issue which usually escalates into somebody settling for mediocrity, making unnecessary changes, quitting, and/or getting fired.

A high level of craft also allows artists to understand how to place panels and panel elements on the page so they're viewed in the preferred order without awkwardly placed balloons, or elongated, twisting balloon pointers.

For writers, where the script is written with intention, acceptance or rejection by artists and editors will be about what they wrote, instead of what they miswrote.

Ultimately, writers and artists can determine whether an artist or writer is somebody with whom they'll want to collaborate, and then develop a working process for that collaboration.

Comics Creator Prep sets a high bar for the level of comics craft, and helps comic writers and artists work and sell with intention.

Your goal inside this classroom should be to work to understand what we discuss, simply so that you may choose whether to apply some or all of it outside this classroom to your craft and career.

And remember, nothing is fixed. There is no single way to create sequential art. There is only the finished work. If it works, it works. If it does not work, then you should endeavor to correct what needs to be corrected to make it work.

As you proceed, sear the following words onto your organic hard drive: *if this was easy, anybody could do it well.*

Chapter 2

Thematic Storytelling:
The Magic Story Bean

Class is in session.

Many of you may wonder what I mean by use of the term "thematic storytelling"....

Blank stares return from everybody in the classroom without a sign anybody is wondering anything.

Simply put, when you understand and successfully apply thematic storytelling you will be able to determine two things: your best ending and how your story needs to set up that ending.

Eyes widen. Attention is suddenly rapt.

That's right, thematic storytelling is *The Magic Story Bean*.

A hand rises in back.

"Yes?" I ask.

"Are you saying that if we apply thematic storytelling to our stories we won't be stuck figuring out the endings?"

"You'll always have to work at it," I begin.

The class moans in unison, realizing there's always a catch.

"But you'll know what those endings need to accomplish in order for them to be the *right* endings."

"Oooooooo," the class says in unison, each mouth making an "O" so small a Cheerio couldn't fight its way into any of them.

Once upon a time, I was at dinner chatting with a producer about movies. I love movies. I love discussing what movies are about.

The producer hadn't seen *Saving Private Ryan*, and wasn't likely to—

why not is an entirely different discussion—so I shared my thoughts about what made the story special.

I saw it the previous summer amidst the hype of it being the greatest war movie since *Sgt. Sliced Bread.*

I left the theater not as impressed as I wanted to be—the hype set expectations so high that *Citizen Kane* would have struggled to reach them—so I saw the film only once, and yet half a year later recounted the struggle of this squad risking their lives to find Private Ryan.

Then I got to the end, where the squad finally found and saved Ryan, but at incredible cost. After the last battle, the Tom Hanks character, Captain Miller, was mortally wounded. Ryan bent over him, realizing he'd be dead if it wasn't for the sacrifice of these brave men, this brave man, and Miller whispered his last words to Ryan, "Earn this."

Honestly, I became misty-eyed just recounting the story, so strong was my experience of reliving the ending.

Next came the coda, the conclusion of the wraparound story, where the old man from the beginning, the man we now know is Ryan, weeps at Miller's Normandy gravesite, still struggling with whether or not he's done enough to "earn this."

Endings prove the theme.

Endings explain what the story is about.

Stories are *about* what you believe to be true.

In some fashion, this makes stories morality plays, or moral arguments.

Your moral argument is your theme.

To clarify: if the point of your story is something you believe, that's your theme, your moral argument.

A hand rises in back.

"Yes?" I ask.

"So, for example, if I believe in 'love,' that could be my theme?"

You cannot have a theme like "love" because that doesn't take a position on "love." You *have* to take a position. You have to make an empirical statement.

For example, you *can* have a theme like "love conquers all" because it takes a position, it states what you believe to be true. It's your moral argument.

A hand rises in back.

"Yes?" I ask.

"So stories can only be about something that's moral?" you ask.

"No, of course not," I reply. "You can have immoral or amoral moral arguments, like 'killing is fun, as long as it hurts the other guy more than it hurts you.'"

"I like that one," you say, already jotting notes for the story in your head. "But are you saying that stories need to teach something or they're no good?"

Absolutely not," I reply. "Sam Goldwyn of Metro-Goldwyn-Mayer once said, 'If you want to send a message, use Western Union.'

"He's still right, at least for not preaching like Barton Fink to the reader or audience."

A theme is the glue that holds your story together and makes it feel complete. *That's* its real value.

If something cuts against the theme then it doesn't belong in your story, at least not that story with that theme. When you've got something that doesn't fit, you've got four choices and only four choices: leave in the thing that doesn't fit, accepting that it undercuts your theme; cut it out; modify the story to fit your theme; or change your theme to reflect its inclusion. But if you change the theme to reflect its inclusion, everything else in the story needs to be examined to make sure it also fits the new theme.

"Will you give us an example?" you ask.

Sure.

If you have a story about a boy and girl who grow up next door to each other, are perfectly suited for each other, have loving parents who approve of the match, get married, have wonderful kids who grow up without dividing the parents, grow old together, and die peacefully while holding hands, this doesn't exactly *prove* "love conquers all," does it?

"Right," you say. "It's not like they had anything to conquer or overcome."

Exactly. If your theme is "love conquers all," you need to create disharmony for the couple from the beginning, make them not so obviously suited for each other, throw everything possible at them, especially the kitchen sink, pry them apart. But these efforts won't and can't ultimately divide them. Why not? Because—and here it comes—love conquers all.

See how stories and themes can be developed together, with one supporting the other?

Now let's return to the perfect-couple story. Since, I did everything possible to *not* give our loving couple real-life problems, we now have a story without a theme. To discern that theme, simply ask, "What *does* the story mean? What *does* the ending say?"

The answer to that question will dictate the theme or moral argument.

In this case, let's try: "life is a bowl of cherries" or "it's easy to get along when everything goes well."

Do all the story points, especially the end, support these themes? They do.

And that's how the end proves the theme.

Is that why I took out the scene where the husband had an affair with his wife's sister? Absolutely. It didn't fit.

Now let's change the story.

Everything else stays, except the end. The couple is near death, and the wife turns to the husband and says, "I never loved you."

Then he says, "I know. That's why I've been having an affair with your sister for fifty years."

Then they die.

Now *that* is a completely different story, all because of the ending. Suddenly it's a story about repressed anger and failed love, about two people going through civilized motions.

Make some more changes, and it's *The War of the Roses*, the darkly comic film about a couple who die in a battle of wills, him for them to stay together and her to be rid of him once and for all.

If your theme is "life is a bowl of cherries," then having a twist ending with the serial killer knocking off our couple simply doesn't make a lot of sense.

Often we don't know what our stories are about till after we've written them.

A hand rises in back.

"Yes?" I ask.

"If that's the case," you begin, "why bother to figure out the theme?"

Great question, perhaps the most important question.

Writing *is* (for most good writers) rewriting. Once a story's done, it's important to determine what it's about so that you can, in the next pass, determine what fits and what doesn't.

Do that, do it well, and you'll be ahead of ninety-five percent of other writers.

For those with access to the Criterion DVD or Blu-ray of the film *Brazil*, check out the commentary track on the edit made for TV, which is appropriately called the "Love Conquers All" version. The commentary track walks you through a completely different cut of the film, which contains only those portions of the story that reflect this re-defining theme.

The cut is an abomination, but the lesson in editing for theme is brilliant.

A hand rises in back.

"Yes?" I ask.

"What if my story doesn't have a theme?"

For those of you who think your story doesn't have a theme, you just haven't yet figured it out. If your story holds together, there will be a theme, even if it's something as familiar as "good will triumph over evil" or "with great power comes great responsibility."

But if your story is a mish-mash of contradictory moral arguments, then the themes are going to fight each other. This means there's some straightening out to do, which there would have been anyway for the story to hold together, even if you weren't looking for thematic focus.

Since most early drafts of stories need some straightening out, the value of identifying your theme is that it helps shape future drafts. Otherwise, you're just cutting stuff you don't like or adding stuff you do like, basically working with your gut as a divining rod.

Sometimes guts are right. They nag at you about things not quite fitting, but wouldn't it be nice to have some gut-support?

That's what identifying and applying your theme will do. It's the Magic Story Bean that will help you keep what works, cut what doesn't, figure out what to do next in your story, determine its best ending, or identify what to fix and how to fix it.

Plant that bean, nurture it with consistent ideas, trim it to fit without damaging its roots, and it will grow into the story you want it to be.

Before proceeding to our chapter assignment, I'd like to introduce your classmates for this semester: *Stephanie, Sam, Lilly, Puck, Hercules,* and *Jules.*

The names of the students have been changed to protect the educated.

Every assignment answer and discussion, here and in later workshops, has been adapted from real questions, real misinterpretations, and real need for clarification, with a goal toward showing you how easily your answers can jump the rails on assignments, assignments so seemingly simple that you have to actually do the work to discover their complexity.

The following guidelines will help you grade the quality of your answers.

1. Review the assignment discussion *after* completing your assignment, not before.

Reason: We learn from our mistakes. You are bound to make some of the same mistakes as your fellow classmates. You are more likely to recognize those mistakes in your own work when you see other people do what you did, then read where they failed, i.e. where you may have failed.

You'll also get reinforcement for what you did well.

2. Wait at least one day before reviewing your answers.

Reason: It's important to create distance from the material so you'll make a more objective determination.

3. Challenge the quality of your answers using the same tough criteria we apply to the quality of the classroom answers.

Reason: You need to be your toughest critic. If you're not, then an editor's assessment of your work will mean more than getting a class assignment wrong; it will mean losing prospective work.

4. As you read each answer from one of the classmates, stop and ask yourself this question: "Did they handle the assignment well?"

If you think did, or didn't, write down the answer—don't just think it—with a clear rationale.

Reason: Writing down answers takes out wiggle room. It commits you to answers that are going to be correct, partially correct, or incorrect. If you believe an answer is correct and our determination proves otherwise then you have gained added insight. If our review of the material aligns with yours then your assessment has gained validation.

Writing down answers also forces you to go slower, forces you to concentrate on questions and answers, forces reflection. All facets of the assignments help you learn and practice what you learned instead of simply getting through these pages to the end of the book. The more you put into this the more you'll get out of it. Make an effort, a complete effort, and you're halfway to being able to apply the age-old truism to your work: *writing is rewriting.*

Chapter Assignment
The interrelation of theme and story

We're taking you out for a thematic test drive. I want you to write:

1. A thematic argument for a simple story.

2. A paragraph or two describing the arc of the simple story that proves your thematic argument.

As an example, let's twist my story about the perfect couple into something different.

Theme: No matter how hard you try, your true feelings will eventually come out, and you'll feel better for showing them.

Story: A boy and girl grow up next to each other, seem perfectly suited, have loving parents who approve of the match, get married, and have wonderful kids who grow up without dividing the parents.

The couple grows old together, are about to die peacefully in each other's arms, when the girl says, "I never loved you."

And the boy responds, "I never loved me, either. That's why I settled for you."

Then they die happily, no longer holding hands.

You can begin with your theme and write the story paragraph or write the story paragraph and figure out the theme. It doesn't matter where you start, as long as the two end up working together.

The story in your assignment does not have to be "good." It simply has to prove your thematic argument.

I know some of you are already considering wildly creative ways to tackle this assignment.

Don't.

Keep it simple.

This is the time to work, not play. This is the time to learn the basics without creative writing complication, to crawl before trying to walk, to walk before running, to understand the principles before trying to bend them to your will, otherwise you will surely miss the forest for the leaves.

In math terms, make this $2 + 2 = 4$, not $4/5 + 4.578/3.74 = y - 4.638/9.567$.

Let's begin.

One day later....

Okay, you finished the assignment (right?), waited a day to mull over whether or not you did it well (right?), and now it's time to review the results.

Who's first?

Puck raises his hand, is the first to leap into the deep end of the pool.

Puck: Just to take this process out for a test ride, I'm beginning with a story we all know.

Theme: There's no place like home.

Story: When nobody listens to her or cares about her troubles, Dorothy wishes she can go to someplace wonderful that's over the rainbow. Then she gets her wish and is transported by a tornado to Oz. Once there, she discovers all is not well. She's become the target of the Wicked Witch of the West, not only for killing the Wicked Witch of the East, but also for gaining the powerful ruby slippers. The threat of death hangs over Dorothy and she now wishes to get out of Dodge and go home. But wishing and getting are two different things, because to get what she wants she'll have to go on a perilous quest. The mysterious Wizard of Oz wants the Wicked Witch's broom. To get that our heroes will have to kill her. With the help of three new friends, each with wishes and needs of their own, Dorothy kills the Wicked Witch and completes her quest. Her friends discover they don't really need their wishes granted, but the Wizard ends up not being able to help Dorothy. That's when, ironically, she discovers the ruby slippers give her the ability to go wherever she wants, so she uses them to go home, where everything is just as she left it.

Puck's grade: **FAIL.**

How does the end of this story—as written here, not as dramatized in the film—reflect this theme?

It doesn't.

"There's no place like home" may be the theme of the MGM musical, *The Wizard of Oz*, but it's certainly not the theme of this version of the story. There's nothing to suggest Dorothy is better off being home, is more loved at home, or that home is an implicitly better place to be. This story is about Dorothy wishing to be places she's not, then paying the price for where she ends up. Even the end doesn't suggest happily ever after. It suggests she's back where she started and has learned nothing from the experience.

My suggested theme for this paragraph is "be careful what you wish for, because you might just get it," or "the grass is always greener on the other side of the tornado."

There is great value in using well-known stories as fodder for this and other assignments; they're a known quantity. But to use them effectively, you need to portray the key aspects of the story clearly and accurately in your synopsis or you'll drown in the deep end of the pool next to poor waterlogged Puck.

Sam: I'll go next, but with something original.

Theme: The starving crew of a becalmed clipper ship learns to share the remainder of their food with stowaway leprechauns.

Story: Crossing from the old country to the New World is never easy, not when you're an Irish immigrant fleeing the potato famine, and certainly not when you're a leprechaun colony searching for new gold to replace the gold you lost. The ship hits a bad patch of weather, or visa versa, and is crippled by powerful winds, then becalmed. Food supplies run short and that's when the crew discovers the leprechauns who have been hiding in the hold and starving. Instead of fighting over the food that's left, the crew, after some argument and fighting among themselves, agrees to share. The leprechauns, restored to strength, use their power to gain back the winds that will send them all to the new world.

Sam's grade: **FAIL.**

The theme reads like a logline, is completely lacking in a declarative statement or moral argument about something he believes to be true.

Sam: This assignment is very subjective. Just because you don't like my theme, it doesn't mean another editor won't think it rings true.

LN: This isn't about me liking or not liking your theme. It's about you writing a theme that clearly reflects your story. "Learning to share" isn't a thematic statement. It's what they *do* in the story.

"It is important to share with others in need, even when you don't have much to share" is a declarative statement. It takes a stand. And your story proves *this* theme.

Keep trying.

Lilly: This one's short and (hopefully) sweet.

Theme: It's more important to be loved for who you are on the inside than the outside.

Story: Mr. Candy Cane is convinced people only love him for what's outside, not inside. That's because nobody's ever tried to get to know him; they only want a sweet, sugary lick. That's all they've ever wanted, and it just wears him away, has made him hard and bitter. Then he meets a girl without taste, a girl who isn't interested in taking a lick. And she doesn't particularly like his bitter attitude. Intrigued by her, Mr. Candy Cane works to change his attitude. She still isn't interested in taking a lick, but she's more willing to talk to him. As they talk, he reveals more and more about his true self, and she comes to like him. She never is interested in taking a lick, because, remember, she has no taste, and has come to love him only for who he is on the inside. Mr. Candy Cane finally knows true contentment.

Lilly's grade: **PASS.**

The story proves the thematic/moral argument.

Stephanie: My turn!

Theme: Even the meanest person in the world can be moved to pity.

Story: Wally is the meanest man in the world, takes every opportunity to say and do the most hurtful things to anybody, whether they deserve it or not, but that's to be expected. It's a requisite for his job as a corporate executive. Wally works in a high-rise, wishes he could fly away, but that's not what he gets paid well to do. One day, after he fires a subordinate for no particular reason, a butterfly flitters into his office then flies back toward the open window to escape. Wally closes the window and watches the poor thing knock repeatedly against it, trying to get out. Finally, it settles on the sill, wings flapping—if it could pant, it would be panting—and Wally sighs. Then he opens the window and the butterfly escapes. He watches it go where he can never go, sighs again, closes the window, and fires another subordinate, just to get the taste of goodness out of his mouth.

Stephanie's grade: **PASS.**

This is a clear, simple story, which reflects the theme nicely. I especially like the part at the end where Wally fired another employee, showing he wasn't redeemed. Had he been redeemed the theme would have needed to be revised to "even the meanest person in the world can change."

See how endings prove themes?

Now, let's flip the assignment. I'd like you to discern the theme of the following story:

Twelve year-old Billy rushes out of his boring old house in search of summer adventure. At first his encounter with men from the future, genetic monsters, and aliens is wild and fun. He manages to successfully defeat all of them through sheer determination and boundless energy. Then he runs into Little Lori, the cutest twelve year-old in the universe, and suddenly his prepubescent brain turns to mush. He can barely move or speak. Finally, she gets bored, or perhaps takes pity on him, and leaves. Relieved to have survived the encounter, Little Billy rushes home to his safe, boring house, where he can regroup and figure out how to talk to cute little girls.

What's the theme of this story?

Sam: To play off our earlier discussion about Oz, I think the theme to this story is, "You won't miss home till after you leave it."

LN: FAIL. Remember, Little Billy is having a great time conquering all kinds of foes, until he meets his Waterloo and runs home to hide, at least temporarily. It's not nearly the movie version of The Wizard of Oz, with Dorothy wondering what happened to Uncle Henry and Auntie Em, and trying to get home as soon as she was parted from it.

Puck: Little Billy learns that a cute little girl can be the most mind-boggling adventure of them all.

LN: FAIL. This is a log line for a story, not a theme for a story.

Lilly: Let's try this one, "When the going gets too tough, even the tough go home."

LN: This one just misses. Just. Had I ended the story at the point where the boy ran home that would be a good answer, but it's not where the story ended so it doesn't quite fit.

Stephanie: "Facing imagined horrors is easier than facing real emotion." Am I close?

LN: Nope. **FAIL.** The horrors in this story were, as written, real, not imagined. I intentionally avoided the implicit imaginary nature of Little Billy's adventures because I didn't want to muddle the theme. Had I written them as imaginary, this theme might have worked.

Here's the thing to consider about writing themes that are intended to reflect stories, whether the stories are short or long: every word and nuance has to be taken into account. The difficulty of writing a theme that corresponds to a story demonstrates how much we need to be mindful of the language we use to craft our scenarios. Word choices affect how our work is perceived, and poor or weak word choices usually create reader perceptions that are different from what we intend.

Hercules: Here's my suggestion, "Even in defeat you can live and learn to fight another day."

LN: PASS. You nailed it. Even though the theme isn't story specific, it fits the specific story. Note how the theme is more closely tied to the end than the adventures that led up to it.

Could there be more than one theme for Billy's adventure? Certainly.

Here's another that works: success can be fun, but failure will make you think.

As the Billy story progresses to outline and script, one of these two, or even another, will be closer to the mark. Can you see how each of these two themes, when developed consistently, will result in very different stories?

Welcome to the wonderful world of thematic storytelling.

These exercises generated much classroom consideration and discussion about writing processes.

No doubt, as you worked through your answers and attempted to determine how well your classmates addressed the assignments, you discovered yourself sailing off a cliff or two.

Perhaps you had difficulty getting non-story specific about themes, wrote loglines, or simply found it difficult figuring out "what it all meant." Or perhaps it was easy, and you're not certain why the others had so much difficulty nailing the assignment.

Here's a possible answer to that question: analytical creators are going to learn thematic writing more easily than intuitive creators.

Starting out, I had a very tough time learning to change my story to fit my goals, and visa versa. Honestly, I didn't even know enough to define my goals. I'd cut scenes or paragraphs, add new ones, or move them around until I found places in stories where they felt better or read smoother, but I didn't have a yardstick with which to measure whether the stories were getting better or simply becoming different.

I was very much an intuitive writer, and it wasn't getting me anywhere fast.

There is only one thing that helped me learn to effectively evaluate whether or not I was getting *some*where: thematic storytelling.

One student noted that an editor might very well like a professed theme, even if it doesn't fit my requisite definition of a theme. My determination about whether or not a theme and story work well together has nothing to do with what I or somebody else might "like." That wasn't the point. The point of the assignment was to determine a theme that truly reflected the story. After having done so, the student would then have an objective yardstick with which to measure whether or not the story, in its numerous incarnations, stays true to the theme.

When you have a measuring stick, an evaluation tool like the thematic argument, it's easier to step back, look at the story within the context of the theme, and make a fairly objective assessment about whether or not the two fit well together.

In theory, that's what you did when reviewing each creator's answers to this assignment.

Sound easy?

Not on your life.

Don't assume you're initially going to be good at this. Remember how hard you worked to get where you are as a writer or artist? Be prepared for a similar learning curve, one that starts nearly from scratch.

This is new to you. It's a different way of thinking about story, and it is going to take a lot of work to make it second nature.

Even if you successfully tackled these chapter assignments, it will be different and difficult applying these techniques to *your* stories and *your* themes. To do this successfully, you need to step back from what you wrote, as if you didn't write it, and be as tough on *your* work as you are on the work of others, especially the work you don't like. You need to make yourself your own backseat driver and Monday-morning quarterback rolled into one. This is how we get better. This is how we learn what does and doesn't fit. Once you know something doesn't fit, it's easier to take it out or change it into something that does fit.

It cannot be repeated too often: the end *proves* the theme.

Thematic storytelling really *is* The Magic Story Bean because you can use it to make an assessment about whether something is *right* or *wrong*.

You have two ways to get to the junction of theme and story: Choose your theme, figure out the best end that fits the theme, and write the story that leads up to it; or, after you've written your story, look to the end as the key to your theme, and revise the story and/or theme to fit. Either way works, though you'll likely be wandering back and forth in the gray zone that exists between the two. It's a process of adjustment. However you approach it, this process provides a quantifiable yardstick, which you can apply to the writing and rewriting of your work.

If you can do this you will be more confident that you achieved your editorial goals and, as an added bonus, you will be able to explain to others what your stories are about.

I have one terrible caveat.

While I began as an intuitive writer, I have a strong analytical streak, which allowed me to adapt more easily into becoming a thematic storyteller. I simply needed to find my yardstick.

Creators who are not analytical will have a more difficult time developing their own process.

Some will never figure it out.

Some won't want to, and some won't be able to, because their brains just don't work that way.

Here's my best suggestion: if you don't analyze, but recognize there are problems with your work, then *learn* to analyze, recognize that you can't keep writing in circles, and do something about it.

Crafting with intention requires you to look at your creation and determine whether or not the work will be perceived the way you intend. If you determine it won't, you'll be able to go back and make whatever changes are necessary for you to achieve your goal.

For writers, "crafting with intention" is the underpinning of "writing is rewriting." If you don't know how your work will be perceived, how do you know what to revise?

Not being able to effectively revise is the death of too many writing careers.

The same is true for artists.

When an artist can't see how some aspect or element of his or her drawing is created with a different or inconsistent sensibility the results are the same: the finished product doesn't fit together, doesn't quite come to life, doesn't feel "right."

Just as with brilliantly intuitive writers, brilliantly intuitive artists who create brilliant work without analyzing don't need to analyze. But artists who can't see the inconsistencies in their work are professionally challenged until they figure out a process that helps them find and resolve their inconsistencies.

So what to do?

Tackle these assignments we've been working on and don't stop just because you got through the chapter.

When you successfully tackle one level of complication, progress to something more difficult—just a *little* more difficult—enough to stretch, but not enough to snap.

Read through the work of others and treat it like an assignment. Examine and analyze everything, especially the works that resist analysis, and remember, it is easier to critique somebody else's work from afar before you can effectively look into a mirror and study the pimples on your nose.

This is only the beginning, because your critical eye needs rigorous training as it continues to turn inward.

This is as true for me as it is for anybody. I still have people reading behind me, and I quiz them nearly to death, certainly to boredom, to get to the heart of their perception. Then I make adjustments.

This will take time—don't fool yourself—probably years to become entirely comfortable with it.

It will hurt, excruciatingly so.

If you're fortunate it'll become fun. (Not the hurting part.)

Regardless, it will seem like the tallest, never-ending flight of stairs you've ever climbed.

But if your intuitive story sense doesn't bring home the bacon (and mine didn't), then you need to develop a new process—whatever it is that works—that will help make your finished product represent your intentions.

This is the best process I can recommend. If it works for you, in full or part, that's great. If little or none of it works for you, at least you've made some progress towards looking for a process that *will* help you reach your intended goal.

However you proceed, your goal should be having your work reflect your intention.

Easier said than written.

Chapter 3

The Comics Panel Time-Master
(or why creators should stop trying
to write comics as movies on paper)

Part One:
How We Read Comics

Most new writers stumble over a particular misconception in their scripts, one that topples editors, artists, and readers like a dominoes daisy chain.

"What's that?" you wonder, truly curious how *one* thing can cause such chaos.

"Time," I reply, "and how it exists in a comics panel."

"Is there time in a comics panel?" you ask.

"Yes and no," I reply, enticing you to read more.

And how much time, or what there is in its place, is entirely up to you, for you *are* (or are about to become) a *Comics Panel Time-Master!*

The comic panel is a marvelous creation.

It contains a single image that represents one or more frozen moments of time, and it's up to the writer and/or artist to determine which moment (or moments) best serve to advance the story within the context of panels that precede and follow.

We could stop right here if there weren't so many ways to mess this up, but there are, so let's get back to basics, the stuff Scott McCloud makes so clear in *Understanding Comics*, the stuff that needs to be embedded at the core of comics craft, the stuff that just can't ever be forgotten or ignored, the stuff that makes comics different from every other medium.

"If Scott McCloud makes it so clear," you ask, "why do you need to bother repeating it?"

"Great question!" I reply.

If creators applied the McCloud tenets, they wouldn't keep making the same mistakes I see time and again. This means one of three things: either they haven't learned the lessons well, don't take them seriously enough, or don't recognize the magnitude of their mistakes. Perhaps they believe this fundamental aspect of the medium, a properly conceived and written panel, is optional or open to personal or stylistic interpretation, when they're really just making poor level-of-craft choices. Regardless, there are short- and long-term ramifications to sloppy scripting.

In the short term, others do work that shouldn't be necessary to fix scripting problems, and the comics get done, perhaps well, perhaps not. If done well, writers get credit for a quality of craft they don't deserve.

In the long term, let's say an editor or artist makes a comic work despite a poor quality of craft in the script. The book gets published, the writer gets more work, becomes known, becomes influential, shares scripts as samples for how to write comics, new writers learn the wrong lessons, and the industry-wide level of craft continues to erode. The flawed script has become a self-perpetuating problem that misleads future generations of writers.

If this reads like a wildly speculative, literary apocalypse, it isn't. Welcome to how we got to where we are today.

We begin by identifying the point where the train jumped the track, in short, why and how scripted panels often fail in their level of craft, then we'll conclude with what *does* work and why.

To state the obvious, something too many writers concede then ignore, comics are *not* film.

Film is ruled by the clock, rolling out story at twenty-four frames per second, unless that film is *The Hobbit*, but the principle remains true. We are captive viewers, experiencing what unfolds through sight and sound. As viewers, we have no control of time, unless you want to get cute and consider the pause and slow-fast buttons on your remote.

In sequential art we view storytelling panels at our own pace. We take as much or as little time as we wish to look at page compositions, images in panels, and to read captions and balloons. We can sit back and ponder each aspect of each element or flip through pages like The Flash.

A movie has a fixed period of time to unfold and a fraction of a movie is a minute, which takes...um, a minute to watch, whether it's all action, all dialogue, a still-camera showing nothing, or a wildly spinning camera showing everything.

In contrast, a fraction of sequential art is a panel. It can take a second, a minute, an hour, or whatever period of time the reader chooses in which to absorb it. That length of time, however, will also depend on the size of the panel and what is in it: how many words, if any, how many balloons, if any, how much or little drawing, if any, tone, if any, and/or color if any. Readers can bask in the beauty of a panel for eternity or give it barely a glance on their way to the next panel.

So where do so many writers go so wrong in trying to write comics like movies (even if they don't believe they're doing so)?

Beginning with what they have in common, comics and film each tell stories with pictures. To further this comparison, movies (or parts of them) are often storyboarded in advance, and storyboards look like a form of comics, even though their intention is different. Comics and film also usually have words, spoken and narrated, or written as dialogue and narration. If you stop at these broad comparisons, ignoring how different sound is from the written word, as well as how different moving pictures are from still images, there really doesn't *seem* to be much difference between the two.

The film script format exacerbates the misconception of real similarity. It requires scene descriptions, names of characters speaking, and dialogue, just like comic scripts. To the untutored comics creator, it makes a *certain* amount of intuitive sense to simply chop up the film script action into smaller bits for comic script action, and dump the dialogue into appropriately placed balloons.

Simple. No big deal, and if there's a problem, the editor or artist will fix it. How many times do you think I've heard this remark from writers who don't realize that it's *their* responsibility to craft their comic scripts well?

Welcome to the first missteps toward learning to write comics badly.

Most untutored comics writers chop up the action into smaller bits, making smaller actions from bigger actions instead of converting action into a series of frozen moments of time. Making this conversion requires understanding *exactly* which images are necessary in a specific order to visually advance a scene or story to meet a dramatic goal.

Let's take a look at a simple and fairly common example of this mistake.

Here's a series of actions: "To save a beleaguered Boy Scout from further jostling, Johnny Action Jr. leaps a picket fence, grabs the two pintsized bullies from behind, clubs one with a Teddy bear, and jams a candy cane up the other's nose."

Here's how I too-often see the action broken down into panels:

1. Johnny Action Jr. leaps a picket fence.

2. He grabs the two pint-sized bullies from behind, clubbing one with a Teddy bear.

3. He jams a candy cane up the other one's nose.

Where did this series of panel descriptions go wrong? One mistake is specific and the other is general.

Take some time to review the question and determine an answer. If you think I'm just testing you and that nothing's "wrong," that's an answer, too.

Have you made your determination? Did you spot the two mistakes? Good. Write them down. Commit yourself to those answers. Like all our assignments, rather than scanning ahead for answers it's better if you figure as much out for yourself as possible.

DON'T CONTINUE READING UNTIL YOU'RE CERTAIN OF YOUR ANSWER.

Done? Good. Please continue.

First, the specific mistake: How can Johnny Action Jr. grab both bullies, an action that presumably requires both hands, while simultaneously clubbing one with a Teddy bear...in the same panel?

Answer: Unless he has a third hand, he can't. If all the "action" elements need to be included, this panel is at least two panels worth of images.

If you didn't catch this mistake, ask yourself why you missed it.

Take a moment and consider it.

Are you done or discombobulated? Please continue.

If you haven't come up with an answer, it's probably this: you're still thinking comics are like film.

Now, what's the general, overarching mistake?

If this was film, each of the actions described in each of the panels has a beginning and an end, instead of being single frozen moments of time, and it's not clear which frozen moments were intended by the description.

For example, in panel one, where is Johnny Action Jr. located in his leap over the picket fence?

If it matters to the writer where Johnny Action Jr. is located in his leap over the picket fence then the description allows for too much misinterpretation. Maybe Johnny is just beginning his leap. Maybe he's in mid-leap just above the fence. Maybe he's just landed and the action lines behind him show the distance of the leap.

While most writers might expect Johnny to be halfway through the action with him having just cleared the fence, is that clear? No. Is it implicit? Perhaps, but only to the writer. Let's say the artist shows Johnny having completed the leap, and the writer says, "That's not what I wanted."

Is it the artist's fault for not being able to read the writer's mind?

This is what happens when untutored writers write action in comics. Their intention isn't clear.

The solution is simple. If writers have specific imagery in mind, they should ignore everything they were taught in creative writing, dump the action verbs and embrace passive verbs. Why dump what is vibrant and alive for what reads like a lump? Because action verbs denote action, which can't be drawn, and passive verbs help pinpoint frozen moments of time.

Now, maybe the writer doesn't *care* where Johnny is in his leap over the picket fence. I've certainly heard enough writers say, "It's not my job to write layouts. That's up to the artist." I've heard artists express the same sentiment. There's a good point here, which we'll get into later in a discussion about different comics script styles, and it is perfectly fair to relinquish certain aspects of the sequential storytelling to the artist...if that's the intention.

However, to keep this discussion on the track, let's go back to my qualification: "If it matters to the writer where Johnny Action Jr. is located in his leap over the picket fence...."

Anybody reading the script will be able to imagine where *they* see Johnny in relation to the picket fence, but what happens when their interpretation of the description is significantly different from what the writer intended to see drawn?

What happens when the writer thought he'd written the description clearly but hadn't?

Maybe the artist is asked to make changes.

Maybe nothing happens, because the artist is used to writers who don't understand how to write visually.

And maybe something happens because the artist is fed up having to deal with writers who don't take responsibility for what they write.

If the interpretation of a written image into a drawn image matters, the writer is obligated to designate the frozen moment of time or at least to impart the dramatic importance of what he hopes to accomplish in the panel. Only then does the writer have legitimate grounds for discussing how well an artist's layout interprets the description.

Why?

If it's worth the time to correct an artist's layout then it's worth the time in the first place to give the artist enough information to create the panel well.

This means it's a writer's responsibility to learn to write with clear intention.

When I critique similar examples of poorly crafted writing, writers usually get the point; they really do. Then they discount the mistakes as minor—mere oversights, really; no big deal, because it doesn't seem to affect the story—and this is where they falter, because in sequential art this kind of poor writing really *is* a big deal.

Why?

When they don't recognize fundamental flaws and work to improve on them in their comics-writing craft they will make the same mistakes again.

And again.

And again.

Why?

Because they need to stop thinking of story in terms of action, and start thinking with their sequential art toolbox.

They need to stop writing movies on paper and start writing comics.

This takes learning, training, repetition, and a dedication to the form.

If that's the problem, what's the solution?

The solution is scary-simple.

And that's what we'll discuss in our next two chapters: controlling time, and becoming a Time-Master.

Chapter 4

The Comics Panel Time-Master
(or why creators should stop trying to write comics as movies on paper)

Part Two:
How Time Flows In Comics

WARNING: This chapter can cause a rise in blood pressure.

Should this occur, please remember three things:

1) I'm going to be obnoxiously redundant on certain points because I want to make sure they get due consideration.

2) Sometimes it takes numerous swings to pound a point through a skull.

3) This will hurt me more than it'll hurt you...er, okay, two things.

Nobody sets out to write comics badly, though some ignore signs that they are doing so, much like a blindfolded man in the driver's seat on a cross-country road trip.

Nobody plans for pages or panels to be read differently from how they intend them to be read.

"Everybody wants to be great at it," you summarize.

"That's right," I say.

"Then where do they go wrong and head south for Antarctica?" you ask, employing my blindfolded driving-man analogy. "Is it a lack of talent?"

"Let's take talent off the table," I say. "We'll discuss that in the future with a number of other ingredients that help creators achieve their professional goals.

"For now, let's focus on what it takes to write a single sequential art panel and have the reader correctly interpret the writer's intention. To do this, there's a two-fold solution.

"First, the writer needs to take off the blindfold."

"Can we dump this analogy?" you ask, your face scrunched into confusion. "I'm not making the connection."

"In short," I quickly reply, not wishing to lose our conceptual purchase, "new writers are often blind to what they write. Each new idea, word, sentence, paragraph, and story is their darling, their baby. They need to take off the blindfold and look at what they wrote for what it is, instead of what they imagine it is. They need to stop being the proud parent defending what they wrote (just because they wrote it) and need to start being Mr. Wilson, Dennis the Menace's neighbor, the guy who grouches about every little fault and winces at every poorly placed comma. Writers need to push back against the material, distance themselves as if they didn't write it, and examine it word for word and concept for concept with this mindset. Only then can creators address whether they accomplished their editorial goals.

"With the blindfolds off writers can now see their stories careening out of control. In this situation, who wouldn't want to learn to use the steering wheel?"

Your face scrunches further into the shape of a question mark and you ask, "You want writers to take driving lessons?"

"Exactly!" I respond. "If they don't know how to steer the script, how can they take it where they want it to go?"

"Let me get this straight," you mumble through clenched teeth. "You want writers to pretend they didn't write what they wrote so they can constantly question whether it's right?"

"Yes."

"And then, after they've fixed it, they should pretend they didn't make the changes so they can once again question whether it's right?"

"Yes."

Completely exasperated, you ask, "Then how will writers know they ever got it right?"

"They won't," I reply, getting to the heart of the matter. "That's why 'writing is rewriting' is such an important step towards becoming a good writer."

To find an endpoint to this process, though, there's another important quote from Voltaire to consider: "The perfect is the enemy of the good."

Translation: you need to do the best work you can and learn to determine when something is good enough.

Should you discover something's not good enough, that readers didn't take from your work what you intended, you need to examine the work again, from their perspective, and work once more to make your writing good enough.

Do this, constantly striving to improve, and in so doing you will improve.

Honestly, you will.

"I dunno," you consider, skeptically. "I know creators who write stuff over and over again, and the work doesn't seem to get better. It gets different but not necessarily better."

"I know," I reply, weeping for the Lost Ones. "That's because they haven't found a working mindset for *how* to improve. When these writers revise their work, they're usually not turning the steering wheel in the right direction, or, worse, when the wheel is turned well they don't know *how* they did it, so they won't necessarily know how to do it well again.

"In short, the good writing was intuitive or accidental, not the result of intention.

"Where inspiration and spontaneity are what prime a comic's pump, or propel it forward, or give it life, it takes comics craft to figure out what a comic is supposed to be and make it happen. *Comics Creator Prep* raises the level of comics craft so creators can fashion their work into what they intend it to be."

"I get it!" you exclaim, actually getting it. "You're saying that we need to figure out what we want to do, work hard with the right focus to do it well, find out whether we did it well, and then, where we didn't do it well, work hard to do it better."

"By George," I exclaim, quoting 'enry 'iggins, "I believe she's got it."

"Okay," you say, excited that we are finally getting somewhere, "I accept that I need to do more than just read these chapters to improve. I need to practice, consider the work, get constructive feedback, then practice again, and continue to do so until I'm old and gray like you."

"Something like that," I mutter.

"My blindfold is off!" you declare. "And I'm going to drive cross-country toward my intended destination!"

"Good for you!" I exclaim.

"Um. So exactly how does this steering-wheel thingy work?"

As I noted at the end of the previous chapter, it's scary-simple, not too different from simply turning the wheel to the right to make the story go to the right, and at the end of this process you will become a Comics Panel Time-Master.

In the previous chapter, we corrected the misguided mindset that sequential art is like film, affirming that it should not be written like film because sequential art panels do not contain motion. Panels contain one or more frozen moments of time.

(If we *haven't* corrected this mindset, then read and reread Scott McCloud's *Understanding Comics,* as well as Part One on this topic, until your eyes bleed. Do not pass Go and do not collect a class credit to proceed beyond this point.)

> **SFX:** (sound of lone pissed-off screenwriter, who doesn't want to deal with the steep learning curve of understanding a new medium)
> STOMP STOMP STOMP
> **SFX:** (sound of same lone pissed-off screenwriter, slamming door on his way out)
> SLAM!

To keep focus, we're going to concentrate on the craft of comics writing instead of the quality of writing. Mixing the apples-and-oranges of clarity-and-quality would blur the lesson. Once we understand how to write clearly then we can concern ourselves with writing well.

Here's a progression of topics we're going to address in this and the next chapter:

- How images read inside sequential art panels;
- How time flows inside sequential art panels;
- Controlling time inside sequential art panels;
- Influencing how much time a reader spends on sequential art panels.

How images read inside sequential art panels
(and why it's important that I be pedantic)

Begin with the following mantra, the scary-simple truth, and never stop repeating it or taking it into consideration: elements inside panels read from left to right.

There are a ton of terrific tricks that can pull the eye in different directions—Brian Bendis is a master of them all—but the important thing to remember, the critical thing to understand, is that these tricks pull the eye *away* from reading left to right...because, in our culture, we read from left to right.

Right-to-left-reading Asian manga originated in another culture, a culture that reads from right to left, so if you wish to work in this discipline reverse the directionality for page turning, page flow, panel flow, and balloon placements.

The real concern is the insidious and stubborn trend in Direct Market comics for word balloons to read inside panels from top to bottom. For example, the first balloon to read in a panel might be on the upper right and the next one in sequence would be on the lower left. This has never been an intuitive way to read comics. It is the decades-old result of artists not placing characters inside panels from left to right, even though that's the order in which scripts indicated the characters should speak.

When this practice began, whether the result of crushing deadlines, where there wasn't time to have pages redrawn or artists refusing to redraw panels because they liked the compositions, editors and letterers were forced to place the balloons in an order that did not read from left to right, so they put them where they could, hoping the reader would figure it out and shift from reading left-to-right to top-to-bottom.

At first, reading these oddly placed balloons didn't make sense. Reading from left to right, characters responded (in the lower left-hand corner) to questions or comments that hadn't yet been asked or stated (in the upper right-hand corner). After this initial confusion, readers read the balloons in the reverse order, now from top to bottom, and the balloons suddenly made sense. Thereafter, when left-to-right reading didn't immediately track readers shifted to top-to-bottom reading. This became a new way to read comics, a legitimate Direct Market alternative.

Then it became more prevalent, accepted, the new natural.

But it isn't natural. This is an entirely learned reading order, which is specific to U.S. Direct Market comics, and it confuses readers outside the Direct Market comics industry.

If you wish to continue writing or drawing comics with this culturally inbred conceit, please consider the following cautionary tale.

Once upon a time, there was an editor who is still fairly well known in the Direct Market comics industry.

This editor looked at a lettered page and asked for two balloons to be moved.

The letterer said, "But the balloons read from left to right. If we make that change they'll read from right to left."

"No," the editor said, "they'll read from top to bottom. This is the

Direct Market. In the Direct Market we read balloons from top to bottom, not left to right."

Yes, he empirically stated that balloons are not read from left to right and insisted on the changes, which the letterer made.

It's a very sad story with a very sad ending.

The comic panel died as a result of malpractice.

In fairness, I've never encountered another editor who mouthed such a preposterous mandate, but a recounting of this exchange reveals the extent to which top-to-bottom panel reading has permeated the Direct Market comics culture.

If you don't care that people outside the Direct Market may not be able to read your comics the way you intend them to be read, then by all means continue writing this way.

SFX: (sound of lone pissed-off Direct Market comics creator, who doesn't like the way he reads comics to be criticized)
STOMP STOMP STOMP
SFX: (sound of same lone pissed-off Direct Market comics creator, slamming door on his way out)
SLAM!

Here's what you should take from this discussion: we read from left to right.

We read books from left to right, spreads from left to right, pages from left to right, panels from left to right, and balloons from left to right.

If you remember and apply this to all things we're about to discuss you will have the makings of a true Comics Panel Time-Master.

Again, how do we read panels?

Correct, from left to right.

This is one of my few requisites in working with creators. Unless creators can intentionally redirect the way we read the panel or page, ala Brian Bendis, the flow of art and balloons inside panels must read from left to right.

Never once has an artist I've worked with objected to this requirement. Every one of them agreed this is how panels are supposed to read, which makes it all the more surprising that most don't get it consistently right, at least not at first. Eventually, with note after repetitive thumbnails note, they come to understand that if the elements inside panels don't flow from left to right I will ask for a layout revision until the end of time.

See why I keep repeating myself? Unless your name is Brian Bendis or you're just as good as he is at manipulating the way we review a comic panel and page, there are no exceptions. Ever.

How do we read panels?

Correct, from left to right.

Here's a sad truth: "We read from left to right" is so obvious, so basic, so ingrained, that many of you will forget to apply it to every aspect of your sequential artwork. Even after this pedantic plea many of you will still not consider it to be your most important editorial tool for becoming a Comics Panel Time-Master.

Do you want to really understand how this medium works?

Do you want to swim effortlessly through this medium the way Scrooge McDuck swims through the money in his bin?

If so, you need to get really anal about this.

You need to become obsessive about this.

"Left to right reading" needs to become second nature, needs to be so ingrained in your sequential art psyche that it pains you to see it abused. If you do not embrace this core concept you will never master the sequential art form, you will never become a Comics Panel Time-Master.

Never.

How do we read panels?

Correct, from left to right.

How time flows in a sequential art panel

Let's explore my oft-repeated phrase: panels contain one or more frozen moments of time.

Here's a description of one frozen moment of time: Johnny Action Jr. is in mid-leap over the picket fence, fiercely racing to stop two pintsized bullies who've pinned a frightened Boy Scout to the lawn. Having turned to see Johnny rushing toward them, Bully #1 is alarmed; Bully #2 is more concerned with demolishing the Boy Scout, his arm cocked back, his fist clenched, ready to deliver a punishing blow to the Boy Scout's face. The frightened Boy Scout anticipates the blow, wincing with his eyes clenched shut. Inside the house behind them, an Angry Little Old Lady leans out her kitchen window, brandishing a rolling pin, calling for the bullies to leave her grandson alone.

For the sake of simplicity, we'll skip specific visual layout direction and trust that the panel will be large enough to contain everything that's described. (We'll discuss later the problem of writing more stuff into a panel than can comfortably fit.)

This panel is a snapshot of a single moment.

It can be drawn.

It is described from left to right.

That's the first thing to consider when writing or rewriting a panel.

Where you consciously describe panel elements in your script from left to right you'll be setting up, in that description, the order in which you wish the elements to be placed, as well as the order in which you intend them to be viewed by the comics reader.

I don't want this most important point lost amid others crying for attention.

If comic script panel descriptions are consistently written from left to right, meaning that you mention the characters and describe the flow of elements from left to right, and note at the beginning of the script that this is your intention, it will be clear to artists how you think panels should be drawn. From this point of clarity artists will be able to consistently interpret intention. Even if artists end up not drawing panels as described, they will still have worked from your intention, rather than their misinterpretation.

This approach to writing panel descriptions also gives artists information, which they can use as a foundation for query.

For example: a script shows Character #1 on the left, speaking first, and Character #2 on the right, speaking second. The next panel is written as a reverse angle of the previous image, with Character #1 *still* speaking first and Character #2 *still* speaking second.

Do you see the mistake?

Take some time, come to a conclusion, write it down.

Done? Good.

Here's the problem: A reverse angle of the art would flip the positions of the two characters, putting Character #2 on the left and Character #1 right. Since balloons read from left to right, how does the letterer show Character #1 speaking first and Character #2 speaking second?

This classic scripting error leaves the artist, editor, and/or letterer to sort it out.

This problem is quantitative not qualitative. The discussion with the writer won't be about "like" and "don't like." It'll be about "works" and "doesn't work" or "clear" and "unclear." In short, it allows for a simple discussion about goals and intention. It allows the writer or artist or editor to fix the script before it becomes the letterer's problem.

This is ideal for a collaborative effort.

This approach to writing panel descriptions with clearly written objectives also gives writers and editors a tool with which to critique layouts. Just like the script examination above, it becomes less about whether an artist got the angle right and more about whether the editorial objective of the panel was achieved.

Forget whether writers—even writers whose work you love—write this way or not. That defense is just a lazy way out of having to do your job of communicating intention to the artist.

SFX: (sound of lone pissed-off comics writer, who doesn't like to be told what to do when it interferes with his personal style)
STOMP STOMP STOMP
SFX: (sound of same lone pissed-off comics writer, slamming the door on his way out)
SLAM!

A hand rises in back.

"Yes?" I ask.

"If professional writers don't necessarily write their panels from left to right, how can you say this is the way to write?"

Great question.

First, not all professional comics writers are Comics Panel Time-Masters. Writers get work for a variety of reasons and their quality level of sequential art craft is only one of them.

Next, and more importantly, I'm not saying this is the way to write comics. I'm saying this is a way to clearly write your panel descriptions, which is the point.

It's your choice how to write panel descriptions. It's your choice what to put into them. I'm merely offering a method that allows for consistent interpretation by artists and editors.

If you work with artists who are terrific at interpreting your current approach to writing, I'm happy for you. If artists don't mind (or prefer) figuring out the order of elements inside panels, I'm happy for you. If editors don't mind working on your behalf to clarify how to deal with ambiguous panel descriptions or don't mind asking artists for layout revisions to fix issues caused by your scripts, I'm happy for you.

If you can make great comics without having to apply any aspect of what we're discussing in *Comics Creator Prep*, I'm still happy for you.

That's your business, not mine.

But if you discover your intention isn't being interpreted well, I've offered some tools with which you may be able to modify your approach and achieve your goals. Like all advice, this is a compass not a rulebook.

For those of you still with us, there's a major advantage to this approach to writing panel description: it clearly orders your intention for a panel. The more you deviate from this, the harder it's going to be for you to keep straight the different frozen moments of time in a panel.

A hand rises again in back.

"Yes?" I ask.

"You just mentioned more than one frozen moment of time in a panel, but you previously described your example as having only *one* frozen moment."

"I did, didn't I?" I respond. "Good catch."

Yes, the image I described is currently one frozen moment.

What happens when we add dialogue?

JOHNNY ACTION JR.: I'll save you, frightened Boy Scout!

BULLY #1: You can't save everybody, Johnny Action Jr.!

BULLY #2: That's right! And I'm going to deliver my punishing blow to this frightened Boy Scout's face before Johnny Action Jr. can reach us!

FRIGHTENED BOY SCOUT: I can't bear a punishing blow!

FRIGHTENED BOY SCOUT: My grandma hates having to scrub the bloodstains out of my clothes!

ANGRY OLD LADY: That's right, you meanies!

ANGRY OLD LADY: New & Improved Super-Suds isn't any better than the crap they were supposed to be improving!

Each character in this frozen moment of time now has dialogue. What is the result?

To state the obvious, where the image is a frozen moment, the dialogue in each balloon takes place over a span of time, beginning with the first word and ending with the last. Less obvious, the balloons point to characters throughout this frozen moment, yet the contents of the balloons aren't from the same time span. They aren't simultaneous; everybody is not speaking at once. They read one after another, in sequence, with characters responding to what characters previously said. In short, the comic panel is multidimensional, with the visual representing one frozen moment of time, and the balloons representing many spans of time.

So how many different spans of time do we have in this panel?

Take your time, write down the answer, commit yourself, and imagine *Jeopardy* music while doing so.

Time's up.

The answer: Five to seven, arguably.

That's right, there are at least five spans of time, roughly one span for each of the characters speaking, though a case could be made that the second balloons attributed to Frightened Boy Scout and Angry Old Lady add two additional spans, making the count seven. (Later, we'll discuss connecting balloons and the additional beats they create.)

In which direction do the spans of time move across the panel?

The hand in the back goes up again.

"Yes?" I ask.

"I don't get the question."

"Where is the earliest frozen moment of time in the panel?" I ask.

"Johnny Action Jr.," the student answers.

"Correct," I reply. "Where's Johnny Action Jr. in the panel?"

"On the left," the student answers.

"Correct," I reply. "Where's the next frozen moment of time in the panel?"

"Bully #1," the student answers.

"Correct," I reply. "Why?"

"Because he responds to what Johnny Action Jr. says."

"Correct," I reply. "Where is the next frozen moment of time in the panel?"

"That would be Bully #2," the student answers.

"Why not the Frightened Boy Scout?" I ask, probing.

"Because," the student replies, "the Frightened Boy Scout responds to Bully #2's comment. If his balloon was placed before Bully #2's balloon, then the balloons wouldn't read in the correct order."

"Good," I say. "So, again, in which direction do the spans of time move across the panel?"

"From left to right," the student answers.

Yes, that's how this panel reads, from left to right, from the earliest span of time to the latest.

Let's try a really simple image.

DESCRIPTION: Johnny Action Jr. has delivered a fierce blow and Bully #2 is flying back from having been hit.

It's one frozen moment of time. Let's add dialogue.

JOHNNY ACTION JR: Take this, Bully Boy!
SFX: (point where the fierce blow was struck) POW!
BULLY #2: OW! That smarts!

The panel now contains three spans of time: the moment before the blow was struck, the moment when the blow was struck, signified by the POW, and the moment of Bully #2 reacting to having been clobbered.

And they read from left to right.

Let's test this left-to-right-reading theory.

What if we flip this image and keep the word balloons and SFX in the same places? Here's how it will look and read:

DESCRIPTION: Bully #2 is flying back from a fierce blow that's been delivered by Johnny Action Jr.

BULLY #2: OW! That smarts!
SFX: (point where the fierce blow was struck) POW!
JOHNNY ACTION JR: Take this, Bully Boy!

It doesn't work, does it? The POW and Johnny Action Junior's line takes place before Bully #2 has been hit, so we're going back in time as we progress, and it doesn't read well.

But something interesting happened: the image can be drawn.

Is it possible it could work without using those particular word balloons and SFX? If so, how?

Take your time, write down the answer, commit yourself, and imagine Jeopardy music while doing so.

Time's up.

Answer: it can work.

Here's how:

DESCRIPTION: Bully #2 is flying back from a fierce blow that's been delivered by Johnny Action Jr.

BULLY #2: OW! That smarts!
JOHNNY ACTION JR: Not as much as Grannie's rolling pin is

going to hurt you, Bully Boy!

In this version, we made Bully #2 flying back the first span of time, eliminated the SFX, and Johnny Action Jr. is reacting to what Bully #2 says, making it the latest span of time.

So how does time flow in this panel?

It flows as it's supposed to, from left to right, from the earliest span of time to the latest.

So we've learned that we can flip our images from "action & reaction" to "reaction & action," but we still need to make sure that any corresponding dialogue sets the earliest span of time on the left, and following balloons, if any, move progressively forward in time to the right.

"So, regardless of how the frozen moment is portrayed, a comics creator *does* need to make certain that the description reads...

"...what's next, class?"

"FROM LEFT TO RIGHT!" the classroom shouts in chorus, completing the thought as though they'd just had it pounded like a nail through their skulls.

"Very good," I reply, my job done.

Now that we know how panels read, as well as how time flows within them, we're armed with the necessary tools to bend time to our will.

As an exercise, write three panels as you wish them to be perceived, with your earliest intended span of time on the left and the latest intended span of time on the right. Then flip each panel, just as you would a picture, and describe it anew so the right is now the left and the left is now the right.

After you've written the panels and flipped them, add dialogue to each, with the realization that, by flipping them, you've chosen a different span of time on the left as your starting point.

A hand in back goes up.

"Yes?" I ask.

"Do we have to add every detail to the description?"

"Of course not," I reply. "Much of what does or doesn't go into description is up to the writer, depending on intention and how much is to be left to the artist's imagination."

For the sake of this exercise, though, please keep your descriptions relatively simple, holding only to the requisite elements, such as location, characters, and objects. We don't need to know that Granny has a wart on her bum.

When writing flipped images from the originals, meaning panels that start with the last images on the right of the previous versions now presented as the first images on the left, use your command of English to make certain that the elements are described in the exact reverse order. If they are not written in the *exact* reverse order, you're not properly flipping the images in your head or on paper, which means they may not end up being perceived as you intend.

For example:

IMAGE 1. In the hallway, a private eye is standing just outside an open office doorway, looking through it toward a desk, but he's paying more attention to the blonde goddess who's sitting behind it and smiling at him.

IMAGE 1 flipped. A smiling blonde goddess sits behind an office desk, looking through an open office doorway at a private eye, who watches her from the hallway.

See how each element is mentioned in the exact reverse order? Doing this well means recognizing that the ordering of elements is more important than jotting down the panel elements quickly. It may take longer to write this way, but your intention will be clearer to the editor and artist. Much clearer.

Now it's your turn. Please begin.

Tick tock. Tick tock.

Done?

Good. Now walk away, come back later, and consider your work before proceeding to the answers presented by your classmates.

Tick tock. Tick tock.

Done?

Good.

Here are three classroom answers, with images and corresponding balloons:

1. A rocket ship is zooming toward Earth.

ROCKET SHIP: This is going to hurt you more than it will hurt me.

EARTH: I hope you hit a volcano!

2. Hansel and Gretel break a piece of siding off the witch's gingerbread house. The wicked witch stares at them from around a corner.
HANSEL: Well, that was a snap. Do you think the owner will mind?
GRETEL: Who would build a gingerbread house without anticipating the occasional nibble?
WITCH THOT: One good nibble deserves another.

3. Mom and Dad sit on a couch, lecturing their son, Johnny, who's responding to what they say, even though he is watching the videogame he's playing on TV.

MOM: Johnny! If you don't listen to me, I'm going to take that remote away from you!
DAD: Just like she took away mine.
JOHNNY: She'll only get *my* remote by prying it from my cold, dead fingers.

Let's stop here for a spot quiz.

QUESTION: Does each of these panels read well?

Please write down your answer, and continue.

ANSWER: There is a problem with the first sentence of number two. "Break" is an action verb. Hansel and Gretel could *just* be snapping it off, and that would require the artist to show some exertion and corresponding body language. They also could have already broken it off and be standing more casually with pieces of siding in their hands. These are two different visuals and either might be fine, but the writer's intention is unclear, because the action verb creates ambiguity.

The deciding factor is Hansel's first line, "Well, that was a snap." This implies that the siding has already been broken off, that it was easy, that it was already accomplished. If we showed them still exerting themselves, then this balloon would read ironically. See how important it is that description and intention be written clearly?

Here's a revision:

2. Hansel and Gretel have each just broken off a piece of siding from the witch's gingerbread house. The wicked witch stares at them from around a corner.

HANSEL: Well, that was a snap. Do you think the owner will mind?
GRETEL: Who would build a gingerbread house without anticipating the occasional nibble?
WITCH THOT: One good nibble deserves another.

Here are the images flipped, with new word balloons:

1. Earth is about to be hit by a rocket ship that is zooming toward it.

EARTH: I hope you hit a volcano!
ROCKET SHIP: I hit whatever I aim for.

2. A wicked witch stares from around a corner of her gingerbread house toward Gretel and Hansel, each having just broken off a piece of siding.

WITCH THOT: One good nibble deserves another.
GRETEL: Why do I get the feeling that this might be a mistake?
HANSEL: What's the worst that could happen?

3. There's a videogame on the TV, which Johnny is concentrating on, even though he's responding to Dad and Mom, who sit next to him on a couch and lecture at him.

JOHNNY: She'll only get *my* remote by prying it from my cold, dead fingers.

DAD: That might be just what happens, son.
MOM: Listen to your father, Johnny. I may be old but I haven't forgotten my ninja assassin training.

Do all the original and flipped panels read well to you? Please review them again carefully, write down your thoughts about whether they pass or fail, and why.
Take your time. Be certain.
Tick tock. Tick tock.
Done?
Good.

Yes, they all read well. Before and after the flip, the dialogue and revised dialogue all advance correctly from left to right, and each balloon fits editorially with the corresponding image it points to.
A hand rises from the back row.

"Yes?" I ask.

"You tricked us!" the student complains. "Before, there was always something wrong with something."

I confess.

I wanted to see if you could look at these examples and be confident they were okay. Looking at something and recognizing that it is good enough can be harder than spotting mistakes.

If you determined the examples read well, you pass.

If you determined something didn't read well, aesthetics aside, weren't sure, or second-guessed yourself into thinking you must have missed something, then you're not yet comfortable enough with knowing what does and doesn't work. That's okay, though. You'll work through it, become comfortable, and get there.

Now, let's review an aspect of the flipped panels and their corresponding dialogues. In each example, note how flipping images allows us to make the last balloons in the first versions the first balloons in the second versions, thus allowing us to advance the conversations from those points?

While you may not choose to use any previously written dialogue in a flipped image, I demonstrated this potential in all three versions because it can come in handy, especially if you need to eliminate panels, combine panels, or start dialogue earlier than originally planned, and still retain a key or beloved balloon or caption.

You now have a working knowledge of how to write panels from left to write, to work with and manipulate the passage of time that occurs with corresponding dialogue and captions.

You've passed your first major test toward becoming...a Comics Panel Time-Master!

Chapter 5

The Comics Panel Time-Master
(or why creators should stop trying to write comics as movies on paper)

Part Three:
How To Direct Time In Comics

WARNING: We're about to jump into the pool. Those of you who have not yet fully absorbed the lessons of *Chapters Three* and *Four*, turn back now and reread them until the gauge in your brain reads *PROCESSED*. Otherwise, possible side effects may include throbbing headaches, confusion, loss of ability to specify and articulate your points of confusion, more confusion, anger over confusion, self-loathing over still more confusion, and a belief that I'm making this stuff more complicated than it really is (because you did not fully absorb the lessons of *Chapters Three* and *Four* until the gage in your brain read *PROCESSED*).

Ready?

"Wait!" you cry. "I need to prepare myself."

"Fine, we'll start with one big toe dipped into the water and summarize to get our bearings.

"What was *Chapter Three* about?" I ask.

"We discussed how sequential art isn't film, with a specific focus on how the passage of time plays an integral part in how the two media are different."

Check.

"And *Chapter Four*?" I ask.

"We covered how comics read and how frozen images and spans of time inside panels progress from left to right."

"What was the purpose?" I ask, harkening back to the follow-up discussions of *Chapter Four.*

"Since most beginning comics writers use continuous time in their panel descriptions, the exercises were designed to get us to think in terms of writing panels as a progression from their earliest to latest spans of time."

"That's right," I say. "Writing from left to right. Writing more than one frozen span of time. Writing them consecutively. Reversing what was written so both directions can be fully understood and applied."

The purpose was to set these fundamental sequential art tools permanently in your toolbox so that you'll be able to bend sequential art storytelling to your will, to write stuff that is less likely to be misunderstood, in short, to write with intention.

Welcome to the deep end of the pool.

As previously noted, a sequential art panel can be read in a glimpse or it can take a significant amount of time to be absorbed, and you already possess the power to determine which it can be. It's just like having a remote control that will slow down or speed up how a reader pays attention to your panel or page.

"I can control time?" you ask, astounded.

You can control how the reader *spends* time, which is almost as cool. Actually, your comics already determine how much time readers spend looking at a panel or page, but in their creation you may not have been aware of this particular result of your writing or art because you weren't manipulating that result with intention.

In this chapter, that's exactly what we'll be doing.

Let's consider the elements that slow down the way we read a panel.

"Wait!" you exclaim. "Does every element inside a panel slow down the reader?"

The major ones, anything that captures our attention, like a prominently placed character, object, implicit action, balloon, and caption: yes.

The minor ones, like a cross-hatched section of the darkest reaches of a deserted alley, the second building in from the right of a cityscape, or an unremarkable face in a large crowd: no.

Where is the dividing line between the two? It slides.

It probably slides toward things that stand out in each panel, which is an added incentive for making the script clear so the artist will know what's important.

"In other words," you ask, already knowing the answer, "knowing what we need to focus on will help us write clearly and with intention?"

"Yes," I say, "but let's do some crawling before trying to zoom like a rocket ship."

A blank page takes the least amount of time to absorb. If we divide the page into four panels, even blank ones, the time it takes to consider their number slows us down. To look at it another way, each one of the four takes individual consideration, which translates into time spent, even if that amount of time is infinitesimal.

It's still a pause, consideration, time, a beat.

It's a beat you created.

Somebody will probably note that if a page is evenly divided into eight, sixteen, or thirty-two equal panels, it may take the same amount time, at a glance, to note they're all empty.

Yes, that's true, too. There's a point where repetition and monotony become an immediately perceivable pattern that will take equal amounts of time to absorb. We'll address this later when we discuss putting panels in sequence, but please don't allow this variance to take your eye off the ball on which we're currently focusing.

For now, consider one fact: Each element of consideration takes *some* consideration.

It's stunningly simple. Adding elements of consideration affects how long each reader will take to consider a panel or page.

Increase the number of elements and you've increased the cumulative amount of reader consideration.

Decrease the number of elements and you've decreased the cumulative amount of consideration.

$1 + 1 = 2.$

$2 - 1 = 1.$

One variable is beyond our control: how much *specific* time it takes a reader to consider something, because everybody reads at a different pace.

We can't make any balloon, panel, or page take two seconds to read or observe. I'm a slow reader and like to look at a lot of different stuff; it could take me three seconds.

For this reason, we must simplify our measuring stick to "adding elements" simply taking "more time," and "subtracting elements" taking "less time."

Let's review a list of elements that will affect the reader's consideration of a panel:

- Prominently placed characters;
- Prominently placed objects;
- Frozen actions, like swooping lines behind a character who's supposed to be running or flying, or a fist that's supposed to be smashing, which lead our eye from one place in the panel to another;
- Compositions, which are intended to lead our eye from one place to another;
- Word balloons, captions, sound effects, prominently placed signage, anything we're directed to read;
- Anything that utilizes drawing or color to capture our attention.

We previously discussed a building in a cityscape as not being something that would normally catch our attention.

What if that building is the only one with lights on?

What if, in an unlit cityscape, there is only one window in that building with a light on?

You get the point: it draws our attention, our consideration, takes time, adds a beat.

You can have as many or as few of these elements of consideration as you wish in a panel.

If you're a creator who plans ahead, it's important to recognize how much relative consideration you wish the reader to spend on a panel, a page, or in a story.

If you're an intuitive first-draft writer, it's important to be able to determine later how much reader consideration your panel might take, within the context of your editorial goals. This way you'll know whether to lengthen, shorten, or maintain that amount of reader consideration.

That's all.

"That's all?!!!" you exclaim. "Your big revelation for us to become Comics Panel Time-Masters is to simply consider how much important stuff we should put in a panel so people will spend more or less time reading it?"

"Yup," I say. "However you get there, you need to make sure the finished panel reflects your intention."

"Will you give us some examples?" you ask.

"I'm glad you asked," I respond.

Please review the following panel descriptions, and come to some

personal determination about how much additional consideration each
added element would require, once that panel is drawn.

Johnny Action Jr. is in mid-leap over the picket fence.

*   *   *

Johnny Action Jr. is in mid-leap over the picket fence, fiercely
racing toward a beaten Boy Scout who lies on the lawn.

*   *   *

Johnny Action Jr. is in mid-leap over the picket fence, fiercely
racing to stop the pintsized bully who has pinned a frightened Boy
Scout to the lawn. Having turned to see Johnny rushing toward
them, Bully #1 is alarmed.

*   *   *

Johnny Action Jr. is in mid-leap over the picket fence, fiercely racing
to stop the two pintsized bullies who've pinned a frightened Boy
Scout to the lawn. Having turned to see Johnny rushing toward
them, Bully #1 is alarmed; Bully #2 is more concerned with
demolishing the Boy Scout, his arm cocked back, his fist clenched,
ready to deliver a punishing blow to the face. The frightened Boy
Scout anticipates the blow, wincing, his eyes clenched shut.

*   *   *

Johnny Action Jr. is in mid-leap over the picket fence, fiercely racing
to stop the two pintsized bullies who've pinned a frightened Boy
Scout to the lawn. Having turned to see Johnny rushing toward
them, Bully #1 is alarmed; Bully #2 is more concerned with
demolishing the Boy Scout, his arm cocked back, his fist clenched,
ready to deliver a punishing blow to the face. The frightened Boy
Scout anticipates the blow, wincing, his eyes clenched shut. Inside
the house behind them, an Angry Little Old Lady leans out her
kitchen window, brandishing a rolling pin, calling for the bullies to
leave her grandson alone.

*   *   *

Note that each successive description doesn't only take longer to read
than its predecessor. Each added element increases important content,
which adds an additional beat, and thus requires additional reader
consideration.

Now, let's add more beats by adding dialogue.

DESCRIPTION: Johnny Action Jr. is in mid-leap over the picket fence.

JOHNNY ACTION JR.: I'll help you, frightened Boy Scout!

* * *

DESCRIPTION: Johnny Action Jr. is in mid-leap over the picket fence, fiercely racing toward a beaten Boy Scout who lies on the lawn.

JOHNNY ACTION JR.: I'll help you, frightened Boy Scout!
FRIGHTENED BOY SCOUT: Man—I really got my ass kicked!

* * *

DESCRIPTION: Johnny Action Jr. is in mid-leap over the picket fence, fiercely racing to stop the pintsized bully who has pinned a frightened Boy Scout to the lawn. Having turned to see Johnny rushing toward them, Bully #1 is alarmed.

JOHNNY ACTION JR.: I'll help you, frightened Boy Scout!
BULLY #1: You can't help everybody, Johnny Action Jr.!
FRIGHTENED BOY SCOUT: I can't bear to get my ass kicked!

* * *

DESCRIPTION: Johnny Action Jr. is in mid-leap over the picket fence, fiercely racing to stop the two pintsized bullies who've pinned a frightened Boy Scout to the lawn. Having turned to see Johnny rushing toward them, Bully #1 is alarmed; Bully #2 is more concerned with demolishing the Boy Scout, his arm cocked back, his fist clenched, ready to deliver a punishing blow to the face. The frightened Boy Scout anticipates the blow, wincing, his eyes clenched shut.

JOHNNY ACTION JR.: I'll help you, frightened Boy Scout!
BULLY #1: You can't help everybody, Johnny Action Jr.!
BULLY #2: That's right! And I'm going to kick this frightened Boy Scout's ass before he can reach us!
FRIGHTENED BOY SCOUT: I can't bear to get my ass kicked!

* * *

DESCRIPTION: Johnny Action Jr. is in mid-leap over the picket fence, fiercely racing to stop the two pintsized bullies who've pinned a frightened Boy Scout to the lawn. Having turned to see Johnny rushing toward them, Bully #1 is alarmed; Bully #2 is more concerned with demolishing the Boy Scout, his arm cocked back, his fist clenched, ready to deliver a punishing blow to the face. The frightened Boy Scout anticipates the blow, wincing, his eyes clenched shut. Inside the house behind them, an Angry Little Old Lady leans out her kitchen window, brandishing a rolling pin, calling for the bullies to leave her grandson alone.

JOHNNY ACTION JR.: I'll help you, frightened Boy Scout!
BULLY #1: You can't help everybody, Johnny Action Jr.!
BULLY #2: That's right! And I'm going to kick this frightened Boy Scout's ass before he can reach us!
FRIGHTENED BOY SCOUT: I can't bear to get my ass kicked!
ANGRY OLD LADY: Go away, you meanies!

*   *   *

Now let's add some additional balloons to really slow it down.

DESCRIPTION: Johnny Action Jr. is in mid-leap over the picket fence, fiercely racing to stop the two pintsized bullies who've pinned a frightened Boy Scout to the lawn. Having turned to see Johnny rushing toward them, Bully #1 is alarmed; Bully #2 is more concerned with demolishing the Boy Scout, his arm cocked back, his fist clenched, ready to deliver a punishing blow to the face. The frightened Boy Scout anticipates the blow, wincing, his eyes clenched shut. Inside the house behind them, an Angry Little Old Lady leans out her kitchen window, brandishing a rolling pin, calling for the bullies to leave her grandson alone.

JOHNNY ACTION JR.: I'll help you, frightened Boy Scout!
BULLY #1: You can't help everybody, Johnny Action Jr.!
BULLY #2: That's right! And I'm going to kick this frightened Boy Scout's ass before he can reach us!
FRIGHTENED BOY SCOUT: I can't bear to get my ass kicked!
FRIGHTENED BOY SCOUT: My grandma hates having to scrub the bloodstains out of my clothes!
ANGRY OLD LADY: That's right, you meanies!
ANGRY OLD LADY: New & Improved Super-Suds isn't any better than the crap they were supposed to be improving!

*   *   *

As you read through each of these panel descriptions, you saw each additional balloon added a beat, some longer or shorter, based on the number of words used.

For those of you looking for a note to post next to your computer screen, this is it: *added complication compounds consideration.*

It's almost so obvious you must wonder why I'm even bothering to mention it.

Would it surprise you to know that too many creators would write that last panel description, the one with all that dialogue, and still believe their story was moving like a bullet train?

Any idea why that might be?

Take a moment, consider the question, and write down your answer, just to commit yourself.

Ready? Okay here's the answer.

Look at all that *"action"!*

Johnny Action Jr. is leaping a fence, a Boy Scout is getting pulverized, and Granny's waving a rolling pin!

Action! Action! Action!

Except there isn't any action in sequential art, and sequential art isn't film.

It doesn't matter how much implicit action there is in the panel. What matters is how much *important* stuff there is to consider, the quantity of which speeds up reading or slows it down, and putting that stuff in or leaving it out is up to you.

Now, you can do it by accident (by not caring or paying attention) or you can do it on purpose.

If you do it by accident, the result will be, not coincidentally, accidental.

If you do it on purpose, you will be a Comics Panel Time-Master.

See how neatly we came full circle to the point?

"So that's it?" you ask. "I read the chapters and now I'm a Comics Panel Time-Master!"

Um...nope, sorry.

You need to practice this stuff.

No practice and no constant consideration lead to no Comics Panel Time-Master gold star on your report card.

"Sounds like there's another assignment that's going to take me away from my videogames," you mutter, just loud enough for me to hear.

"You bet there is," I say, brandishing the cheeriest of smiles.

Our assignment for this chapter is as follows:

Write a panel containing a foreground and background element. Read it. Consider it.

What follows may read repetitively, but please don't just scan it and say, "I get the idea." Take each paragraph to heart, and follow the directions. If you do this, you really will absorb the point of this instruction.

Add one character to the panel, doing whatever you wish, to the panel. Read it. Consider it.

Then add another character. Read it. Consider it.

Add another character. Read it. Consider it.

Add another character. Read it. Consider it.

Add a last and fifth character to the panel. Read it. Consider it.

Note that it took longer to absorb what was in each successive panel.

Now add a balloon, with a short sentence, and point it to one of the characters. Read it. Consider it.

Add another balloon, with a short sentence. Read it. Consider it.

Add another balloon, with a short sentence. Read it. Consider it.

Add another balloon, with a short sentence. Read it. Consider it.

Add another balloon, with a short sentence. Read it. Consider it.

Note that it took longer to absorb what was in each successive panel.

Now add more dialogue to one of the balloons, at least another sentence. Read it. Consider it.

Add more dialogue to a different balloon, at least another sentence. Read it. Consider it.

Add more dialogue to a different balloon, at least another sentence. Read it. Consider it.

Add more dialogue to a different balloon, at least another sentence. Read it. Consider it.

Add more dialogue to a different balloon, at least another sentence. Read it. Consider it.

Note that it took longer to absorb what was in each successive panel.

Now split one of the balloons into two balloons, in a way that makes sense. Read it. Consider it.

Split another balloon into two balloons, in a way that makes sense. Read it. Consider it.

Split another balloon into two balloons, in a way that makes sense. Read it. Consider it.

Split another balloon into two balloons, in a way that makes sense. Read it. Consider it.

Split another balloon into two balloons, in a way that makes sense. Read it. Consider it.

Which set took longer to read, the groupings with the split balloons, or the previous version with the dialogue grouped together in the single balloons?

Some readers hardly notice this, can never really differentiate, but the version that takes longer to read is the split version. Even though shorter dialogue groupings are easier to read, splitting balloons requires our eyes to move from one balloon to another, so it still adds a beat.

Further, two balloons connected by a stem read more quickly than two separate balloons pointing to the same character. Not having the eye drawn directly to the second balloon by a connecting stem adds a beat, albeit not a very long one. The farther you move the two disconnected balloons from each other correspondingly increases the length of the beat.

Some years ago, I once got into an argu...um, discussion with an editor about this. My script called for separated balloons, and the letterer connected them with a stem. I noted that this had lost a beat on a gag. The editor thought I was crazy. On this topic, he's probably right, though I might skew more toward the word *obsessive*.

It's probably not important to the fate of the universe that the stem stayed.

What is important, though probably still not to the fate of the universe, is that I knew and cared how a reader would perceive the work.

What do you believe is important?

If it's to write and draw with intention, if it's to become a Comics Panel Time-Master, this is what it takes: consciously considering how each elemental option will affect the pace of each panel.

"So that's the trick to becoming a Comics Panel Time-Master?" you ask. "Simply figuring out how much consideration I want a reader to spend inside a panel, then making sure I put in some combination of stuff that correlates to this?"

"Yes," I reply.

"But how do I know what's too much or too little?"

"Well," I answer, "that depends on the goals of the panel in relation to the ones that precede and follow it, all, of course, within the additional context of the page and the story.

"This is why we're learning to walk before we blast off in a rocket ship."

"Well, if we don't yet know the context of the panel, what's the point in doing the exercise?" you ask.

"Because when you actually *know* how much consideration you *need* from a reader in a panel, for whatever reason you need it, you'll know why you're writing what you're writing."

"By adding or subtracting stuff, whether they're balloons or characters or implicit actions?" you ask.

"Yes," I reply, liking that I get to answer with only one word.

"These are my tools for crafting, with intention, the time a reader takes to consider a panel?"

"Yes," I reply, repeating myself again, still liking it.

"That way I can review what I wrote or drew and make an estimated determination about whether I accomplished my goal for that panel...or not?"

"Yes," I reply, nodding to emphasize the point.

"So now I have the rudimentary sequential art tools I need to become a Comics Panel Time-Master?"

"Yes."

"But knowing the tools isn't the same as knowing how to use them, is it?"

"No," I say, happy to break the monotony.

"Thus the need, especially at first, for constantly examining my work in this context?"

"Yes," I say, for the final time. "Class dismissed."

"Yay!" everybody cries in unison.

"And don't forget to do your homework," I add.

"Boo!" everybody cries in unison.

CHAPTER 6

YOUR OWN PRIVATE WORMHOLE
PART 1: ALL THE TIME IN THE WORLD

"We're going to discuss what happens between panels," I announce boldly.

"You mean where nothing happens?" you ask, taken aback.

"Oh, something happens," I confirm, with confidence. "And if you combine this with what we learned about becoming Comics Panel Time-Masters, you'll have two of the most important tools necessary for thinking like comics creators instead of like filmmakers."

"You're going to make my head hurt again, aren't you?" you whine, wincing in anticipation.

Ignoring the question and yet confirming the result, I ask, "How many of you did your homework and became Comics Panel Time-Masters?"

Six thousand hands go up.

"Yay for the six thousand," I say. "This will be smooth sailing for you folks."

"What about the rest of us?" you ask.

"Whitecaps and gale warnings," I reply, already mourning the Lost Ones who didn't even think to bring life preservers for this deepest part of the pool.

In sequential art, we can jump from any time and place in one panel to any other time or place in the next panel.

It's like having your own private wormhole.

We make these jumps instinctively and don't even have to click our ruby slippers three times to get there.

However, utilizing this wormhole has become so automatic, so instinctive, that we spend too much time on cruise control. Worse, our cruise control is so-often set to the "think like a movie" setting we're not taking full advantage of the medium in which we're working.

This discussion has one goal: to switch your default setting to "think like a comic."

Just that.

And that's why I'm approaching the use of time between panels from a different direction.

I want to scramble how you currently use this tool. I want you to stop and consider its use *each and every time* until you've cast off the default setting of using it like film with CUT, FADE, DISSOLVE, or PAN.

For those of you crying out in dismay, don't worry, there's nothing wrong with using comics versions of CUT, FADE, DISSOLVE, or PAN, if they accomplish your sequential art storytelling goals, but to write with intention (a phrase you've read from me once or twice before) you need to open your toolbox wider and consider all the available sequential art storytelling tools. Then if you still choose to "think like a movie" at least you're doing so with intention.

To reach this point of consideration we need to understand and learn to control our ability to create a wormhole.

That means discussing the full range of options, and then we get to work on some creative writing exercises that will firm up those flabby sequential art muscles.

"Flabby?" you protest.

"Underdeveloped?" I rephrase, hoping to mollify.

"I suspect there's going to be more homework," you mumble.

"I suspect you're getting better at reading that crystal ball," I respond cheerfully.

Let's start by separating the use of time and space by working with one, then the other, then both.

One of the narrative strengths of the sequential art medium is that it allows you to travel seamlessly through time, to make the next panel in a sequence one second later or earlier, or a million years later or earlier. You can even keep it the same moment in time if that's what you wish. You can go any-when you want or need to in as few or as many panels as you like.

Sounds simple, doesn't it?

Yes, deceptively so, because it's easier to say than to do well.

Does it matter how much time passes between panels?

Often the answer will be "no," especially in a dialogue-driven sequence or, just as often, when you're delineating images from key moments of physical action.

In these cases, though, you're still passively determining how much time has passed between panels, but that's because it's not the thing on which you need a reader to focus, and that's okay.

However, sometimes it's critical for the reader to know that the gap between panels is the hour somebody is waiting in his cell for the moment when he'll be taken to the execution chamber, or the three minutes the egg in boiling water takes to be ready, or the million years that pass for an impatient pebble to move an inch.

When you have a time machine that allows you to intentionally determine the amount of time that passes between panels it's a valuable tool to keep near the top of your toolbox.

So let's play.

"Play?" you ask in wonder. "Like something that will be fun?"

"More like something that's really work," I reply. "But if you don't enjoy it then maybe it's time to pursue that career as a stockbroker."

I can't quite catch the mumbled two-word response.

We begin by advancing small measurements of time from panel to panel.

Let's start with a single panel that contains sixteen seconds: A man sits in a police station interrogation room. In the first balloon he thinks: "One second, two seconds, three seconds—when are these guys going to show up?" In the next balloon he thinks, "I can't take it anymore! It's been sixteen whole seconds!"

It's not elegant, but it's sixteen seconds, right?

And it is, of course, expository and silly, which is fine, if expository and silly is the intention.

Now let's use our wormhole on two panels, making their combined length of time sixteen seconds.

PANEL ONE: A man waits in a police station interrogation room. A caption reads: "12:30 a.m."

PANEL TWO: A caption reads: "Sixteen seconds later." The man is standing and screaming, "I can't take it anymore!"

The two panels clearly and seamlessly jump from one moment of time to the next. It's also pretty funny, if dramatically unbelievable.

Let's say it's important the reader believes the man can fall apart so quickly or at least feel the impact of passing time more dramatically. (Just to establish an editorial context for how it *could* be made more acceptable and dramatic to a reader, imagine some version of this scene being drawn by Will Eisner for *The Spirit*.)

To dramatize this man's weak-willed nature, imagine sixteen panels on a page. The first fifteen panels show him sitting in the same position, and a clock in the background advances a single second for each panel. At first he's confident and cocky, then becomes increasingly concerned, and finishes with torrents of fearful perspiration streaming around his wildly panicked eyes. Finally, in the last panel he's standing and screaming, "I can't take it anymore!"

We have shown, in sixteen story-seconds, a man transforming from confident and cocky into a frantic wreck. We believe it because we experienced each one of those grueling story-seconds.

Now let's make this sixteen seconds take even longer to review, which will help connect us to each agonizing second the man is experiencing.

Go to your sequential art toolbox and pull out your accredited Comics Panel Time-Master techniques.

Rather than using a background clock, something a reader may or may not pay close attention to, let's track the sixteen seconds in a series of captions, increasing the count by one second in each successive caption, and just to draw attention to what's different, each of the second-counts will print red, so the reader's eye will be drawn immediately to those number changes: "12:01:**01**", "2:01:**02**", etc. This addition slows down how we read the page. Read the caption; look at the art. Read the caption; look at the art. Read the caption; look at the art; etc.

If that's too clinical for your taste, use words instead of numbers in the caption box: One second. Two seconds. Three seconds. Etc. This takes a little longer to review than the version with numbers, albeit, not much longer...but longer is longer, and it would extend our perception of the man's increasing level of anxiety.

To really push the amount of time it takes to review the sixteen seconds of story these sixteen panels contain: continue using captions to count the seconds with words, continue showing the man's increasing anxiety, then add thought balloons in panels one through fifteen, with the man wondering why he was arrested, wondering whether they've discovered he didn't vote in the last election, wondering if they know he still has a thing for his first-grade teacher, wondering what the cops are going to do to him, wondering if their rubber hoses will hurt as much as he's heard, etc., until he breaks down in panel sixteen, and cries, "I can't take it anymore!" With a balloon in every panel expressing increasing levels of anxiety we know this version of the sixteen-panel page will be the longest for the reader to review.

Let's examine our options.

We have one panel, standing alone.

We have a two-panel sequence, which is only going to work if it is set up beforehand or afterwards, because they certainly don't deliver a self-contained dramatic experience, as written.

We have a sequence with a clock in the background, but the reader may only pay attention to the man becoming increasingly anxious until he breaks down. This is quick, and the reader will get the idea.

We have a time calculator advancing one second from caption to caption, with either numeric digits or words, both clearly demonstrating how time advances as the man goes to pieces. These captions add beats to the sequence, as well as increased dramatic tension.

Finally, we have the version where we get to read the man's thoughts as each agonizing second advances. The added and perhaps more important advantage is that we can use his thoughts to advance a narrative. He can be reflecting about what brought him to this place or anticipating correctly or incorrectly what will happen next.

To clarify, let's make this the first page of a new Spirit story. The man, middle-aged, middle-class Mike Morton, spends this first sixteen-panel page of the story speculating about which among a range of recent minor infractions is the reason for his arrest. Page two begins his story, in flashback, with him at home, getting ready to go out for the day. His stereotypically bossy wife, Margie, stops him at the door, dictating a laundry list of chores he agreed to do, and she tells him he's not leaving the house until the chores are done. In the next series of panels, Mike gets madder and madder and madder, keeping the anger bottled up, not saying anything. We can see he's ready to blow, but then, in the next panel, Mike strolls out his front door, whistling a merry tune, and we, the readers, wonder what happened between the two panels. Then his outing takes an immediate turn for the worse, where an inadvertent misdemeanor leads to another and another and another and he is soon on the run from The Spirit. Catching Mike should be easy, but The Spirit is having one of those days, where each attempt to capture Mike goes wrong with increasingly disastrous and slapsticky results. Mike's a slippery sucker, but finally The Spirit corners him on the ledge of a building, where there's no way out but down, which Mike is ready to try. Before Mike can leap to his death the Spirit makes a heroic grab, and this brings us to the last page where Mike is in the interrogation room after his sixteen seconds of increased anxiety. He's still puzzled about why The Spirit was so determined to capture him, as are we, the readers. The mystery is solved when The Spirit and Dolan show up, advising Mike he's being charged with the murder of his wife, the one crime he never even considered as a possibility for his arrest. Without a shred of remorse, Mike insists that killing her was entirely justified, that he did the world (and himself) a favor. Then he asks to be tried for one of his other crimes instead, perhaps jaywalking, for which he'd happily spend the rest of his life in prison. The Spirit and Dolan are understandably dumbfounded and this is where we end the sad tale about Mike and Margie Morton.

Compared to the other versions, do you see how the nine-panel page with thought balloons does a better job than the other versions of setting up and advancing this particular story?

Does this mean this sixteen-panel version is the best version for all occasions? Of course not.

Let's return to the two-panel version and add a panel at the end to give the first two panels a storytelling context.

PANEL ONE: A man waits in a police station interrogation room. A caption reads: "12:30 a.m."

PANEL TWO: A caption reads: "Sixteen seconds later." The man is standing and screaming, "I can't take it anymore!"

PANEL THREE: The man has collapsed, his head in hands, weeping. A cop stands in the open doorway, disgusted, holding a tray with two steaming cups of coffee. The cop says, "Stop blubbering, you big weenie! I told you I'd be back in a minute."

As a set-up for this "story" or gag, the two-panel version works fine. If the set-up for the gag is the sixteen-panel version with thought balloons, the gag is probably diminished. It makes getting to the payoff not quite worth the effort. However, one of the other versions that simply counted the seconds from one to sixteen might have worked fine, because we could have scanned more quickly to the end.

Which is better? It depends on where the writer of this story intends to go with it, how much space he or she has, how much the pacing of this needs to be fast or slow, and that's the point of this discussion.

Determining which version is best depends on your editorial goals. The importance of these sequences to the pacing of (and placement in) your story is the ultimate barometer.

There's never one solution—there are trillions—and now you know how to select from them the one that will best fit your needs.

As Bullwinkle J. Moose once said (actually he repeated it a million times in continuous reruns), "And now for something completely different!"

Let's jump one hundred years from one panel to another.

PANEL ONE: A man sits in a crowed doctor's waiting room. He thinks, "I think I'm going to throw up."

PANEL TWO: Now in a space-aged version of the same doctor's waiting room. The caption reads, "A hundred years later." The nurse stands by the open door, says, "Next." The room is empty of patients, except for the skeleton of the same man, still dressed in the same clothes from the previous panel (so we'll know he's the same man), and perhaps the hair is fashioned the same, too, just for comedic effect. The skeleton peers angrily at her through eyeless sockets, and thinks, "I think I'm going to throw up."

Our assignment for this chapter is for you to create two panels with a specific amount of time having passed between them. It doesn't matter how little or how much time, but the goal is for the reader to know exactly how much time has passed from one panel to the next.

The assignment: Without changing the location so much as an inch, I'd like to see two panels so the reader of the finished panels will know they take place a specific number of seconds apart, two panels that take place a specific number of decades apart, and two panels that take place a specific number of centuries apart.

Do not repeat in any of your three choices your use of balloons, captions, objects, or storytelling devices for showing the passage of time.

If you use captions in one panel of an answer segment you can't use captions in the next panel. You also can't use captions in any other answer segments.

"So I've got to really consider all my different options," you conclude.

"That's right," I respond. "In these three answer segments, you've got to use six different devices for showing time passage between panels. And wouldn't it be nice if you could find a way to avoid any of the ones that I've shown you?"

"And doing this will help my...um, underdeveloped muscles?" you ask.

"It will help turn them into those of a sleek sequential art powerhouse, ready to bound forth from the sequential art gate," I reply.

"Wow," you say.

"Wow, indeed," I reply.

Let's get to work.

One day later....

Okay, you wrote your answers (right?), waited a day to mull over whether or not you wrote them well (right?), and now it's time to see how the rest of the class tackled the assignment.

Who's first?

Puck raises his hand.

Puck: Here are my answers, and I kept them simple, just to make sure I got them right.

1. Thirty seconds difference between panels:

> **PANEL ONE:** It's morning. An egg sits in a bird's nest.
> SFX: (sound coming from shell) tap tap tap

> **PANEL TWO:** It's still morning, thirty seconds later, and a baby bird has emerged from the broken shell.
> BABY BIRD: Chirp.

2. Three decades difference between panels:

> **PANEL ONE:** 1920. A young soldier is marching alongside other veterans down a crowded city street in an Armistice Day parade, and he speaks to an old soldier next to him, a Civil War vet.
> SIGN: (a banner across the street) Armistice Day Parade
> SOLDIER: This is my first parade, pops, but it sure won't be my last.

> **PANEL TWO:** 1950. The young soldier is now middle-aged, but he's

still marching alongside other veterans down a crowded city street in the Armistice Day parade, and he speaks to the young soldier next to him.

SOLDIER: This is my thirtieth parade, and it still makes me proud.

YOUNG SOLDIER: Me, too, pops.

3. Four hundred years difference between panels:

PANEL ONE: 1776. A cheering group is outside Independence Hall.

CAPTION: 1776.

MAN: Hurrah for the Declaration of Independence!

PANEL TWO: 2176. There's nobody outside Independence Hall, because it's now nothing but rubble, and looks like it was nuked, since the landscape in the background is nearly flattened. There's a tattered banner draped above the remnants of a doorway.

BANNER: Happy 400th Birthday, America!

Before we discuss where Puck succeeded or failed, please review his answers and make your own determination.

Okay? Done?

Puck's grade: 33% success—**FAIL.**

The good news first: Congratulations to Puck for not repeating a single time-passing technique. Also, he followed the assignment and didn't change the location in any one of the three answers.

Now let's assess the merits of each answer.

1. Thirty seconds difference between panels.

In the second panel description, Puck informed the script reader that thirty seconds had passed, but nobody reading the finished comic will have a clue as to how much time has passed.

This is a comic writer's most common mistake.

That bears repeating.

This is a comic writer's *most* common mistake: informing the script reader about something that is supposed to be apparent in the finished comic, but doing so in a manner that fails to make it clear to the readers of the finished comic.

The purpose of a panel description is to inform the artist and editor about visual goals and, perhaps, if the writer is so inclined, intention. But this is information for collaborators. Where it's a description of something physical, like the time on a clock, it conveys information to the reader. Where it's a timeframe, like 1920, which informs the artist of the period that needs to be drawn, no reader is going to look at a drawing of a newly constructed building or style of clothing and think, "Oh, it's 1920, not 1921." If it's important for the reader to *know* it's 1920 then the writer needs to use something from his or her sequential art toolbox that conveys the specific year.

Does it matter whether the comic reader knows that thirty seconds passed for the baby bird to emerge from the egg? Probably not. But the assignment was for Puck to show that a specific number of seconds have passed and in this he failed completely.

When it does matter to Puck that readers understand a specific amount of time has passed then failing will matter.

Hopefully Puck has learned his lesson.

2. Three decades difference between panels.

This is Puck's moment of glory. He informed the artist of the timeframes that needed to be drawn and used balloon dialogue to inform the comic reader that three decades had passed between panels.

Does the reader of the finished comic know that the first panel was 1920, and the second was 1950?

No.

Was it part of the assignment for the comic reader to know *when* the panels took place?

No.

The assignment clearly stated that the goal was to show the reader of the finished comic how much time had passed between panels, and Puck kept his eye on the ball.

3. Four centuries difference between panels.

On the face of it this would appear to be a simple and clearly correct answer, but how do we know when the second panel took place?

We don't know, and that's where this answer fails.

The panel could take place a year or five years after the destruction.

Had the writer used the caption in the second panel, and had it read, "Four hundred years later...." then the goal would have been achieved.

This is how simple it is for a writer's intention to jump the rails and for readers to not glean what is supposed to be gleaned.

If your three conclusions to Puck's test answers did not correspond to these answers ask yourself, "Why not?"

The answer is likely that you weren't considering each detail and how it did or did not delineate the passage of time to the prospective reader.

Now turn that same level of scrutiny to *your* answers to this assignment.

Did you succeed or fail? Are you as tough on yourself as I was on poor ol' Puck? If so, you'll come to the right conclusions and be that much closer to having learned to control the passage of time in sequential art.

More importantly, apply this level of scrutiny to all your future writing, and your readers will perceive from your panels exactly what you want them to perceive.

Now, how would you like to learn to ride a wormhole?

CHAPTER 7

YOUR OWN PRIVATE WORMHOLE, PART 2:
THE CASE OF THE BEFUDDLED PASSENGER

It's a shame you can't get frequent flyer miles for what we're going to discuss.

Your hand goes up.

"Yes?" I ask.

"Does this mean we don't have to stay in one place, like in the last chapter?"

"Yes," I reply.

"Does it also mean we'll get to go anywhere we want to?" you ask hopefully, your eyes sparkling with anticipation.

"You're very quick," I answer, "and I only have a few important travel restrictions."

"There's always a catch," you mumble.

Yes, there's always a catch.

You currently use this particular sequential art tool, this wormhole through space, with wild abandon. It's one of the coolest things about creating comics, one of the things that no other medium does as well as comics, and only prose does less expensively.

From panel to panel, you jump from one place in a room to another place in the same room, from one room to another room, from one city, country, or world to another. In one panel you're in a Los Angeles restaurant, and in the next you're suffocating without a helmet on Mars.

You have done this so often that you already know how to do it.

You're proficient at going anywhere you wish to, willy-nilly, but there's an important consideration that's often overlooked, and when it is overlooked your passenger ends up befuddled about where he or she landed.

Your hand goes up.

"Yes?"

"I have a passenger?" you ask, confused.

"All creators have passengers," I answer cryptically.

Your passenger is your reader.

As we discovered last chapter, when traveling through time you often leave your passenger, the reader, confused about how much time passes between panels.

When traveling through space, you're like a skier swooping straight down a slope in Stowe, Vermont, blinking and shooshing on a different type of slope in Zermatt, Switzerland, blinking and traversing a completely different type of slope in Vail, Colorado. Your passenger doesn't have a clue which slope you're on in any given panel, but you miss this because *you* know where you are.

Leaping willy-nilly from a location in one panel to another location in the next panel is fine for the sake of willy-nilly-ness, but when you intend for a passenger-reader to know where Dorothy's landed it's completely irresponsible to show little people dressed in funny outfits dancing near a dead old lady with a black dress, striped stockings, and ruby slippers, and have Dorothy wondering whether she's still in Kansas.

Too often readers get to a place in the story and wonder, "Where am I?"

Your hand goes up.

"Yes?" I ask.

"I always state my location in my script," you declare defensively.

"Yes, you do," I respond, "but that's in the description portion so the artist will know what to draw. When you change location do you stop and think that the passenger-reader might need to know that location?"

"Sometimes," you answer, your hand slowly lowering.

That's right, sometimes.

To clarify, sometimes you *won't* want the passenger-reader to know where the story has landed. Sometimes you'll *want* them to ask, "Where am I, because this certainly doesn't *look* like Kansas?"

Other times, you may show a thief caught by police in the first panel and behind bars in the next panel. In this case, it's probably not important to know the bars are in the city jail. Then again, it might be important for the passenger-reader to immediately know the thief is in Sing Sing, implicitly conveying that the thief has been tried, convicted, and sentenced. Conversely, you also might prefer the passenger-reader to *think* the thief is only in a city jail and not reveal he is in Sing Sing until after you've shown, in succeeding panels, hundreds of other cells.

Editorially, landing the passenger-reader into a temporarily mysterious location can be a powerful storytelling tool, but it's a tool that should be used intentionally, not accidentally.

Often—again, too often—creators *intend* for the passenger-reader to know exactly where the story has landed, but doesn't do the work to make it clear.

The resulting disconnection between the creator's intention and a passenger-reader's reality leaves the passenger-reader wondering where they've landed. Momentarily confused, they waste valuable concentration trying to get their bearings while the creator is simultaneously trying to get the reader to focus on the next part of the story that's unfolding.

With attention split the story jumps the rails.

At this point a passenger-reader stops, steps back, reexamines the sequence that led to the point of confusion, maybe even glances ahead to get his or her bearings, and probably figures out the creator's intention. Then, with the story back on track, the passenger-reader moves forward.

But the damage is done. Valuable concentration and intended story pacing are lost, all because the passenger-reader didn't understand what the creator wanted him or her to know.

Setting aside when and where it's important for a creator to inform a passenger-reader about a panel location let's simply state: where it's editorially important to do so, it's the creator's obligation to let the passenger-reader know where he or she landed. Phrased another way: only confuse your reader on purpose.

Pretty obvious, isn't it? But keeping constant vigilance on what a reader will perceive is so much easier said than done. With this in mind keep handy an important cliché: it's better to be safe than sorry.

There are many sequential art tools at the your disposal and we're going to explore their potential use through a series of exercises that will take the passenger-reader from any real or imaginary place to any other real or imaginary place, making certain he or she is comfortably aware of each landing location.

To clarify, you can move from any real place to another, any imaginary place to another, from one dimension to another, or you can switch types of destinations in any way you wish, and travel from an orc-infested Hobbiton to a Walter-Mitty daydream. The only boundaries are the editorial parameters and your imagination.

But please learn to toddle before you blast off to Mars.

If your answers don't meet the editorial criteria of the assignment, then you will have befuddled another passenger-reader and won't have yet learned to write with intention.

The goal of this assignment is to solidify sequential art fundamentals through constant repetition so that your passenger-readers will perceive exactly what you wish them to perceive.

Does "wax on...wax off" ring any bells?

Here's the assignment:

1. Beginning with a tricky one, write a different location in each of two panels, making each location clearly understood by any moderately informed passenger-reader. You cannot use balloons, captions, or signage to identify or label the locations.

2. Write a different location in each of two panels, making each location clearly understood by any moderately informed passenger-reader. You are free to use captions and signage, but do not use character thought or word balloons to identify either location.

3. Write a different location in each of two panels, locations that will be clearly understood by any moderately informed passenger-reader. Use a caption in panel one, and another in panel two that creates a conceptual bridge for the two. E.g. if the panel one caption reads, "Cairo is hot," and the panel two caption reads, "but the North Pole is not," the two panels are conceptually tied together by the second caption, and both locations are identified.

4. Write a different location in each of two panels, locations that will be clearly understood by any moderately informed passenger-reader. A character of your choice will be in both panel locations, and what he/she/it says or thinks in the panel one word or thought balloon should conceptually connect to his/her/its word or thought balloon in panel two. E.g. if the miserable penguin in a panel one thought balloon thinks, "Cairo is hot," then thinks in panel two, "but the North Pole is not," the two panels are conceptually tied together by the thought balloons, and both locations are identified.

Also, you are not limited to the sequential art tools I noted, as long as the necessary ones for each portion of the assignment are utilized. E.g. I don't care if there are characters in #2, or even balloons in #2; I simply want to make sure you use a caption bridge as the location identifier in #2.

If each location in each panel is not made immediately clear to the reader-passenger, then it is an automatic **FAIL**.

So keep it simple and start developing those muscles.

Wax on...wax off.

Let's make your sequential art shine.

Have you completed the assignment?

Did you wait to review your answers in the light of a new day, just to make certain they are correct?

Are you sure you aced this?

Good. Let's review some of the classroom responses.

Who's first?

Hercules raises his hand.

Hercules: This assignment was a piece of cake.

Me: Well, the proof is in the pudding.

Hercules: So this assignment was a piece of pudding?

Me: Let's see.

1. TWO LOCATIONS, UNLABELED.

PANEL ONE

We're in the New Orleans French Quarter during Mardi Gras. People are roaming the streets in costume, and everybody's partying.

PANEL TWO

We're at the Grand Canyon. It's a hot, dry day, we see the cliff's edge nearby, but from our close angle, can't see the bottom, but we know it's a long drop.

2. TWO LOCATIONS, LABELED WITH CAPTIONS OR SIGNAGE.

PANEL ONE

This small introductory panel shows us Hollywood Blvd. The street is busy, with lots of cars and people. The sidewalks are crowded. There's a street sign half a block away.

SFX: (street sign) Hollywood Blvd

PANEL TWO

Spring Street in downtown Los Angeles, skid row, a littered sun-washed street, with vagrants lying on the sidewalks or milling about.

CAPTION: Skid row.

3. TWO LOCATIONS, USING CAPTIONS OR SIGNAGE TO CREATE A CONCEPTUAL BRIDGE.

PANEL ONE

This introductory panel shows us Hollywood Blvd, near Mann's Chinese Theater. The street is busy, with lots of cars and people. The sidewalks are crowded.

CAPTION: Too many people come to Hollywood looking to make it in the movies...

PANEL TWO

Spring Street, skid row, a littered sun-washed street, with vagrants lying on the sidewalks or milling about.

CAPTION: ...and end up playing rolls they never imagined on Spring Street.
CAPTION: Welcome to the City of Angels, where all the world's a stage.

4. TWO LOCATIONS, USING WORD AND/OR THOUGHT BALLOONS TO CREATE A CONCEPTUAL BRIDGE.

PANEL ONE

Midtown. In a New York City office on the thirtieth floor, a man sits behind his desk, depressed.

MAN THOT: It's nothing but work work work in this town. I can't wait to go on vacation.

PANEL TWO

A man sits in a Waikiki Tiki bar. The same man is sitting a table in a tropical bar, an untouched drink in front of him, depressed.

MAN THOT: It's nothing but play play play in paradise. I can't wait to go back to New York.

Hercules's grade: **FAIL.**

He missed three out of four. Can you locate the one he got right? Can you see where the others miss?

Study his answers closely. Come to a conclusion about what they will or will not communicate to the reader of the finished comics.

Done?

Okay, here's my assessment.

This was indeed a piece of pudding with lots of tasty ideas, but most of them are too mushy. Very little of what the assignment required was accomplished.

1. In his first half of this answer, a reader might speculate that the street party was in the New Orleans French Quarter, but it's not certain. Without signage, is there a single image in the French Quarter that's so recognizable that any moderately informed passenger-reader would be certain of the location? Nope.

The second half of this first answer has a similar issue. Written as shot close to the edge of the Grand Canyon, nothing in this image suggests a longer aerial view that might help us identify it. Even if there had been a longer shot showing a perspective of the Grand Canyon with which we're more familiar, it still might be problematic, because most people only know that the Grand Canyon is a gigantic crack in the ground leading to a river far below. Coming back to what's described, the point of view really kills our potential to identify this image. Showing the Statue of Liberty at an odd angle likely won't matter, because a reader will still know it's the Statue of Liberty. But showing the edge of a cliff and a long drop does not, in itself, bring to mind the Grand Canyon. For all we know, the image in this panel could be the Martian canals.

So if it is important from the first for a reader to know the location of an image inside a panel, where that location does not have well-recognized iconography, identify it.

2. These two panels demonstrate the most frequent identifying mistakes I see in comics writing.

The first panel is described as a small panel with lots of traffic. The street sign identifying this as Hollywood is half a block away. If drawn as written, the sign won't be readable. If the artist is paying attention to the need for a reader to understand that this is Hollywood, he or she will bring the street sign to the foreground where it can be easily read, and the writer's intention will have been rescued.

The second panel is more subtly incorrect. While you might consider this a judgment call, because the panel caption does note that it *is* skid row, the writer's intention for the reader to know the location, presumably *which* skid row, has not been realized.

3. This is the one that Hercules got correct.

The first panel artfully identifies this panel as Hollywood. The reader is then led into the second panel, which depicts life on Spring Street and what can happen to people who lose their dreams and then themselves.

4. This one uses thought balloons to repeat previous mistakes.

The panel description describes the locations, but the character only refers to New York at "this town," and Waikiki as "paradise."

Interestingly, the second panel makes it clear that the first panel took place in New York, which might be acceptable editorially, but misses on the assignment parameters.

"I can do better," says Hercules.
"Show me."

1. TWO LOCATIONS, UNLABELED.

PANEL ONE
We see the four Presidents carved into Mt. Rushmore.

PANEL TWO
We see the Eiffel Tower in Paris, France.

2. TWO LOCATIONS, LABELED WITH CAPTIONS OR SIGNAGE.

PANEL ONE
This introductory panel shows us Hollywood Blvd. near Mann's Chinese Theater. The street is busy with lots of cars and people. The sidewalks are crowded.

CAPTION: Hollywood, California.

PANEL TWO
Spring Street in downtown Los Angeles, skid row, a littered sun-washed street with vagrants lying on the sidewalks or milling about.

CAPTION: Spring Street, downtown Los Angeles.

3. Already successful.

4. TWO LOCATIONS, USING WORD AND/OR THOUGHT BALLOONS TO CREATE A CONCEPTUAL BRIDGE.

PANEL ONE

A man sits behind his desk, depressed.

MAN THOT: It's nothing but work work work in New York City. I can't wait to go on vacation.

PANEL TWO

The same man is sitting a table in a tropical bar, an untouched drink in front of him, depressed.

MAN THOT: It's nothing but play play play in Waikiki. I can't wait to go back to work.

*   *   *

Please review Hercules's corrected answers.
Has he resolved the issues?
Are you certain?
Would you bet money on whether he has or hasn't nailed it?
Take some time; come to your conclusion.
Ready?
Okay. Let's begin.

"Now, *that's* a piece of cake," I say.

PASS.

Hercules kept it simple, kept his eye on the ball, and communicated his intention clearly to the reader.

A hand rises out of the darkness from the back row.

"Yes?" I ask.

"I don't understand why the first answer was correct in the second version but not in the first version."

Great question.

In the do-over, answers two and four were clearly correct, and answer three was previously correct, so let's examine the answer one revision.

We already discussed why the French Quarter in New Orleans and the Grand Canyon answers were "wrong," why they missed the mark. In the revision, Hercules successfully identified two locations, Mt. Rushmore, which *is* a location, and the Eiffel Tower, which is in Paris. Any moderately informed passenger-reader should recognize each of these locations.

The student in the back asks a question. "So you'd expect a reader to know the Eiffel Tower is in Paris?"

Presuming the passenger-reader isn't a child who's understandably not yet uneducated enough to make the connection, I do expect a moderately informed reader to know the Eiffel Tower is in Paris.

Still, this brings up an interesting point, a topic that should be addressed.

How should we identify our prospective passenger-reader? Do we play to the masses that are only barely paying attention, who need their hands held to make sure they follow what's going on in the story, or do we create for those who will look for the subtleties and undercurrents of the story, those who are willing to be involved in the work, in this case, to the ones who will easily connect the Eiffel Tower and Paris?

The answer to this depends on our goals. Yes, it always comes back to goals.

If the work is intended for young children then it does need to be created so young children will perceive what's going on.

If the work is Hi-Lo (high interest level, low reading level), then content needs to be created to appeal to a teen, but with a simpler use of language.

There's no one-approach-fits-all solution, but the broader question being asked is: "Should we write up or down to our readership?"

A Producer-Who-Shall-Not-Be-Named once made a revealing statement about making movies. It's a rule of thumb, a guideline, an observation that has been disproved countless times but remains a rule of thumb because we have also witnessed its results: the more expensive a movie is the dumber it needs to be.

Rather than wasting time in a discussion about why we despise that truism, let's examine why it exists.

Ticket sales transform into income. Income pays back investment. A greater investment translates to a financial need for a greater number of tickets to be sold.

To be obvious, in order to recover an investment and become profitable, a film costing 200 million dollars needs to sell a lot more tickets than a thirty million dollar film. To sell a lot more tickets the expensive film has to be perceived as having the potential to appeal to a lot more people, and the presumption by producers who adopt this philosophy is that most people aren't that smart or don't want to work when watching a movie. The expectation is that these moviegoers just want to munch on popcorn and be blown away by what's being handed to them on a silver (not very challenging) screen. To achieve this result the 200-million-dollar movie needs to be crafted for the largest common denominator. It needs to be simple or, using the producer's misguided word choice, "dumber."

Simple isn't necessarily dumb, which is why "dumber" has quotes. Simple can quite often be smart, but where that's the result it's not the intended result by the people forking out the 200 million dollars. All they want is their money back, plus interest.

Coming back to the question of whether we should write up or down to our passenger-reader, it is each creator's personal and business decision. Where H. L. Mencken once wrote, "Nobody ever went broke underestimating the intelligence of the American people," I believe in smart writing, writing that involves the passenger-reader, rather than in writing that ham-fistedly delivers expository content so a passenger-reader won't have to wonder about subtext.

Regardless, whether creators wish to write up or down to their passenger readers, they still need all their storytelling tools to craft the intended result.

If a creator believes their intended passenger-reader won't know the Eiffel Tower is in Paris, France, and if it is important for the passenger-reader to know this, then the creator should include a caption that reads: "Paris, France."

This discussion may seem so basic that it shouldn't need to be pursued at such length, but when simultaneously working with numerous story aspects, including location, character, pacing, even necessary exposition, there is a creator-tendency to snap into Default Mode, to put down what has been practiced, what has become instinctual.

That's why it's important to synchronize Default Mode with intention. Wax on...wax off.

Chapter 8

Silence Is Golden

We've spent no small amount of time discussing how comics are *not* like film.

To summarize, trying to write comics like film creates numerous craft-related problems, not the least of which is that intention often doesn't translate into the desired result.

We've discussed how time and the pace of reading flows inside panels, how much or little time there can be between panels, how to leap from one place to another through *Your Own Private Wormhole*, and how to create all of this with intention so readers have the best opportunity to perceive what creators wish to convey.

But we haven't yet discussed how comics *are* like film.

"Yay!" shouts the classroom film fans.

"Yay, indeed," I reply, fully aware that I appear to be cutting against the grain of my own *"comics aren't film"* thesis by suggesting we can apply film techniques to determine visuals for sequential art. Actually, I'm simply acknowledging a contextual overlap between the two media, and focusing on it so creators can take advantage of specific cinematic (i.e., visual) storytelling methods.

In a later section on script styles, I'll elaborate more on David Mamet's book, *On Directing Film,* and the influence it had on my approach to comic script writing. However, there's a brilliant process outlined in it for how to determine exactly what's required in a series of shots (in the case of comics, "frozen images" inside a series of panels). As conceived, these shots allow readers to connect contextual dots and advance a visual narrative that involves readers in a way that a lazier approach to visual storytelling does not.

In this chapter, we're going to briefly discuss this distillation of Eisenstein's theory of film and how it translates to comics.

In an excerpt from a 2010 memo to staff writers of *The Unit*, Executive Producer (and playwright, screenwriter, film director) David Mamet wrote (I'll summarize) that film is a visual medium, yet most of the writing for TV "sounds like radio." He encourages (pushes, actually) his writers to let the camera tell the story, to "do the explaining." Mamet offers a fascinatingly simple methodology to accomplish this: "pretend the characters can't speak, and write a silent movie." The result, he promises, will be "great drama."

Mamet further describes the current use of narration, speech, and exposition in TV writing as a crutch, suggesting that it holds writers back from fully exploring the dramatic possibilities of the medium. And then he tells them that making this shift, training themselves to write visually, does not come naturally, implying that success will only come with hard work.

Much of what Mamet wrote here translates well to the sequential art medium. Not everything, of course, because our use of the written word in dialogue and narration doesn't necessarily decrease the potential for great sequential art stories or storytelling.

In his memo, Mamet pushes writers to abandon narration and speech as the first solution for reaching dramatic storytelling goals. Mamet understands that the eventual use of dialogue and narration is likely, if not inevitable, even where the goal is to create a "silent" film, if for no other reason than that most silent films have title cards (white text on a field that was usually black) with some dialogue or narration.

"If he knows folks will ultimately need to use dialogue and narration," you ask, "why does he suggest withholding it?"

"I'm glad you asked," I answer. "It's because of his use of the term 'crutch.'"

"What's wrong with that?" you ask, a defensive tone creeping into your voice.

"Nothing, if you're writing a stage play," I reply.

Most comics scripting from beginners goes like this: write the talky or narrative stuff, break down how the balloons will separate into x-number panels planned for a page, then figure out the best possible images to go with them. It's the primary default for comics writers who don't think visually or don't *first* think visually. That's the crutch. It's the natural default, the way too many comics writers teach themselves to write comics, even though it doesn't take full advantage of the visual storytelling medium.

When you use dialogue and narration as the first resort for unfolding a drama, the images then get attached to support them.

Too many writers, especially ones who aren't artists (and this refers even to working professionals), begin their scripts by blocking out the dialogue.

In a medium that remains primarily visual, blocking out space with dialogue as a default process to begin storytelling is too easy...or as easy as dialogue ever gets. It's a crutch that doesn't allow writers the opportunity to consider how they might explore other dramatic possibilities. Simply put, writing dialogue, then adding images to fit, immediately eliminates too many potential, and perhaps better, storytelling opportunities.

Why would you ever want to do that, except that it's a default, that it's what you're used to, and that it's easier than learning new ways to write comics?

"What if starting with dialogue is what I'm best at?" you ask.

"You're always going to be better at something you've been practicing than something you've never tried," I respond. "Once you've got the hang of it, how do you know that using a more balanced storytelling process might not make you a better comics creator?"

"I don't," you confess.

"Which is exactly why we're going to give you the chance to find out," I reply, "in the same way David Mamet gave his TV writers the chance to find out."

When you tackle storytelling from this purely visual approach, you're involving the reader in every element inside the panel, from character acting to camera position and focus.

Readers can't just read the balloons and captions to figure out what's going on. They need to involve themselves more fully; they need to examine what's going on in each panel, within the context of the ones that preceded it.

Ultimately, it's unlikely that a writer using one approach to every script would produce the best results in every script. Each story comes with its own set of challenges, and writers need to approach those challenges with all the potential storytelling options at hand.

So we're going to work on adding visual storytelling to your toolbox.

To explore its potential we're going to reverse the dialogue-and-narration-first default, and work on telling stories only with images. Later, after you've acclimated to this new approach, you'll be able to block out scenes with the necessary images, and then be able to add, where necessary or simply preferred, the requisite dialogue and/or narration to fill out the narrative.

But first we're going to learn to play with the new tool.

I return to *On Directing Film* as a masterwork for how to choose images that will help you visually advance story.

Referring to TV in the '80s, David Mamet suggested (for some very interesting reasons) that the visual presentation stayed on everything characters did, but that film utilized juxtaposed uninflected imagery, cuts between different images that get put together in a specific order to form a narrative. The result of the latter approach to advance a narrative is that it requires the viewer to think, to interpret the order of the images and come to a conclusion about what they mean, to become involved in the story, instead of just watching a character do whatever the character is doing, while simultaneously explaining everything he's doing and why.

For example:

In TV, in one shot, a man enters a building, walks down a hallway, opens a door, and walking into a classroom. There's not much thinking involved in understanding that.

But in film, we see a man entering a building, shoes walking on a hallway floor, a hand on a doorknob, then, from inside the classroom, the man walks through the door, entering a classroom.

Instead of seeing every letter from A to Z and not having to pay much attention to what's going on, we're seeing A, J, R, Z, and we connect the dots to follow the narrative.

That's my *Reader's Digest* version of Mamet's thesis, which is based on Eisenstein's theory of film.

My best comics correlation for this process is that it's a writer's version of the Plot Method, otherwise known as the Marvel Method.

In the Plot Method, the writer gives a story synopsis to the artist, the artist then draws the story, making it as visually interesting as he or she can, then the writer adds word balloons and captions to have the story make sense.

It's the primary difference between Marvel and DC Comics storytelling from the '60s. Marvel was Plot Method and DC was Full Script Method.

Each approach has strengths and weaknesses.

The weakness to the Plot Method is that the artist must be a good sequential art storyteller. If he or she is not, if he or she cannot unfold the drama without a script, the drawn pages often require the writer to use too many captions and too much expository dialogue for the damned thing to make sense.

I'm not fond of the Plot Method approach to creating comics, but that's a personal choice, because some great comics have been created in this manner, most notably the Silver Age work of Jack Kirby, Steve Ditko, and Stan Lee.

On the contrary, I *love* Plot-Method writing.

I love unfolding image upon image without dialogue: holding focus on a scene that allows us to explore what's different between panels; panning or changing focus, which allows for a slight increase in visual drama or a reveal; panning *and* changing focus, which brings us a dynamic shift in tone or a reveal; cutting from close-up to long shot (or visa versa) of a character in different locations, allowing us to show great passages of time; or, in contrast, holding focus on a character in a series of shots with different background locations, keeping our attention focused on the character.

There are too many wonderful opportunities and options to list.

For now, though, let's simply acknowledge the potential for brilliant wordless storytelling in masterpieces like Raymond Brigg's *The Snowman*, Shaun Tan's *The Arrival*, and Peter Kuper's *The System*.

And that's what we're going to practice.

Without a single word balloon, thought balloon, caption, or block of floating text, write two *wordless* sequential art pages, containing at least five panels per page.

The sequential art toolbox is wide open, even to the use of signage and sound effects. Excepting the limitations described above, you're free to do whatever you wish, with the following provisos:

1. Write each panel from left to right (because you're a Comics Panel Time-Master).

2. Write with intention (because that should be your goal as a creator).

3. Have the two pages make sense in some way as a wordless progression. It doesn't have to be a story, but it should make some kind of sense.

Here's a simple example:

PAGE ONE

PANEL 1

Centered left and right in the foreground of the panel, a rock sits on the near-molten material, with a gushing volcano in the background.

PANEL 2

The rock is on the cool ground, with sparse flora in the background.

PANEL 3

The rock is on the mossy ground, with little prehistoric creatures scuttling about.

PANEL 4

The rock is on the grass, with monstrous dinosaurs battling in the background.

PANEL 5

The rock is on the frozen ground, with dinosaur skeletons in the background.

PANEL 6

The rock is on the cold ground, with a wooly mammoth in the background.

PANEL 7

The rock is on the grassy ground, with early man chasing a deer in the background.

PANEL 8

The rock is on the hard-packed ground, with Romans chasing Goths in the background.

PANEL 9

The rock is on the hard-packed ground, with, in the background, Romans being chased by Goths in the opposite direction.

PAGE TWO

PANEL 1

The rock is on a concrete street, with two groups of 21st century people arguing with each other in the background. Each side holds protest signs, and it doesn't matter that we can't read them.

PANEL 2

The rock is on the concrete street, with a nuclear explosion in the background.

PANEL 3

The rock is on the cracked concrete street, with desolation in the background, and dingy dust still not settled, hangs in the air like putrid fog.

PANEL 4

Motion lines under the rock show that it has stood up on the cracked concrete street, its three thin legs long and spider-like, with desolation in the background.

PANEL 5

The rock stands on the cracked concrete street, stretching one of its legs to the left, with desolation in the background.

SFX: (The stretching) urrrrgggghhh

PANEL 6

The rock stands on the cracked concrete street, stretching one of its other legs to the right, with desolation in the background.

SFX: (The stretching) gurrrgggghhh

PANEL 7

The rock is on the cracked concrete street, and motion lines show that it is stepping to the right, now clearly no longer in the middle of the panel, with desolation in the background.

SFX: (The stepping) step step

PANEL 8

Now off-center in the panel, motion lines from above show that the rock has lowered back down to the cracked concrete street. Its legs are folded at the joints. Desolation remains in the background.

PANEL 9

The rock is sitting on the cracked concrete street, still off-center in the panel, its legs hidden. It smiles, with desolation in the background.

*   *   *

This two-pager was written for this assignment in about a half hour, so if you simply concentrate on the assignment basics and don't over-think it, it can be quick and easy.

Here's another two-page script, something that's slightly more complicated. It's a revised two-page excerpt from my *Once Upon A Time Machine* anthology story, *Silver-Hair & the Three Xairs*. The artist is my ol' pal, Scott Roberts, who created *Patty Cake*, and worked on the *Rugrats* (writing and pencils) and *Prince Valiant* (color) comic strips.

PAGE ONE

PANEL 1 (big panel)

Establishing shot on another planet, with strangely colored ground, tree-things, and sky, perhaps with two or more moons, so we'll know we're not on Earth. Silver-Hair, a cute little six year-old, is skipping happily up a "walkway." The oddly shaped "walkway" is contoured more like a swale for something to flow through than like something on which somebody is intended to walk. It leads to a strangely shaped alien abode. At a glance, the abode obviously doesn't accommodate a human shape or size. Perhaps the thing that looks like a door is round or oblong, rather than tall. "Round" or "curved" are the predominant design shapes for the creatures that built this, which is in obvious contrast to the rectangular or sometimes-triangular nature of human design. I'm thinking "round" or "curved" because the aliens will be revealed (at the end of the story, not here) to be sometimes-gelatinous and sometimes-fluid, and perhaps they're pear-shaped, so round and cupped (like a fruit bowl) would be more naturally comfortable for them to sit, sleep, or relax.

PANEL 2

Silver-Hair has just pulled the "door" aside—it's like a draped flat-noodle (something that's vertically and horizontally flexible, not solid, maybe like heavy window drapery) that is hung rather than hinged—and she has to duck low to be able to peek inside.

PANEL 3

Inside the alien abode, Silver-Hair has just stepped inside, looking in wide-eyed in childish awe at...

PANEL 4

...the huge, open space that is unlike any room she's ever seen. She's walking through the space, looking up (still in awe) at all the stuff that might or might not be furniture. It's attached to or hanging from the walls and ceilings; it's stuff that indicates the creatures living here don't JUST live on the floor like people. We should wonder what they are.

PANEL 5

Silver-Hair is looking in a different direction than in the previous panel, so we know she's really scoping out the place. While doing this, she's walking toward something we MIGHT think is a sitting area, but let's not make this visualization too on-the-nose, because it probably isn't a sitting area (and nope, I don't know what it really is for, because, like her, I'm just an ignorant human).

PAGE TWO

PANEL 1

Still checking out stuff, she eases her fanny onto a sofa-like cube suspended a few inches above the ground (and nope, I don't know how it's suspended; it simply seems to be floating).

PANEL 2

Her alarmed attention is quickly switched to the problem at hand, which is that she can't seem to un-stick her fanny from the cube. She's pushing back from it, but the cube is stretched out of shape to keep itself attached to her.

PANEL 3

Now the attached portion of the cube has SNAPPED off to send her flying away from it, humorously head over heals.

1 SFX: (the point where SH and the cube have parted) snap!

PANEL 4

Lying with her back on the ground like Charlie Brown after having missed kicking the football, she's pissed, and at this moment we just KNOW this is a kid that doesn't like to be crossed; definitely more Calvin than Charlie Brown or Pippi than princess.

PANEL 5

The perfectly innocent cube hovers inches above the ground. Up on one of her knees, Silver-Hair is suspiciously eyeing the cube. A sphere is nearby, on the ground behind her.

PANEL 6

Silver-Hair's a real candidate for the ADS Hall of Fame, as her attention is now locked onto the sphere.

PANEL 7

With understandable skepticism, she pushes a finger into the surface of the sphere and it gives a little like a sofa cushion.

PANEL 8

Silver-Hair is watching closely, eyes narrowed, to see that her finger hasn't stuck after she has pulled it back from the sphere. She's obviously being more careful; if I was generous I might even say she's learning, but that's yet to be determined.

PANEL 9

Silver-Hair carefully eases her fanny onto the sphere, and we see it giving a little to her weight, then...

(BONUS PANEL FOR THOSE WHO WANT TO KNOW WHAT HAPPENS NEXT)

PAGE THREE

PANEL 1 of 9

...she has fallen so far into the sphere that all we can see are her flailing arms and legs. Bill Watterson would've loved drawing this image.

1 SFX: (the point where SH has collapsed into the sphere) schluupp

*   *   *

And that's where we'll leave our struggling little interplanetary adventurer.

This was just part of a story that has ten out of twelve wordless pages.

My first page here is actually the fourth page of the published story, so I tweaked the first panel to fit this assignment. I added a bonus panel for interested readers whom might want to know what happened next, but I could've easily just stopped at the end of page two to satisfy the assignment parameters.

So far, both script examples kept the main characters in each panel. Neither takes that next more adventurous step towards utilizing Mamet's more advanced juxtaposed-uninflected-image storytelling techniques.

For this or future exercises, when you're feeling comfortable with basic wordless storytelling, add one complication to the assignment. Write two wordless sequential art pages that contain at least five panels per page and don't repeat the use of any location, character, or object in two *successive* panels, while maintaining a cohesive narrative.

Here's an example, which took ten minutes of free-associating and focusing on never repeating an image in successive panels. Then I took another ten minutes to add atmosphere and expression.

PAGE ONE

PANEL 1

At night, on a rain-drenched, city street that is dimly lit only by a couple of working street lamps, Henry is walking confidently down a sidewalk.

PANEL 2

A mugger hides in the darkness of an alley.

PANEL 3

On the sidewalk, Henry stops.

PANEL 4

The mugger peers out of the alley, light catching his beady eyes.

PANEL 5

On the sidewalk, Henry has jammed a hand into a pocket, looking puzzled.

PANEL 6

The mugger is back in the shadows, his back pressed against a brick wall, eyes squeezed shut.

PAGE TWO

PANEL 1

On the sidewalk, Henry is now checking inside his briefcase.

PANEL 2

The mugger peers out of the alley again, light catching his anxious expression.

PANEL 3

On the sidewalk, Henry has a hand on a hip, obviously perplexed.

PANEL 4

The mugger continues to peer out of the alley, also perplexed.

PANEL 5

Henry walks back the way he came, annoyed.

PANEL 6

The crook now sits in the darkness of the alley, his hands covering his face.

*   *   *

Your hand rises.

"Yes?" I ask.

"I thought the assignment was not to repeat the location," you comment.

"That's right," I confirm.

"But aren't the alley and the street at the same location?" you ask.

"Are they?" I ask.

"But the crook is looking at Henry, nervous about the impending mugging," you say, "so that's the same location, right?"

"Do I ever show Henry and the mugger in the same panel?" I ask.

"No," you concede.

"Do I ever write that the alley is right off the street?" I ask.

"No," you concede, realizing the point of contention might not exist.

"So how do you know that the alley and the street are same location?" I ask.

"Because of the way you flipped back and forth between the two," you reply defiantly.

"Have you ever seen the film, *Silence of the Lambs*?" I ask.

"Yes," you answer, accessing your organic hard drive.

"Remember the scene toward the end, where the FBI are surrounding the house that the serial killer is supposed to be inside, juxtaposed with the serial killer inside a house?"

"Yes," you answer.

"Remember the point in this sequence where the FBI guy pushes the doorbell?"

"Yes," you say, recalling what happens next.

"The serial killer answers the door, right?" I ask.

"Right," you confirm.

"And who's at the door when he answers it?" I ask.

"Agent Starling," you answer, "who was in a different town than the FBI, following up another lead."

"Right," I say. "This was a masterful sequence, where we are made to believe, simply through the use of juxtaposed, uninflected storytelling, that the house the FBI had surrounded was the same house that the serial killer was inside."

You follow my logic and conclude, "So in your script you led the reader to believe that Henry and the mugger are at the same location, when they may or may not have been."

"Right," I confirm. "I presented the images, and you connected the dots, which is what I intended you to do."

Here's my best suggestion to the more adventurous among you: at first, try this simply. Don't do anything fancy. Just write two pages that make sense. If you're successful, stretch a little on the next one, and so on. This isn't about accomplishing this exercise once and thinking you now understand everything about this kind of storytelling. This is about doing it over and over, at will, so you get good at it, so it becomes natural, so you can do it well anytime you choose to.

Wax on...wax off.

Be creative, have fun, and don't worry about anything except the constraints of the assignment. If there's a story, there's a story, but don't anguish over it. You only have one goal: to properly address the assignment and tell a story visually so that it's perceived by the comics reader the way you want it to be perceived.

One last tip: I strongly recommend you avoid the bane of every beginner's script: camera angles. Don't get tricky. I know you can imagine a two-page scene well enough without them. This is about specifying a series of wordless images. The more time you spend on minutiae, the more you'll likely lose the flow of images and/or jump the sequential art storytelling rails.

What's a PASS? Addressing the assignment correctly, so that a drawn interpretation of the script can be made by the artist and perceived as you intended by the finished comic's reader.

What's a FAIL? Not completely addressing the assignment, or where any aspect of the script can't be drawn by the artist and/or perceived as you intended by the finished comic's reader.

Who's the arbiter?

For this discussion, it will be me. After you've left the classroom, it will be the hard-nosed editor inside yourself, then, ultimately, your real hard-nosed editor or readers.

Let's begin.

Okay, so you've written your two pages and followed the assignment, keeping to its parameters, right?

Great! Now, let's ask for a volunteer from our class to show us what he's written. Who's first?

Hercules raises his hand. "I'll go first."

PAGE ONE

PANEL 1

In a bedroom, we see a husband in pajamas, sitting on top of covers in bed, with his back propped up against pillows and the backboard. His legs are crossed. He aims a TV remote control in one hand, pointing it past his wife, who is sitting up, under covers, reading a book by the light from the lamp that sits on the bed stand to her left. The TV is the thing the husband is pointing the remote at, and it is not on. Next to the husband, his nightstand is piled with stuff, books, magazines, and household gadgets.

PANEL 2

This is a close-up of the husband's finger pushing the power button on the remote.

PANEL 3

The TV is still off.

PANEL 4

The wife is perturbed, her head turned to look at her husband.

PANEL 5

The husband is annoyed as he looks down at the remote.

PANEL 6

Close-up on the husband's fingers, as they hold the remote in such a way that we can see the lower portion of its reverse side. The piece that is supposed to hold the batteries in place is not there, and a place where one of two batteries should be lodged is empty. One of the batteries is missing!

PANEL 7

The husband sets the remote on his nightstand, amidst the rest of the mess, while he is in the process of turning to get out of bed, with one of his two feet near the floor.

PAGE TWO

PANEL 1

The husband is now standing next to the bed, and he's lifted up the top sheet and blanket to see if that's where the battery fell out.

PANEL 2

His wife is now turned to get out of her side of the bed, her legs on the floor, her expression showing annoyance. Meanwhile, the man is crouched down on the floor on his side of the bed, his head low enough to look under the bed for the missing battery.

PANEL 3

This is a view looking toward the husband peering at us from underneath the bed. In the foreground, we can see un-vacuumed dust bunnies, a lost cat toy, a discarded paperback that is open with its spine up, but there's no battery to be seen. On the far side we see the husband squinting toward us, peering into the dark to find the battery. No luck! The camera is actually on the other side of the bed, so that we can see the wife's feet in the foreground, which are now on the carpet.

PANEL 4

This shot is close on the wife's index finger depressing the TV's ON button.

PANEL 5

The wife stands next to the TV, her arms crossed, a wry expression on her face. The television is on, showing a baseball game in progress. The husband peers over the top of the bed, his eyes slightly widened in surprise.

PANEL 6

The husband and wife are back in bed. She's reading her book, and he's happily paying attention to the game on the TV. The forgotten remote lies with the rest of the junk on the husband's nightstand... right next to the missing battery.

*   *   *

Please carefully review Hercules's script. Spend some time with it and make notes on every minute aspect of that consideration. Your job is to make a complete determination of whether or not the script stays within the parameters of the assignment, and especially to conclude whether it can be drawn as written and still represent the story that was intended. Let's be clear about that second point. If an artist were to draw what was indicated in the panel description, would the finished comic convey the writer's intended story?

Do you think it would?

Not sure?

I'll give you a hint: it wouldn't.

Now figure out why it wouldn't and note what you, as a writer, artist, or editor, would do to fix it. The more time you spend with this, the more you will get from this assessment, and, moving forward, the more it will help you with your own work.

Successfully completing this assignment, as well as a successful review of Hercules's script, requires a comprehensive level of craft on the topics we've discussed to this point.

Have you made your assessment and written your notes?

Have you caught everything there was to catch?

Would a revision based on your notes make a workable script?

Ready? Good. Let's begin.

Macro to micro....

First, the craft level of this script is fairly typical of what I see from too many comics creators, even ones with a few professional jobs under their belt.

Per the assignment, it misses on almost every level, except that it does not contain any dialogue or narration. In this aspect, the most obvious part of the assignment, it succeeds. The story is amusing and ironic, so kudos for that, too. Also, there's a nice use of juxtaposed uninflected imagery here with the hands on the respective buttons. Hercules has done a nice job of presenting images that will involve the reader.

However, if the script were drawn as written, much of what was intended would be lost.

Since the story in this two-page script is clear, keeping our focus on it will help us identify and fix the problems.

This is the story about a husband trying and failing to find the missing battery to his remote control so that he can turn on the TV. He's so lost in the search that he forgets that the purpose of a remote control is to make things easier, not harder, a point made perfectly clear when his wife gets out of bed and turns on the TV by pressing its ON button. With her point made, he can watch his baseball game and she can now go back to reading.

Does everybody agree that this is the story that was intended?

A hand is raised.

"What about the missing battery lying on husband's messy nightstand?" you ask. "That's where Hercules finished his script. Isn't that important enough to include?"

"Great point," I note. "Hercules obviously intended the missing battery to be the punch line to his story, the Rosebud to his *Citizen Kane*, so let's revise the concept."

This is the story about a slob of a husband trying and failing to find the missing battery to his remote control so that he can turn on the TV. He's so lost in the search that he forgets that the purpose of a remote control is to make things easier, not harder, a point made perfectly clear when his wife gets out of bed and turns on the TV by pressing its ON button. With her point made, she can now go back to reading and he can watch the baseball game, all the time unaware that the missing battery was lost in the clutter of his nightstand, right next to where he set down the remote.

The story now has two punch lines, one about finding the simplest path to a problem, and the other about not being able to find something out in the open, because it's lost in the clutter.

These two points don't fit well together. The second point muddles the first and the first undercuts the second. At this point, neither is the controlling idea in the script, and the story suffers for it.

If we eliminate the reader seeing the battery, along with any aspect of the husband's messy habits, the irony of the wife turning on the TV is clean and simple.

However, if the man continues searching for the battery, even after the wife turns on the TV, then the story becomes more about the obsessive search for the lost battery than its intended purpose. This revision reveals a disorganized, unfocused man who can't see the forest for the trees, and who, conversely, can't see the battery amidst the mess.

Either one of these stories is fine. I think Hercules would be wise to revise his story concept in either direction, but fixing his story is not why we're here, though we've given ample notes for how that can be done. Right now, our goal is to determine Hercules's intention, identify where the script is and isn't working to convey it, and fix it.

Does everybody agree with that revision of the story concept?

No hands go up. Every head nods.

Okay, we've identified the intention; now let's tackle the script, panel by panel.

I'm presenting each panel below, followed by its critique.

PAGE ONE / PANEL 1

In a bedroom, we see a husband in pajamas, sitting on top of covers in bed, with his back propped up against pillows and the backboard. His legs are crossed. He aims a TV remote control in one hand, pointing it past his wife, who is sitting up, under covers, reading a book by the light from the lamp that sits on the bed stand to her left. The TV is the thing the husband is pointing the remote at, and it is not on. Next to the husband, his nightstand is piled with stuff, books, magazines, and household gadgets.

CRITIQUE: This image establishes the location and introduces both characters, but it violates the left-to-right scripting guideline portion of the assignment.

"Is that really so important?" you ask. "Or are you just being anal about a panel that wasn't written the way you wanted it written?"

"Let's see," I answer.

Hercules clearly wants us to take special note of the nightstand, likely because he's going to pay off this part of the image in the last panel on Page Two. However, based on how the rest of this panel is staged, this messy nightstand will be on the left side of the panel, not the right, yet the writer clearly wanted this to be the final image we perceive or remember.

"Why can't the nightstand be on the right-hand side?" you ask. "Maybe that's where Hercules wanted it to be."

"Maybe it is," I answer. "Let's explore this question."

If Hercules intends the messy nightstand to be on the right, then the TV is on the left, nearest to the wife's side of the bed, and that means everything else is written backwards from right-to-left. Presuming Hercules tried to follow the assignment, it's more likely that the nightstand was an afterthought added later or as something important placed at the end to capture our attention. The problem with the latter is that it may leave that impression with the person who reads the script but won't leave that impression with the person who reads the finished comic.

"And we come back to my first question," you ask. "What's the big deal if he tossed it in later, as an afterthought, or wanted to get the artist's attention. The artist will know where to put it."

"Maybe the artist will, and maybe the artist won't," I reply.

Remember, the panel description is written so an artist will know the writer's intention. In this case, the artist might draw the panel with the nightstand on the left or the right.

"So what does that matter?" you ask.

"It might not matter at all where the nightstand is placed in this panel," I answer, "but it will certainly affect where everything else is placed in relation to it, here and in following panels."

Is that important? Let's see.

In numerous panels, we see the husband doing something and the wife reacting to it, or visa versa, with the wife doing something and the husband reacting to it. Even though it's perfectly fine in comics to show a reaction to an action on the left and the initiating action on the right, as written in this script, the person acting is supposed to be on the left, and the person reacting is on the right.

Put them in a field filled with daisies and switching who does something (on the left) and who reacts (on the right) is not an issue. We can view them from any angle in the field and easily flip who's on the left and who's on the right to get the desired order for action and reaction. But the location in this script is a room filled with furniture. The bed is probably not in the middle of the room to allow such flexibility of camera movement, nor is it going to move from wall to wall to suit the storytelling, and the characters do not move far from the bed. In fact, the bed is central in every panel that contains both of them in it. (We'll leave the sub-textual analysis to Freud.)

Sketch a quick overhead diagram of the room, as described in Page One, Panel One, showing the husband's nightstand against a wall on the left, then the bed, with the messy headstand against the same wall. The husband is on the left side of the bed (as we look down at it), within reach of the messy nightstand, and the wife is on the right side of the bed (as we look down at it). Next to the wife's side of the bed is the wife's nightstand with her reading lamp. Next we see the TV on the right side of the diagram, with its back against a perpendicular wall, facing the wife's side of the bed.

Done? Good.

Looking at this diagram from the base of the bed, the nightstand is on the left and TV is on the right.

Does anybody dispute this?

No hands are raised. Most heads make a subtle shake back and forth.

Okay, so what happens when we want to show the wife, on her side of the bed, doing something first, and the husband, on his side of the bed, reacting to what his wife has done?

To accomplish this, she needs to be on the left and the husband needs to be on the right.

Does anybody dispute this?

Most heads make an even-more-subtle shake, sensing that the boom is about to be lowered.

Viewing the diagram from every possible angle, do you see the only options we have for viewing this potential image are a down-shot from above or a view from *behind* the bed, a bed that is shoved up against the wall?

"What if the view is from behind their pillows?" you ask.

"Yes, that's a possibility, too, with them so large in the foreground that the nightstand and TV had better not be part of the intended image. For facial expressions, at best, we get side views."

From any of these perspectives, to have the wife on the left and the husband on the right, it would be a challenge to draw. And wouldn't an artist love you for writing it?

"So maybe we don't write that panel," you suggest.

"Too late," I say.

Boom.

Let's take a glance at *Page Two, Panel Five:*

PAGE TWO / PANEL 5

The wife stands next to the TV, her arms crossed, a wry expression on her face. The television is on, showing a baseball game in progress. The husband peers over the top of the bed, his eyes slightly widened in surprise.

To clarify, in this panel, in order from left to right, we first see the wife showing her triumphant wry expression, then the TV turned on, and then the husband reacting to the TV that was manually turned on. From left to right, this is the order of how we are supposed to view these elements.

Does anybody disagree with this?

"Couldn't we first see the husband surprised, then the TV turned on, then his wife with her wry grin?" you ask. "Couldn't that work, too?"

"Yes," I answer. "That could be the order of elements in the panel. If we do that, with the wife on the right, instead of on the left, the wife's wry grin is the last thing we see. It has become the visual punch line of this panel, and it does work nicely. However, presuming Hercules intended us to view the panel as he wrote it, which was from left to right, the man reacting to the TV having been turned on is the visual punch line, which also works nicely.

"Either is valid. Do we all agree, though, that they would leave different impressions with the reader?"

Every single head nods slowly in agreement.

I ask, "So how is the artist supposed to know which version fits with Hercules's intention?"

"Can't the artist decide which works best?" you ask.

"Yes," I answer, "and that often happens. But that result doesn't fit our current goal, which is to write a script in such a way that the artist will know and can draw what was intended. If we look at how Hercules wrote Page Two, Panel Five, and we accept that he was writing from left to right to show the artist the order in which to present the images, do we agree that the wife is on the left and the husband is on the right?"

Every head nods, even more slowly, still absorbing the points of contention.

"Looking at the diagram, do you all agree that trying to view Page Two, Panel Five from behind the pillow or bed would be awkward, if not impossible, to draw?

Every head nods, embellished by an unsolicited sigh or two.

"And do we all agree that a down-shot is certainly going to be awkward, at best, and would not allow us to get a good view the characters' important facial expressions?"

More nodding. More sighing.

Well, then, as the saying goes, "Houston, we have a problem." (For those who don't know the quote, watch *Apollo 13*, once for the reference and a couple dozen more times for pleasure.)

Problem: the intention of the script is in conflict with its staging. One or both will lose out, to varying degrees.

Problem translation: Just because something can be written, that doesn't mean it can be drawn.

Solution: In the revision, Hercules needs to become more aware of all the visual elements in his script, as well as how they can be drawn and perceived. If that means Hercules needs to diagram elements in a room or draw rough stick-figure thumbnails of a page in order to understand what can and cannot be achieved, that's fine. A comics writer doesn't need to know how to draw, but he or she does need to know how to visualize well enough so that the script can be drawn.

"Point taken," you note. "Are we done with this script?"

"You wish."

"Okay, are we ready to move onto the next panel?" you ask.

"You wish."

While left-to-right panel staging is the greater consideration in this panel, we should address another aspect of the panel description that may be (or may not be) a point of concern, specifically the part that reads: "... we see a husband in pajamas, sitting on top of covers in bed, with his back propped up against pillows and the backboard. His legs are crossed."

Can this be drawn? Absolutely.

How much of this is necessary? Well, we come back to the question of intention.

Hercules has written a clear image of the position in which this character is posed, and that's a good thing.

An artist might draw this exactly as indicated or take from this the *sense* of the overall image and improvise, either of which is a fine and necessary part of the collaborative process.

But what if Hercules wants the husband to be in this exact position? What if Hercules feels his vision is compromised if the artist draws the husband in a slightly different position or under the covers instead of on top of them? Is Hercules's vision compromised by an artist staging the husband differently?

A hand slowly rises from the multitude.

"If that's what Hercules wanted, then yes, I think his vision for how the panel should look is compromised."

"Fair point," I reply. "Is the intention of the script, the point of the story, the goal of showing the husband relaxed in bed and ready to watch TV, compromised by the artist making this change?"

"Um..." you answer.

"Exactly," I reply. "Um."

We will discuss later how to negotiate through the collaborative process, as well as how to determine what is and isn't important in the visual interpretation of the script. For now it is fair to say that an artist needs to be allowed fair interpretation of the material, as long as the main visual clues, pacing, and story points are retained. Anything less could result in a writer cutting off his nipple to spite his chest.

I ask: "How could this description have been written to convey the broader vision, without getting so specific that it might stifle the artist?"

You answer: "The husband lies comfortably in bed."

"Good," I respond. "That is all a broader description needs, and it allows for an artist to find his or her best interpretation of that image."

Another student asks, "But what if the character isn't in a comfortable position? Wouldn't it have been better for Hercules to simply describe the position?"

"You might think so," I answer, "but not necessarily. If the husband is lying stiffly in bed, instead of comfortably, it's much easier to make an observation about the overall demeanor than about whether the legs are properly crossed. This approach to a discussion can take much of the ego out of the collaborative process and keep the focus on whether the art accomplishes the overall professed goal.

"Notice, by the way, Hercules's description never explicitly describes the husband as being comfortable in his position; it's implicit. So what happens if the husband is in the exact position that's described but doesn't appear to be comfortable?"

"Um..." the student says.

"Um, indeed," I reply. "The artist can simply say, 'I drew what you described.'"

How panel descriptions are written is a personal choice. There are many good reasons for "going Alan Moore" (and describing everything) or "going Denny O'Neil" (and keeping the focus only on what's most important to advance the narrative).

There is no right or wrong, as long as the approach allows for an artist to discern the writer's intention. Where the writer fills panel descriptions with detail, if it can be drawn as described, that's fine, and if it's a broad-strokes description that allows for an artistic interpretation of the minutiae, that's fine, too.

The point here, and later when we discuss different approaches to formats and panel descriptions, is that the writer understands the benefits and the tradeoffs.

Could Hercules have benefited by adding that the husband is in a comfortable position on the bed, before describing that position? Absolutely. It's always good to keep the bases covered.

Onto *Page One / Panel Two!*

PAGE ONE / PANEL 2

This is a close-up of the husband's finger pushing the power button on the remote.

CRITIQUE: "So you're okay with this panel description, right?" I ask.

"Right," you reply.

"Wrong," I answer back.

How do we know it's the power button that's being pressed?

"Well, the button is labeled 'ON'," you answer.

"But the husband's finger covers the button," I respond, "and presumably the 'ON' label, too."

"What other button could it be?" you ask.

"Maybe he's raising the volume or changing the channel," I respond.

"But the TV isn't even on," you note accurately.

"You're right," I reply. "So maybe it's implicit that he's trying to turn it on."

"Exactly," you say.

"So the reader of the script knows that it's the power button that's being pushed, but the reader of the finished comic will see a finger on the remote and need to conclude that's what's going on. Right?"

"Um...right," you answer.

"Is this difference going to make a difference in this instance? Will it change the perception of how the comic is read? Probably not. But that's not the point. The point is that this is another instance of something that's written in the script that's not necessarily going to be absolutely clear in the finished comic.

"And that's something to be concerned about. That's something for the writer to be aware of in the future so that he or she doesn't make a monumental slip when it does matter.

"How would you fix this panel description?" I ask.

"Simple," you say. "'This is a close-up of the husband's finger clicking the remote.' We might add a CLICK sound effect to carry the point home."

Now the script reader won't be getting important story information that's deprived from the reader of the finished comic. If you want to cover all the bases, here's a variation: "This is a close-up of the husband's finger clicking the remote. From this, and the CLICK sound effect, the reader should conclude the husband's is trying to turn on the TV."

See how this explains what we hope the reader will glean from the drawn panel? See how this helps the artist know what the writer intends?

Next panel.

PANEL 3

The TV is still off.

CRITIQUE: "How about this panel description? Is it working for you?" I ask.

"Yeah," you reply. "I think so."

"Me, too," I respond.

PANEL 4

The wife is perturbed, her head turned to look at her husband.

CRITIQUE: "What about this one?" I ask.

"Well," you answer, "as written, the wife would be on the left and the husband would be on the right. We already discussed the nature of what we'd need to do to make that work, didn't we?"

"We did," I reply. "How would you fix it in this panel?"

"Well, there are two options. The first is to flip it so the husband is on the left and the wife is on the right. This way we see what he's doing and then that she's annoyed by it."

"How would that read?" I ask.

"Simple," you say. "'The husband is studying the remote with a perplexed expression. The wife looks at him, perturbed.'"

"I like how you added the husband doing something, but doesn't this addition make the next panel redundant?"

"Oh, right," you mumble.

"You said there were two options," I add.

"The alternative is to keep the husband out of the panel. This way we don't have to worry about switching the angle from which we're viewing her."

"And how would that read?" I ask, encouraged by the response.

You answer, "The wife is perturbed, her head turned to look in the direction of her husband, who is off-panel."

"Good."

PANEL 5

The husband is annoyed as he looks down at the remote.

CRITIQUE: "This panel is fine," you state.

"I agree."

PANEL 6

Close-up on the husband's fingers, as they hold the remote in such a way that we can see the lower portion of its reverse side. The piece that is supposed to hold the batteries in place is not there, and a place where one of two batteries should be lodged is empty. One of the batteries is missing!

CRITIQUE: "Is this one also working?" I ask.

"Yes," you answer.

"What about the part that reads, 'One of the batteries is missing'?" I ask.

"The writer is noting the conclusion the character and the comics reader will come to," you answer. "I think it's a good way to show what's important about this panel to the artist."

"I agree," I reply.

PANEL 7

The husband sets the remote on his nightstand, amidst the rest of the mess, while he is in the process of turning to get out of bed, with one of his two feet near the floor.

CRITIQUE: "And how well is this panel written?" I ask.

"Um..." you reply.

"Yes," I answer. "Um, indeed."

I'd say this is a tendency by the writer to be thinking in terms of film, not comics, where there's conceived a series of actions, rather than a single frozen image. The result is a classic case of a writer trying to do more than can be reasonably accomplished and perceived by a reader in a single panel. The focus on what the husband is doing is split. He's putting something down and trying to stand up, but hasn't yet stood up. At best, if drawn as described, it will make an awkward drawing. Since setting down the remote is the more important of the two actions, story-wise, the artist will likely show the husband sitting on the side of the bed, with his feet on the ground, and setting down the remote. This will eliminate the superfluous act of turning to get out of bed.

There is a really simple way to avoid writing yourself into this kind of cinematic trap, but first, a caveat: most rules can and should be broken under the right circumstances.

If writers want to avoid potential action conflicts like the one in this panel, keep in mind a simple rule of thumb: don't try to have a character concentrate on more than one physical thing in a single panel.

In this case, have the character put down the remote or get out of bed, not both.

"Interesting rule," you say.

"Pick up any comic," I respond. "Simply look at the characters in the panels. Don't read the balloons or try to follow the stories; just look at the characters and what they're doing. Now, how many of the character drawings show a character concentrating on more than one thing at a time?"

"Does leaping out of a helicopter and shooting a gun count as two things?" you ask.

"Is the character concentrating on his shooting or his leaping?" I ask.

"The shooting," you answer. "He's already leapt out of the helicopter and is in mid-air."

"Is he concerned yet about the process of leaping or where he's going to land?"

"No."

"Then the leaping part is behind him, the landing part is ahead of him, and at this point he's only concentrating on the shooting. It's not any different than having a character shooting and running."

"But that's still two things," you answer.

"Yes, it is," I concede, "but which is he concentrating on?"

"The shooting," you answer, "because he's already running."

"If he were just beginning to run, or leap out of a helicopter, or get out of bed, and if any of these was his focus, how easy would it be to have him also concentrate on shooting a gun?"

"Um," you say.

"Exactly," I respond. "It's the 'not having a character concentrate on two things at the same time' that's important, not 'having the character do two things.'

"This is a *KISS* rule, something to keep in mind so that you won't get more caught up in your writing than what can be effectively drawn."

"KISS?" you ask.

"Keep It Simple, Stupid," I answer. "No offense."

PAGE TWO

PANEL 1

The husband is now standing next to the bed, and he's lifted up the sheet and cover to see if the battery fell out there.

CRITIQUE: "Does this panel work for you?" I ask.

"Yes," you answer.

"What about the part that describes his intention?" I ask. "How does a comic reader know he's looking for the battery?"

"It's implicit," you answer, "and it helps the artist know why the husband is checking under the sheets."

"I agree," I reply. "It's like Page One, Panel Six. Describing a character's intention can be a terrific writer's tool, as long as the reader can discern that intention from the drawn comic. Adding it is like advising the artist, 'This is what I want the reader of the comic to take from this.' It becomes the touchstone for the intention of the panel, and that's what this is all about, communicating intention."

"And this comes back to Page One, Panel One, too," you begin, "where Hercules could have noted the husband's demeanor as 'casual.'"

"Exactly," I respond. "Noting intention complements panel description and helps an artist fully understand the goal."

PANEL 2

His wife is now turned to get out of her side of the bed, her legs on the floor, her expression showing annoyance. Meanwhile, the man is crouched down on the floor on his side of the bed, his head low enough to look under the bed for the missing battery.

CRITIQUE: "Any thoughts on this panel?" I ask, knowing that you know we've been here before.

"We're back to the problem of needing to put the wife on the left and the husband on the right," you note.

"That's right," I confirm. "How would you fix it?"

You ponder the staging options. "Can we view this from the wife's side of the bed, closer to the wall so that she's to the left and husband is on the other side of the bed to the right?"

"We can," I say, "and that's a nice creative solution. So, where is the husband positioned on the other side of the bed?"

"Um," you say, "on the floor, looking under the bed."

"Right," I say, "so we would have to be viewing this from a pretty high angle to see both of them, wouldn't we?"

"We would," you answer, "but the reader might not easily see what the husband is doing. Is there a simpler solution?"

"There is," I say. "The simple alternative is to flip it so the husband is on the floor, looking under the bed for the battery, and then show her responding to this. At this point in the story, I think it actually makes cleaner storytelling sense, too. He does something, which is still looking for the battery, and she reacts to it, being pissed as she gets out of bed.

"Just to clarify," I add, "in another script with more staging options the reverse can work, too, and often effectively."

"How so?"

"Assuming that putting the wife on the left can work, staging-wise, first show her, annoyed, and then show him, the source of her annoyance. It adds a beat of consideration by the reader."

"What kind of a beat?" you ask.

"Well, it's a moment where the reader looks at her and asks, probably in a microsecond, 'Why's she pissed?' The different staging creates that question in the reader's mind, thus adding a beat of consideration.

"The order of 'which goes first, the action or the reaction?' is an incredibly valuable storytelling tool. Like any tool, even though..."

"It needs to be used with intention," you say, reading my mind and finishing my sentence.

"Exactly so," I reply. "Do you have any concern about the part of the description that indicates the husband is looking under his bed for the missing battery?"

"Nope," you answer. "It declares the husband's intention, and the visual corresponds well to it."

"I agree."

PANEL 3

This is a view looking toward the husband peering at us from underneath the bed. In the foreground, we can see un-vacuumed dust bunnies, a lost cat toy, a discarded paperback that is open with its spine up, but there's no battery to be seen. On the far side we see the husband squinting toward us, peering into the dark to find the battery. No luck! The camera is actually on the other side of the bed, so that we can see the wife's feet in the foreground, which are now on the carpet.

CRITIQUE: "What are your thoughts about this panel?" I ask.

"Something feels wrong," you answer.

"Right," I respond, "With one major aesthetic concession, it cannot be drawn without significant modification, so the reader cannot perceive what the writer indicated."

"What's the major concession?" you ask.

"We'll get to specifics later, but to make this work the rest of the story art or color would have to be boxed into a very specific corner."

"But the panel seems so simple," you say. "Where's the problem?"

"Let's take it step by step. "How is the left-to-right description working for you?"

"Um...I don't see anything that's left-to-right here."

"Correct," I respond, "because there isn't any. This panel is intended to be read from back to front. Does that work?"

"Why from back to front?" you ask.

"The back is mentioned first and the front is mentioned last. Does that work?"

"No," you answer. "No matter how it's written, readers are going to see what's in front of the panel before their eyes check out what's in the background."

"Agreed," I reply. "Then presuming this was written from front to back, can the panel be perceived as the writer intends?"

"It seems pretty straightforward," you answer.

"It may be written clearly, but let's take a look at what Hercules wrote. From foreground to background, please describe what's in this panel."

You answer: "Feet in the foreground, stuff under the bed in the middle-ground, and the man looking at us in the background."

"That's what I see, too," I say. "Let's tackle each one of these focal points.

"The wife's feet are in the foreground. Are they big or small?"

"Big," you answer, "because the perspective would make them so."

"Correct," I say. "The feet probably take up a huge portion of this panel. They don't really help to advance the story, because the wife could still be sitting with her feet on the floor or standing. The panel would have to be very tall for us to discern the difference, but let's keep going.

"Looking at the stuff under the bed, there's a lot of it, some of which is very specifically detailed, like the open, discarded paperback."

"Is there a problem with the detail?" you ask.

"Not really," I answer, "not that it's significant one way or another to this story, except to indicate that there's stuff under the bed. The specific detail of the stuff doesn't matter. What matters is that we can see that the missing battery isn't here."

"So what's the problem?" you ask

"The answer to one simple question. Is the space under the bed fully lit or dark?"

"Um..." you say.

"Right," I say. "Um. To recognize all this stuff, the area under the bed would have to be lit well enough to identify it. Have you looked under your bed lately?"

"Can't it be dark or dingy under the bed?" you ask.

"It can and should be," I answer. "If it's dark, can we see that the lost battery is not there?"

"No," you answer. "From this viewpoint, even if there was some indirect lighting, everything under the bed should be darkly shaded or colored or close to silhouette."

"Right," I say. "But the panel description says that the battery isn't there. How is the artist supposed to show that if what's under the bed can't be easily recognized?"

"Can't the artist or colorist take some license and light the area?" you ask.

"Yes," I answer. "And that's the only way the writer's intention can be achieved in this portion of the panel. However, that means the entire shading or color scheme in this story needs to be based on how the artist or colorist handles this panel. It really puts the artist or colorist in a corner, at least if he or she wants the lighting in this panel to be consistent with the lighting in the rest of this story."

"So it can be done," you conclude.

"With a significant sacrificial limitation to the rest of the story, yes," I reply. "Do you think Hercules was aware of this when he wrote this panel?"

"Probably not," you concede, "or he would've indicated the lighting here and throughout."

"Right," I conclude, "meaning that, in this panel, he inadvertently affected how the rest of the story needed to be drawn and colored, providing the artist or colorist would've figured out what we've figured out."

"Either way, it's not ideal," you say.

"Agreed," I reply.

"Now, what about the husband peering at us from the other side of the bed?" you ask. "Is that okay?"

"I like that image," I answer. "Actually, I like the idea for this entire panel image. The problem is that, without significant aesthetic compromise, it can't convey to the reader of the comic what Hercules wants it to convey."

"Well, if the area under the bed is dark," you conclude, "all it shows is that he's looking under the bed."

"Right," I say. "Now, that might be enough for Hercules. If all he wanted to convey is that the husband is searching high and low for the lost battery, then that goal is achieved in this panel..."

"...but that's not what Hercules wrote," you conclude, "meaning that his intention cannot be easily achieved without a significant compromise, of which he is likely unaware."

"That's correct," I say. "Let's move onto the next panel."

PANEL 4

This shot is close on the wife's index finger depressing the TV's ON button.

CRITIQUE: "So, are you feeling the déjà vu?" I ask.

"I am," you answer. "With the finger covering the button, the reader can't know it's the 'ON' button."

"Right," I reply. "In general, it's sloppy writing. In this case, it may not affect what the reader perceives in the finished comic, but this kind of mistake can end up derailing an entire story by muddying the perception of what is supposed to be a crystal clear image."

"How would you fix this and still keep it simple?" you ask.

"Easy," I respond, embracing the challenge. "This shot is close on the wife's index finger pushing a button on the TV."

"But how is the reader supposed to know it's the ON button?" you ask.

"In this panel," I answer, "maybe it doesn't matter that the reader is supposed to know it's the ON button, but the description now represents something that can be perceived as drawn. However, if you feel the need to show the TV is being turned on, you can add something to the art description, perhaps the old-style picture tube's little white dot that appears at the center of a TV screen to indicate that something is happening on it. Or, if you simply feel the artist needs to know what this panel description is about, you can add: 'In the next panel, the reader will know it was the ON button that was pushed.' See? Simple."

Clearly frustrated, you ask, "Is it really this hard to write comics?"

"No," I answer. "It's this hard to write comics well. Where most writers understandably want to focus on story, it takes practice and a focus on the craft to execute a story well. As previously discussed, when something is written poorly or sloppily, it's usually the editor or artist who gets saddled with fixing the problems, providing they get fixed at all."

"So if a writer doesn't know what he's doing, he or she should constantly work to improve, rather than being defensive about what isn't working," you say. "And if a writer knows what he or she is doing, then why shouldn't he or she do it well in the first place and save everybody the unnecessary aggravation?"

"Right," I answer. "I'm not sure there's such a thing as a perfect script, but the more a writer knows about what can and can't be drawn, and the more a writer knows how the visual interpretation of the script will be perceived by the reader, the more likely the finished comic will be a reflection of his or her intention. I think that's a lofty and achievable goal."

PANEL 5

The wife stands next to the TV, her arms crossed, a wry expression on her face. The television is on, showing a baseball game in progress. The husband peers over the top of the bed, his eyes slightly widened in surprise.

CRITIQUE: "We discussed this panel earlier," you say. "The wife and TV being on the left means we'd have to view these images from an awkward angle."

"Right," I respond. "Given the options, I'd follow the lead we discussed in another panel. The simple solution is to flip the reading order so the husband is on the left and the wife is on the right. In this version, he would be responding to something we haven't yet glanced right to see, then we'd see the TV turned on and the wife's wry expression."

You ask, "What if Hercules definitely wanted to show the husband's wide-eyed expression after showing the TV? How could he do that?"

"Simple," I answer. "Add more panels. If that's what we really need to do, space allowing, I'd use three panels in this one's place, each one fairly narrow. After the panel showing the wife pushing the TV button, the next panel would show the husband looking over the bed to see what the wife is doing. She isn't in this panel. The next panel would show the TV on and the wife's crossed arms and wry expression. The third replacement panel would repeat the layout from the first replacement panel, the only difference being that the husband is now wide-eyed in surprise. Keeping the angle on the panel from the panel he was previously in, allows the reader to note the differences between the two, in this case his change of expression."

"Can't it be done in two panels?" you ask.

"Sure," I say. "I made it three because I wanted to show the husband reacting to the wife pushing the button. It also set up the layout for the last panel, but this is a pacing preference. You could easily take out my first replacement panel and retain the goal of showing the husband's reaction after showing the TV turned on."

PANEL 6

The husband and wife are back in bed. She's reading her book, and he's happily paying attention to the game that's on the TV. The forgotten remote lies with the rest of the junk on the husband's nightstand...right next to the missing battery.

CRITIQUE: "And how is this last panel working for you?" I ask.

You answer, "Well, as we previously discussed, it doesn't work from left to right at all. The most important image is the lost battery, and if we keep the husband on the left and the wife on the right, then the battery is the first thing we see, not the last. Since we can't easily flip their positions in the room, I'd follow the suggestion you made to fix the previous panel."

"Agreed," I say. "Make it two panels. How would you do that?"

"Simple," you answer. "In the first panel, show this longer view with the nightstand, husband, wife, and TV reading from left-to-right. In the next panel, show a close shot of the battery amidst the mess on the nightstand, which solves another potential problem, which is that it'd be pretty hard to spot the battery next to all the other junk on the nightstand."

"Good catch," I say. "That's how I'd handle it, too. Hercules will likely have his own ideas, but for the purposes of this discussion, we've identified what isn't working and offered constructive solutions."

Now that we've completed the Evisceration of Hercules, turn that same wicked scalpel inwards, not to commit seppuku, but to consider your own two-page story and address what needs to be fixed. As you do so, keep in mind that old adage and repeat it to yourself like a mantra: writing is rewriting.

This will help your script reflect the comic you intend it to be.

Not just this one; all of them.

Chapter 9

Inside Balloons: Sequential Art Punctuation & Word Emphasis

Does it make us feel defensive that Mark Twain and Charles Dickens didn't combine question marks with exclamation marks?! Are we bothered that William Shakespeare and Dorothy Parker didn't use multiple question and exclamation marks to note greater emphasis???!!!

It shouldn't.

Until we accept that sequential art stands alone as a medium, that it does not function or read like prose or poetry or plays or screenplays, and has its own unique toolbox that works for it in a way that other media toolboxes do not, then we are bound to feel and behave like awkward, unwanted literary stepchildren.

But that is not who we are. We simply need to take our cue from Hans Christian Andersen and accept our kinship with the ugly duckling, recognize we are swans, and stop bothering to compete with our stepbrothers and stepsisters, the ducks.

Just like with prose, poetry, and other literary, stage, film, and art forms, our use of tools and language changes with time, tastes, and the market. Even as we experiment with and embrace new techniques, aesthetics, and tools, the old ones do not go away. They sit in the toolbox, waiting to be used. For this reason, little is standardized about comic book punctuation and word emphasis, except that it's not standardized. This can lead to creator and reader confusion, perhaps not anywhere near my level of confusion with astrophysics and cricket, but we're going to note and address consistencies and inconsistencies of use, as well as misperceptions of intent.

A hand rises in back.

"Yes?"

"So are you going to show us the right way to use punctuation and word emphasis?"

"No. We're going to discuss how they're used today, where many uses originated, how they're often perceived by others, and then I'll leave it for you to decide how and when to do what you think is appropriate."

"That's an interesting switch," you remark. "In previous chapters, you've laid down guidelines for how stuff works and disdained certain industry practices, like top-to-bottom-reading panels. If a reader cannot clearly understand the use of punctuation and word emphasis, why backslide on showing the right way to use them?"

I'm not backsliding. Remember the Comics Creator's Creed? "I have all the sequential art tools at my disposal, and I will use them to ensure that the finished version of my work is perceived as I intend it to be perceived."

Everything in your sequential art toolbox has a purpose, even top-to-bottom-reading panels, which may be preferred by a particular type of creator, editor, and/or fan. (What I think of that result is irrelevant; what the creator thinks of that result is everything.) Throughout, I've set down guidelines for how sequential art tools work, but with the explicit or implicit understanding that these guidelines are starting places. Effectively deviating from them requires knowing how a prospective collaborator, editor, and/or reader will perceive these deviations.

I am not going to offer simple answers and simple rules. You could browse online and get numerous single-sentence or short summaries for how somebody else thinks you should address comics punctuation, but much of that gives you direction without the benefit of historical usage and rationale.

Here, we're going to discuss and challenge dogma, and then you can figure out for yourself what works for your project.

The key to the effective use of punctuation and word emphasis, like the key to the use of any sequential art tool, is to tailor them to the needs of the creator, the project, and the prospective readership. Ideally, these needs will be in synch. However, where a creator understands that his or her use of punctuation and word emphasis, like the use of any sequential art tool, may not be understood or interpreted the way he or she intended, it still remains his or her decision to use them.

It's important to note the creator may not have the last word on this or any other crafts-related topic, just as I am not the last word. Where somebody else gets a vote, perhaps a partner, an editor, or a publisher, he or she may or may not agree with a particular use of the toolbox. How it gets resolved is the subject of future chapters, but for now it's important to note the result of such disagreements will be acquiescent, collaborative, unsuccessful, or dictatorial.

As Stan Lee wrote, *'nuff said*.

The use of punctuation and word emphasis in comics is personal, based on a combination of traditional, inconsistent, intuitive, and historical usage. It's personal in a way that's similar to prose writers not completing sentences. Which is fine. Except good prose writers don't pack together a lot of exclamation points! While good comics writers sometimes do!!!!! Do you see good prose writers combine punctuation marks? Rarely. But do good *comics* writers combine punctuation marks???!!! Sure, but it's not requisite. Which brings us to the use of ellipses...

--and double-hyphenated dashes, which aren't actually dashes but are often used like them.

Next we come to word emphasis, and *making* the determination to *use* it or *not* use it. And *where* we use it, we get to sort through the options for using it *well*. Providing such a way *exists*.

Confusing?

Of course it is.

Let's straighten this out by taking an anecdotal trip into the past with Mr. Peabody's Wayback Machine.

We begin with punctuation.

To get there, we travel back to the early part of the 20th Century in the United States. Comic books didn't yet exist, comic strips ruled the newspapers, and comic strip characters were among the first and most popular licensed properties.

The sequential art form had been born here and abroad, and cartoonists were still making most of it up as they went along. Sure, balloons with pointers and panel borders had become conventions, certain genres captured the public fancy and were endlessly imitated and produced, just like today, but this was still the Wild West of Creative Invention, and the sequential art sandbox was still being built, along with its use of language, which was still being formed.

Sometimes there was no punctuation to end the last sentence in a balloon; the words just stopped as though the period was implicit. And sometimes the same cartoonist in the same strip used a period to end the last sentence in a balloon. What was the distinction between the two ways to end a sentence? What differentiation did the cartoonist hope to impart? Frankly, this one still eludes me, and sometimes it's simply difficult to discern the intent.

But the medium was new and there weren't any rules for how it worked, so new sequential art storytelling and grammatical tools were constantly being invented, explored, evolved, and kept to be used again or cast aside.

However, there was one constant to the use of punctuation in early strips, whether it was grammatically correct or not: the punctuation usually fit the images.

This provides a key to unlocking the mystery for why it is perfectly okay for comic strips to fiddle with how punctuation is used. Comics are a graphic medium, and early creators melded their use of lettering, grammar, and balloons with the rest of the art. Whether consciously or unconsciously, they understood that it all needed to work together, that the visual use of lettering and grammar could be more important than an academically precise use.

In short, the use *looked* right, and that's what counted.

That's what became correct.

For example, the traditional use of an exclamation mark is for a short sharply spoken statement. Like this! But in comics, where we *see* somebody shouting, even where the sentence that's being shouted is long, a period just doesn't *feel* right, because the character is SHOUTING!!!!! The use of one or more exclamation marks visually corresponds to the character's tone, and conveys a sense of volume. It melds. It looks right, where a period at the end of that long sentence probably wouldn't look right.

To accompany the added punctuation for shouting, lettering was often drawn larger than what was spoken normally in a previously lettered panel. Anybody looking at it could intuitively understand that the size of the lettering corresponded to a raised voice.

Imagine being the one to invent this convention. You're sitting at your board and have drawn a character that's shouting. You letter the shouted words normal-sized, but it just doesn't look or feel right. And then it hits you! *Louder equals bigger!!* It's so brilliant in its simplicity that it takes my breath away just thinking about it.

Now what happens when a character is shouting a question? Doesn't an exclamation mark *feel* like it needs to be added to match the visual and tone of the character shouting?!

These are the type of issues early comic strip creators encountered and addressed. Some stuff stuck and some stuff didn't.

As cartoonists codified their comic strip toolboxes, a new aspect of the medium evolved from comic strip reprint magazines, most notably, Superman in *Action Comics* #1. To us, he's the Man of Steel. From a publisher's perspective you could call him the Man of Cheap Paper, Poor Printing, and Inexpensive Talent, the first of many vehicles created in the quest for a quick buck.

Early comic books were printed on coarse, pulpy paper, which soaked up ink like a sponge. The ink smeared, bled through, and spread out; colors were poorly registered. To avoid ink running together into a muddy mess, halftone line screens were low, meaning same-color dots were placed farther apart than in higher quality printing so they couldn't easily bleed into each other. High quality printing on a smooth or coated paper stock was usually 133 or even 150 lines (or rows) per inch. These closely spaced dots are hard to see without a magnifying glass or printer loupe. A mid-range halftone screen was 100 lines and still too close together for printing on newsprint. Newspaper and comic book screens were typically 65 lines per inch, which kept the printed dots farther away from each other, but were also easier to see without magnification, a result for which Roy Lichtenstein should be grateful.

A hand rises in back.

"Yes?"

"Thanks for the print production history lesson, but what does this have to do with punctuation?" you ask.

"That's a great question," I respond. "Directly, it has nothing to do with punctuation. Tangentially, in story terms, it's the inciting incident, the thing that caused something else to happen."

Because comic book printing was so poor, the simple period could drop out, making it hard for a reader to tell where one sentence ended and the next one began. Anecdotally, the simple solution was for letterers to end sentences with exclamation marks, which were more easily printed and seen than the disappearing periods.

A hand in back shoots up like molten lava erupted from a volcano.

You ask, "Are you saying that the multi-decade predominant comic book use of exclamation marks instead of periods is the cultural result of poor printing that no longer exists?"

"Anecdotally (from industry veterans who got it from a previous generation of industry veterans), yes."

"Oh."

Knocks your socks off, doesn't it?

Understanding the origin of our tools helps us make decisions based on current goals rather than dogma. Still, exclamation marks now have a place in the comics culture. In some contexts readers expect them; it often feels right to read them. In other contexts, they're like ancient artifacts that have lost their purpose.

As previously mentioned, we also retain sequential art punctuation from the early days of newspaper comic strips, notably the combined question marks and exclamation marks, which still do the job of corresponding to the image of a character shouting a question.

Traditionally, the shouted or insistent question ends with "?!", the question mark to indicate that a question is being asked and the exclamation mark to indicate the tone in which it's being asked.

There is a relatively recent variation, "!?", with the exclamation mark first and the question mark second.

While consulted comics-industry professionals seem to agree the purpose of "!?" is identical to "?!", this flipped ordering does not read the same to me. It's a personal response, but this variation bugs me. It *feels* like an exclamatory remark with a questioning tone, and I've yet to figure out a sentence or situation where this can be well utilized. Some consulted comics-industry professionals agree that it doesn't look right, and others don't differentiate it from the flipped version or seem to care.

This is a great example of how our use of sequential art punctuation continues to evolve. The "!?" will either find a prominent place in the toolbox or fade with diminished use.

Next we come to the double-hyphenated dash.

We set aside our Wayback Machine, don our deerstalker hat, and employ our magnifying glass to seek clues to uncover this mystery.

A hand slowly rises above a wall of blank stares.

"Yes?"

"What mystery is that?"

"Why do comic books use a double-hyphen (--) instead of an en-dash (–) or an em-dash (—)?"

Your face contorts into something resembling dried fruit. "There's more than one kind of dash?"

Welcome to the world of editors, typesetters, proofreaders, and style guides; it's a world defined by the cliché, "the Devil is in the details." For this discussion, not only is the Devil in the building, he's bowing under the spotlight.

You often hear a hyphen on the keyboard referred to as a dash. It's not a dash; it's a hyphen.

An em-dash is as wide as the letter "m", thus the name.

An en-dash is as wide as the letter "n", also not a coincidence.

We see the most obvious em- and en-dash usage in prose as parenthetical remarks or segues—how they differ from parentheses is another discussion—but if you haven't previously studied them you'd be surprised by their other uses. That last sentence contains an em-dash that butts right up against the words before and after it, without spaces.

A variation of this usage – something that looks like this – has a space on either side of the dash, and this is where an en-dash should be used.

I'll leave it to your own studies and *The Chicago Manual of Style* to sort through the uses and misuses of the hyphen, the en-dash, and the em-dash.

For this discussion, we focus on their predominant use in comics, which is to conclude the abrupt halting of a sentence.

In prose, abruptly halting a sentence would require an em-dash that butts right up to the last word, like this—

Traditionally, in comics, we use double-hyphens instead of an em-dash, like this--

There is no concrete or even anecdotal reason for why comics started using double-hyphens instead of dashes, but there is an interesting theory (hello, *Ockham's Razor!*) that may be the simplest explanation, a theory several comics creators arrived at independently, so it's both a common-sense hypothesis and history lesson.

Before computers, the typewriter keyboard contained the full character limit of what could be typed in a manuscript, with only lower- and upper-case options for each key. While the keyboard did not have an en-dash or an em-dash, it did have a hyphen (to the right of the "0" in lower case).

When writing prose for a manuscript, the way to indicate a dash was to put two hyphens next to each other, like this: --

Typesetters understood this manuscript designation. When they saw it, they typeset a dash.

The theory is that early comic book letterers did not understand this designation, and simply lettered everything as it was presented in the manuscript.

A hand in back shoots back up like a second blast from the angry volcano.

You ask, "Are you suggesting that the multi-decade predominant comic book use of double-hyphens instead of dashes might be the cultural result of comic book letterers not knowing how to interpret what was typed in manuscripts?"

"Yes."

"Oh. Wow."

Indeed. But it's just a theory, albeit the only theory that makes sense.

Regardless, the double-hyphenated dash has a significant place in the sequential art toolbox. To me, it has a more organic look in a hand-lettered style than the em- or en-dash, but that might simply be cultural bias.

The persistent hand rises like a shark fin from the sea of perplexed expressions.

"Yes?"

You ask, "If a creator simply prefers the double-hyphenated dash, why bother with conjecture about its origin?"

Forewarned is forearmed.

One of these days you may come across an editor or proofreader from outside the comics industry who'll insist on an em- or en-dash. If that person comes from the world of education, it's likely to be a losing battle with the firing of the first shot, but at least you'll be able to explain where the double-hyphenated dash might have come from. It's so much better than saying, "Because that's the way we do things in comics."

Aesthetics, instead dogma, is a much more interesting discussion.

Next we come to the oddly variable use of ellipses.

There's no history lesson associated with this usage. It's simply the continuing tendency by comics creators to punctuate what they believe looks right inside balloons, whether their high school English teachers or university professors would approve or not. Still, after we're done you may wish to consult your resources and well-thumbed-through copy of *The*

Chicago Manual of Style.

Ellipses (...) are most commonly used to indicate a pause...like this...or that something has been excised from a sentence. Representing the latter use, you'll often see quotes from people begin or end with ellipses, showing that it was only a portion of the original quote. It would read like this, "...showing that it was only a portion of the original quote."

In comics, we often see ellipses following the last words at the end of a balloon or caption, as though the character or caption was pausing mid-thought. When that's the case...

...the next balloon or caption begins with ellipses to show you it's the continuation of the thought.

Ellipses are also used in comics to indicate that the end of a sentence in a balloon or caption has trailed off.

The most common example might be a caption that reads something like this: The next day...

Sometimes a character's words trail off to nothing, with no continuation, like in a balloon that reads: Um...

In *Chicago Manual of Style* Land, where there's no continuation of the sentence, these ellipses should be followed by a period to indicate the sentence is finished, like this.... You rarely see this grammatically correct additional period in comics.

Occasionally, though, you'll see two periods (..), which are used to show pauses or a trailing thought at the end of a balloon. In this case, we've returned to the realm of comics creators making up punctuation that feels and/or looks right.

Cartoonist Dan O'Neill uses double-periods to separate different thoughts in extended monologues, as well as to end trailing thoughts. Actually, he uses them so often that they read like paragraph breaks, which comes in handy, since the traditional paragraph break in comics is to start a new balloon, and O'Neill likes his balloons large and filled with words.

Cartoonist Charles Schulz used several versions of sequential periods in *Peanuts.* Speculatively, I think he used their number to match the intended length of a pause. If he wanted a short pause, he'd go with two periods. Longer pauses could be three or four. Look at his strips and see if you don't come to the same conclusion about the effect of their use.

I like this idea of equating the length of the pause to the number of periods.

Imagine a balloon containing only five periods. Wouldn't this be informing the reader that a character was lost for words?

What if the character had ten periods in a balloon? Does that feel like a longer span of time or is it just too much?

What if the character had two balloons with five periods in each one? I think they'd feel like a longer span of time than the one balloon with ten periods.

What if the character had a half dozen balloons with only two or three periods in them? Doesn't that seem to represent a character completely lost for something to say?

What if the balloons had no words or punctuation in them? Does this accomplish the same result or is that a character whose voice can't be heard?

You get the idea.

Mix the tools; get different results.

Returning to my earlier thesis, comics are a visual medium, and the visual use of punctuation often looks and feels more right than grammatical correctness.

The trick to the use is predicting the reader response, and then being sensitive to it.

A hand rises in back, no doubt overwhelmed by the potential of the period.

"Yes?"

"Sometimes I see ellipses used to connect a sentence from one balloon to the next, and sometimes I see double-hyphenated dashes doing the same thing. What's the difference between these uses?"

Great question.

Most working comics pros will agree that a double-hyphenated dash is for an interruption (No--wait!), and ellipses are for a pause (I...I don't know).

The most common example of an interchangeable use occurs when a sentence is clipped short at the end of one balloon--

--and continued at the beginning of the next balloon.

This sentence would more often have ellipses at the end of the first balloon...

...and continue them again at the beginning of the next balloon.

The difference between the two is a matter of timing, whether there's an intended pause--

--in the sentence...

...or not.

Most current comics use the ellipses to extend a sentence from one word balloon to another, but that's because most writers intend a pause at the splitting point.

Think of it this way: for a slow stop or pause, use ellipses; for a quick stop, like being interrupted, or no pause between the words, use a dash.

Keep these differences in mind...

...and you'll never be at a loss for which one--

--to use.

The next slice of our punctuation pie is the inconsistent use of quotation marks or open- and close-quotes.

A hand slowly rises in back with the purpose and hunger of a freshly wakened zombie.

"Yes?"

Convinced your prey is cornered, you ask, "How can the use of quotes be inconsistent? Isn't it a case of using them or not using them (like in this sentence)?"

"I am so glad you asked," I reply.

The most common inconsistent use takes place in captions boxes.

Where the caption boxes are simply a first-person narrative, you usually don't see quotes, just as you don't see them in the first-person narrative of a book or story.

Where there is dialogue in a caption box (for whatever reason), the dialogue begins with an open-quote. In America it looks like this ("), and in the UK, Canada, and other British-influenced countries the open-quote looks like this (').

I explain further, "In prose, when a character is finished speaking, there are closing quotes, like this (") or this (')."

I paused to demonstrate the point.

"When a character continues to speak in a subsequent paragraph, there are no close-quotes at the end of the first paragraph.

"The next paragraph begins with another open-quote, and there are no close-quotes until the character has stopped speaking."

Now comes the tricky part.

"When a character is speaking in a first caption box, and there is continuing dialogue in the next caption box, you will often see close-quotes at the end of the first caption box..."

"...even though the dialogue continues in the following caption box."

"If this was prose, it reads like there's more than one person speaking."

"This can be very confusing."

"It's as if there's something between the caption boxes that allows the writer to put close-quotes at the end of each caption box."

Your hand skyrockets up.

"Yes?"

"You said, 'It's as if there's something between the caption boxes that allows the writer to put close-quotes at the end of each caption box.'"

"Yes."

"Can't the visuals we're presumably seeing between caption boxes substitute for the prose we read between blocks of dialogue?"

Interesting thought.

As we've discussed, sequential art is a graphic medium, and we continue to adapt the rules of punctuation to fit the comic. With this in mind, though, comics creators need to be aware how their work can be misperceived.

Personally, I trend towards using quotes the way they're used in prose, because it doesn't require the reader to stop and think about who's speaking in the next panel.

Other writers clearly have different perspectives.

Tangentially, there's been an interesting evolution in caption boxes: color-coding to whomever is speaking.

For example, one character might speak in white lettering on a black field, another character could have black lettering on a blue field, and still another character could have black lettering on a pink field. The advantage of this use is to have the reader understand that several characters are speaking in succession, without reader confusion about who is speaking at any given time. Corresponding to our topic above, color-coding captions also allows a reader to understand that it is the same character speaking in successive captions, regardless of close-quotes use.

This is yet another addition to our toolbox, which, like so many tools that came before it, was clearly designed to address potential reader misperceptions.

Sometimes you'll even see the character's head inside the caption box, so there's no misunderstanding at all about who's speaking.

Whether your use of quotation marks, ellipses, or dashes is traditional or untraditional, be clear and consistent in the use. Otherwise, the reader will trip up, and the story flow will be interrupted.

Where the story flow is interrupted, fix it.

Clarity is king, and everything else is subordinate.

Now let's take the tarp off Mr. Peabody's Wayback Machine, which is getting surprisingly heavy usage.

Why do you think comics use bold-faced italic on certain words in a sentence?

You answer, "So we'll know how to read the intended word emphasis or inflection."

Correct.

There's a long tradition in comics of emphasizing certain words in sentences, usually with a bold-italic.

When do you think it started, and why?

"Why?" you ask, puzzled, before stating the obvious. "So we'd know how writers wanted their sentences to read."

"That may be why writers *chose* to emphasize certain words, but word emphasis, in itself, doesn't have a *predominant* history of use in prose or any other medium, not even comic strips, so why would early comic book creators have perceived a need to *use* this word emphasis technique as much as they did?"

"Um...." you say.

Exactly. Like with the use of exclamation marks and double-hyphenated dashes, discovering the reason word emphasis began may lead to its contemporary relevance or irrelevance.

Remembering that comics are a graphic medium, anecdotal reporting suggests that early comic book editors thought the large blocks of lettering in word balloons looked too gray. They wanted more pop (or contrast) in them to catch the reader's eye, so they added boldface or bold-italic to certain words. Sometimes the words chosen were simply character names, but more often they indicated word inflection so a reader would understand how the writer wished a sentence to read.

You ask, "Are you saying that the multi-decade predominant comic book use of word emphasis is because editors didn't like the way balloons looked with lots of words in them?"

"Anecdotally (from industry veterans who got it from a previous generation of industry veterans), yes."

"Wow."

Indeed.

Even though the predominant use of word emphasis is on the wane, it has an important place in our toolbox. Popping words inside balloons contributes to a "mainstream" comic book look. Words *not* popping says something, too, often that it's not "*just* a comic book."

If you choose to use word emphasis, next comes the question of how to decide which words to pop.

Each writer has an ear for how a sentence should read. The problem is that editors have ears, too, often with a different sense of voice.

That's certainly been my personal experience.

Back in my Stone Age, one editor was certain I'd chosen the wrong words to emphasize in a script. He instructed me on how to choose the right ones, and we had quite a long chat about it, leaving me pretty confused. Thereafter, I became insecure about deciding which ones were "right," constantly second-guessing myself as I switched emphasis back and forth from one word-choice to another. It became the most aggravating part of my sequential art process.

It wasn't until years later I realized there is no "right."

Just as an actor reads lines from a play or script with her/his own emphasis, making that performance unique from any other actor's, so it is for writers choosing how their characters will speak.

Here's the visual set-up in the last panel of a comic strip: Lucy holds a football, standing next to Charlie Brown. He lies on his back after having the football snatched away from being kicked.

Lucy says, without word emphasis: "It's not really a football, Charlie Brown. It's a metaphor for your life."

Here's a simple example with bold-italicized emphasis: "It's not really a football, ***Charlie Brown.*** It's a metaphor for your life."

Here's a way to put emphasis how different words in the sentences: "It's not ***really*** a football, Charlie Brown. It's a ***metaphor*** for your life."

Now here's another way to emphasize the line: "It's not really a ***football,*** Charlie Brown. It's a metaphor for your ***life.***"

No version is right or wrong. They simply impart a different inflection.

If you're at a loss for which words to emphasize, read the different versions aloud to determine your preference.

It's also up to you to determine whether every sentence or just the occasional sentence should have word emphasis.

My best tip on this topic: if an editor tells you your usage is "wrong," listen to her/his reasons. If they are because he/she has a different ear, then there's a proprietary issue at stake, which we'll discuss in a later chapter. If the editor's reason is that something isn't working (like so many bold-italic words that the sentence has become sing-songy), then it's advice intended to help you achieve your goals, and that's a different discussion.

Here's an example of this last point: "It's not ***really*** a ***football,*** Charlie Brown. It's a ***metaphor*** for your ***life.***"

Is that too much? Try saying it aloud and see if you don't agree. Regardless of the conclusion, it's a fair discussion.

Now we come to something that is more the result of punctuation, but it's important for knowing how to prepare a manuscript.

We set Mr. Peabody's Wayback Machine to when you took typing class. In my case, this was the first semester of 7th grade: Fall, 1964.

In typing class, before the Digital Age, you were taught to type two *SPACEBARS* after a period.

Why?

A reluctant hand rises above the surface of the Sea of Confused Faces. "Yes?"

You guess, "So there would be more than one space after a period." "That is correct."

Aesthetically, there should always be more than a single word-space after a period. The easiest way to achieve this in a manuscript or a letter was to type two *SPACEBARS*.

There was another practical reason typists were taught to put two *SPACEBARS* after a period. Without the added *SPACEBAR*, it could be difficult to differentiate a period from a comma, especially since typewriter ribbons were inexact at best in making their mark on paper. Typing the second *SPACEBAR* confirmed to the reader that a period preceded it, instead of a comma.

Taking another trip in Peabody's Wayback Machine, we arrive in a strange and distant world, one that existed before digital design and production, one that had yet to even hear of the Compugraphic phototypesetting system, an expensive and cumbersome machine that allowed anybody to set their own type. Its fonts were on filmstrips that spun at high speeds inside a light-free compartment, flashing letter-images onto photosensitive paper. You could actually run two font strips at a time without having to change strips. It was amazing! The Compugraphic was a transition between hot type and digital.

I see nothing in response but dull stares.

Hot type is a term for physical fonts that were assembled, letter by letter, to create galleys. The galleys were cut up and pasted onto mechanicals, which is another antiquated term for a board with all the type and art components pasted onto it with wax or glue. The finished mechanicals were exposed to film, processed and cleaned up by technicians, and ultimately used to make printing plates.

We've traveled back to the ancient world of print production. It's the late '70s, where *Star Wars* is still fresh and the highest watermark of cinematic special effects since *2001: A Space Odyssey.*

We take this most important trip to see if typesetters also added two *WORD-SPACES* after a period.

What's your best guess?

No reply, not even a tentative hand venturing above the horizon. There is, perhaps, an uncomprehending shrug.

Typesetters put a wider amount of blank space after a period than the space they put between words, but this after-period space was not twice the width of between-word space. Writers typing two *SPACEBARS* was simply another example of a manuscript designation that showed typesetters what was required.

Faces are scrunched, wondering whether I have lost my perspective and am becoming nostalgic.

Here's the difference between then and now.

Then: typesetters used manuscripts as a guide, but they were the ones to put in the actual type. Like with double-hyphenated dashes, they interpreted two *SPACEBARS* accordingly, making the finished type look the way it should, with a space after periods that was wider than the space between words, but less wide than a double-space between words.

Now: writers produce the document that is ultimately used for producing the finished digital type. Their text gets flowed or cut and pasted into the appropriate InDesign or Quark document. The upshot is that writers no longer need to type two *SPACEBARS* after a period in their manuscripts, because digital font design automatically adds the correct amount of space after a period.

If a writer types a second *SPACEBAR* after a period, that space doesn't look the way it should in the final product. Because of this, somebody has to take out all those second spaces in a manuscript. Based on personal experience, I can tell you it's a pain.

Still, writers are resistant to making changes from how they learned to type; it's muscle memory. I hope this particular trip down memory lane has shown that it's in the best interest of the finished book to add one *SPACEBAR* after a period and create a new muscle memory.

Here's a practical tip for how to take double-*SPACEBARS* out of a manuscript: do a *SEARCH* and *REPLACE* of the entire document. *SEARCH* for *<TWO SPACBARS>*, *REPLACE* with *<ONE SPACBAR>*, and *REPLACE ALL*. Repeat this process until there are no more double-*SPACEBARS* to replace.

IMPORTANT NOTE: this *SEARCH* and *REPLACE* technique only works if you *TAB* for paragraph indentions. For those who indent paragraphs with multiple *SPACEBARS* (like you were taught in typing class), do not try this *SEARCH* and *REPLACE* technique, because it will completely mess up your manuscript.

We've covered a wide range of related topics, many of them conflicting and ambiguous.

However you decide to use punctuation or word emphasis in sequential art, remember that the use should not be so pronounced that it calls unnecessary attention to itself. You don't want it to distract from what's important: the finished comic.

As always, let informed intuition be your guide. Know your tools and you'll know how best to use them to meet your goals.

In order to minimize any confusion readers may have about your use of punctuation and word emphasis, especially compared with how other creators may use them differently, simply set your ground rules for use as early as possible in your comic and then stick to them. Be consistent.

Consistency is your pal.

Chapter 10

Writing For the Page Turn

When I begin blocking out a sequential art story or book, one of my first semi-casual questions is, "Does the story begin on a right- or left-hand page?" The publishing standard is a right-hand page, but never make assumptions about what a publisher, anthology editor, or book designer will do with pagination. This might not seem like a top-tier concern, but therein lies the great misconception.

A hand rises in back.

"Yes?" I ask.

"What misconception is that?" you ask.

"While it's somewhat important to know whether a double-page spread begins on an odd- or even-numbered page," I respond dryly, (and wouldn't it be fun to discover after you've written the script to discover the left-hand side of your double-page spread starts on a right-hand page?), "it's critical for page turns."

Your hand pops up in back.

"What's a page turn?" you ask, planting your big toe onto the teeth of my Response-O-Meter.

I'm glad you asked.

Open the comic of your choice, somewhere in the middle so there's a sequential art page on the left and the right.

When you start reading the left-hand page, your peripheral vision picks up the right-hand page whether you like it or not. Any number of things on that page can draw your eye to them, from the layout, characters, large elements on the page, or color that pops; it could be anything.

Only one place is guaranteed to be a reveal, something your peripheral vision can't pick up, and that's the first panel on the left-hand side of a new spread.

How can you use this to your advantage?

Before you turn the page from one spread to another, you may or may not have some editorial expectations of what you're going to see. The last panel of a right-hand page sets up the anticipation.

And then you turn the page.

And then you see or read what's there.

Maybe the reveal is a change of location, a shift to other characters in the story, a story twist that wasn't expected, or something visually exciting. Maybe it's a double-spread illustration of two gigantic battling robots, or something that jumps out, shouting, "Boo!"

To pound home the nail, here are some simple examples:

Last panel on a right-hand page: A jet lifts off from a runway.

Next panel, after the page turn: Angled down shot from behind the plane, as it flies towards New York City.

If we weren't previously aware of its destination, we suddenly realize where that plane is going.

Last panel on a right-hand page: A briefcase leans against a wall near a crowded NYC street corner, with SFX reading, "tick...tick..."

Next panel, after the page turn: This is a double-page spread, a long shot that pulled back and up from the previous image to show a bomb has exploded, blowing everything and everybody out of its path.

The first panel set up a briefcase that was ticking, and the double-page spread revealed what was in the briefcase. Even if we thought it was a bomb, did we think it was that big a bomb?

Your hand rises in back.

"Yes?" I ask.

"Does the reveal always have to be visual?"

A reveal can be whatever you want it to be, even just the answer to a simple question.

For example:

Last panel on a right-hand page: A woman looks surprised, as a man kneels in front her, holding an open ring case with a huge diamond ring. He asks, "Will you marry me?

Next panel, after the page turn: The woman smiles with arms crossed, saying, "Not a chance." The man is now the one who looks surprised.

A reveal can combine visual and verbal, too, the central idea being that the new thing isn't revealed until after the page turn.

Again, for example:

Last panel on a right-hand page: It's night in a suburb, and a woman leans out a light-filled doorway, singing her plaintive song to the night, "Where oh where has my little dog gone? Where oh where can it be?"

Next panel, after the page turn: This is a variation on the classic painting showing a group of dogs at a poker table. The bulldog says to the Chihuahua, "Your mommy's calling."

With editorial planning and a publisher's cooperation, the page turn is an opportunity to surprise the reader.

Your hand rises in back.

"Yes?" I ask.

"What do you mean by 'a publisher's cooperation?'"

To quote and translate from a Robert Burns poem, "The best-laid plans o' mice an' men often go awry." Here's sad proof to that adage.

During my tenure at Platinum Studios, I edited *The Weapon*, written by Fred Van Lente, with art by Scott Koblish. (You won't see my name listed as the editor, even though I edited the script, hired Scott to draw it, and worked with him on the layouts to get the storytelling straight. The editors noted in the credits took the book to finish, but I oversaw the script and visual storytelling.)

The Weapon was initially projected to be a sixty-four-page, magazine-sized (8.5 inches by 11 inches), stand-alone graphic novel. Then the formatting gods changed their minds from what had originally been agreed to and scripted; it was now a comic-sized, four-issue miniseries.

Fred had moved onto other projects, so I modified the one-shot script with sixty-two large pages into four comic books, each with twenty-two smaller pages. Since the larger magazine-sized pages contained more panels than could comfortably fit on a regular comics page, panels needed to shuffle backwards, and book breaks needed to be established, giving each comic a recognizable arc, all while working to maintain as much of

Fred's original pacing as possible.

Fred, being the great writer that he is, had carefully planned some explosively funny gags to be revealed after page turns.

Shuffling back pages, while maintaining any of these reveals after page turns, was your basic editorial nightmare, but consider the consequences of failure: if I didn't get these images to the top of left-hand pages, readers would glimpse the gags ahead of time, and they'd be spoiled.

The repagination on the script was successful, and Scott Koblish did a great job laying out the pages. The gags were nicely revealed at the top of left-hand pages, and even though that was the end of my involvement on this book, it's not the end of the story about what can still go wrong.

A right- or left-hand story lead-in isn't the only factor that affects where the rest of the pages fall in a book, especially if there are chapter breaks and/or advertisements.

In the first published issue of *The Weapon*, a couple pages after Fred's first explosively funny gag was nicely revealed, there appeared a single-page ad for another Platinum comic. Not a double-page spread ad or two ads back-to-back that would have maintained editorial left- and right-hand page pagination. It was just a one-page ad, tossed in by somebody who didn't know or care what he or she was doing. It totally threw off the editorial layout, and the next left-hand-page reveal shifted back to a right-hand page, making it not that much of a visual surprise to the reader.

Fred's gag was blown because somebody wasn't paying attention or didn't know better.

There's a moral to this story, one you've read before: the Devil is in the details.

I'll add: everything is connected, so sweat the small stuff. Somebody who doesn't is lazy, incompetent, or ignorant, and everybody pays the price.

Now we're going to practice some visual reveals from the last panel of a right-hand page to the first panel of a left-hand page.

"Yay," the class mumbles.

This is going to be easy and difficult; easy, in that writing for the page turn is entirely subjective, and difficult, in that writing for the page turn is entirely subjective.

There is no "right," but there may be "better" and "worse," which is still entirely subjective. So we're going to concentrate on what "works" and "doesn't work/accomplish the goal of the assignment."

Your assignment: write three page turns and their reveals. Each version will have two panels, the last panel of a right-hand page, followed by the first panel, a reveal, on a left-hand page.

The first example should show a dramatically different visual change, while keeping the same setting in both panels. The change can involve the addition or subtraction of character, character action, objects appearing, moving, or leaving the scene, in short, anything that demonstrates a dramatic or humorous change from panel to panel.

The second example should show a completely new location from the first panel to the second, but they should be conceptually connected in some way, any way you choose. Can you show the Hollywood hills and sign in panel one, and the Eiffel Tower in panel two? That's not enough. But if you show a woman walking through Hollywood in one panel, and suddenly walking down a street in Paris in the next, with her comparing the two locations then you've accomplished the goal of the assignment. You can also show a soldier pressing a button on a toggle stick in one panel, followed by, after the page turn, a missile headed toward a terrorist camp; just make sure you find a way to conceptually connect the two images. As another example, just to show assignment flexibility, you can show the soldier pressing the button in panel one, then, in the next panel, having a terrorist say, "Do you hear something? Is that a rocket?" You can see that the two images *feel* connected.

The third example should set up an expectation of any kind in the first panel, then *not* pay it off in the second panel. It should extend the tension from panel one by completely switching the point in the second panel. For example, you can show that soldier pressing the toggle-stick button in panel one, then, in the next panel, have a terrorist ask, "Who are we fighting for?" Do you see how we're yet to see the result of the pushed button? Another example is to show a paratrooper leaping out of a plane in panel one, then showing a terrorist camp in panel two. We see the second panel and *wonder* how they might be connected, even though they're not yet connected.

Have fun with these assignments, and let's discuss the results tomorrow.

Welcome to tomorrow.

Have you completed your assignment? Did you review your answers to make sure they work well?

Good.

Who's first?

Jules raises her hand.

ANSWER 1:

LAST PANEL ON A RIGHT-HAND PAGE

Angle on Henry the Detective, talking to a man who stands next to the open rear door of a car. The man looking at Henry is dressed in a rumpled suit, and, from this angle, we cannot see in the backseat.

HENRY: I promise we'll find out who did this.
MAN: Did what?

NEXT PANEL, AFTER THE PAGE TURN

New angle. Henry is pointing to the backseat, and the man has turned to look where Henry is pointing. Turning has revealed that there's a blood-drenched stain on the man's shirt. This angle also reveals a body sitting in the backseat, with a blood-drenched stain on its shirt, and we can see the corpse's face and clothes well enough to recognize that they're identical to the man Henry is talking to.

HENRY: That.
MAN: Oh, crap.
MAN: (connected to balloon above) I'm dead, aren't I?

ANSWER 2:

LAST PANEL ON RIGHT-HAND PAGE

On a rough, rain-drenched sea, a boy is at the tiller, steering a thirty-foot sailing craft through white-foamed waves. The boy's expression is alarmed, because he sees a vast wave ready to break over his boat.

BOY: AAAIIIEEEEEE!

NEXT PANEL, AFTER THE PAGE TURN

The same boy sits in a tub, taking a bath. He has gleefully used two hands to throw a toy sailboat in the air, along with a lot of water, much of which is flying out of the tub.

BOY: AAAIIIEEEEEE!

ALTERNATIVE TO ANSWER 2: We could switch the order of these images, and that would work, too, depending on whether we want the fantasy or reality version to be the visual reveal.

ANSWER 3:

LAST PANEL ON RIGHT-HAND PAGE

In a restaurant, a man kneels in front of a woman, presenting an open jeweler's box and the sparkling diamond ring inside.

MAN: Will you marry me?

NEXT PANEL, AFTER THE PAGE TURN

On a New York street, another man is rushing from the open door of a cab toward a restaurant.

*   *   *

How did Jules do on this assignment?

Lilly raises her hand.

"Yes?"

Lilly says, "I think she did well."

"I agree."

Another hand goes up.

"Yes?"

"Why is the third one okay?" Sam asks. "The second panel is supposed to completely switch the point, and I don't think it does."

"Why not?" I ask.

Sam says, "Because there's a man rushing into the restaurant to try to stop the engagement."

"Where does the script say that?" I ask.

"Well, it doesn't say it explicitly," Sam answers. "It's implicit by how these two panels work together."

"That's right," I answer. "It's implicit. It extends the tension, makes us wonder why he's rushing into the restaurant. To break up the proposal is the first thing that comes to mind. But we don't really even know if it's the same restaurant, do we?"

"Um," Sam says.

"Right," I say. "The second panel doesn't necessarily pay off or even extend the first panel, but it does create an expectation, per the assignment."

There are so many ways to use the page turn to your editorial advantage that I wanted you to get a taste for its potential.

There's more to a page turn than simply changing from one scene location to another, or paying off a question with its answer.

When you ask yourself on each and every potential reveal, "How can I turn this (pun intended) to my advantage?" you'll be digging deeply into your editorial toolbox.

The only limits are in your imagination.

Part Two

Working With Others

Chapter 11

Script Formats:
Style Has Substance

There is no right way to write comics.

You can follow the path of what's been done, what's required, or make it up. Your approach simply needs to be clear to (and fit well with) those with whom you're working.

Some scripting formats are ingrained in the comics culture, while others are tailored to the needs of writers, artists, editors, books, and/or publishers.

The script breaks into two primary components: the content that is presented for interpretation by an artist; and the manner in which the content is written/created. The former is the substance, otherwise known as the story (if it's fiction); the latter is the style, the manner in which the story is crafted.

There are styles that work best for you and ones that work best for your prospective editor and/or collaborator. It's ideal when you both prefer the same style, but we'll address later what adjustments can be made when that's not the case.

Let's begin with what works best for you.

There are three basic comic script styles, each with multiple variations we'll also get to later. They are:

1. *Full Script:* this most used script format includes panel breakdowns, panel descriptions, dialogue and sound effects.
2. *Plot Method:* this approach involves writing a plot outline, which

can be rough or detailed. The artist is free to break down the story however she or he chooses. When the story is drawn, the writer adds balloons and dialogue.

3. _Thumbnail Method:_ the most hands-on approach to writing comics, creators sketch (roughly or tightly) the panels and characters onto the page, and write dialogue into the balloons.

We'll discuss the pros and cons of each format later, but let's begin with variations on writing the more traditional _Full Script_ approach to writing comics.

While there is no one way to approach writing a full comics script, during my tenure at Platinum Studios, I witnessed a lot of tendencies among beginning writers, so let's begin there.

Even though sequential art is a visual medium, most comics writers tend to begin by writing narration and discussions between characters, then dividing the balloons with panel breaks, then figuring out images to add to each panel.

Welcome to the best way to write a really talky comic.

Sometimes this approach is fine, and sometimes it slows down a comic that's supposed to read like a speeding bullet.

Consider another way to write comics, especially when you need that comic to read like a speeding bullet.

In the '90s, Disney Publishing launched its own Disney Comics line, hiring, among others, David Cody Weiss, who offered me the chance to put my money where my Mouse was. I wrote my first two first Mickey Mouse comic stories, which have since been reprinted in _Walt Disney's Vacation Parade_ #5 (Gemstone, July 2008).

Disney also launched _Disney Adventures,_ hiring comics editor and writer Marv Wolfman to edit the comics-half of the magazine.

I wrote numerous comic stories for Marv, including the magazine's first graphic novel, a three-part Mickey Mouse adventure called _Space Mickey and the Throgg Ray Wars._

Writing the third and final installment of this graphic novel changed my approach to comics scripting.

My approach had already shifted from sketching thumbnails to scripting. I typed better pictures than I drew but there was a downside to this approach I had not yet fully absorbed. Thumb-nailing comics allows you to immediately judge how pages read. But when you script, write a million word balloons and indicate that they are to fit inside a teeny-weenie panel set next to a million other teeny-weenie panels on a teeny-weenie page, then you won't see how well or badly it will turn out until it's too late, unless you've got a great sense of the use of space or an editor who knows enough about what he or she is doing to write you a stern note to do better.

After scripting two action-packed, twenty-four-page installments of *Space Mickey and the Throgg Ray Wars*, I was left with a hundred pounds of story resolution that needed to fit into a twenty-four-pound bag.

I knew the story, knew what needed to be in it, scene for scene, but each scene had the potential to be bigger, bolder...and longer. If I approached the third part the way I had the first two—beginning at page one, then two, then three, and so forth—there would have been too many word balloons in the panels, too many panels per page, the page count would have run long, and I'd end up in Self-Editing Hell trying to make it all fit and read well.

I was stuck.

Luckily, the Italian artist was taking forever to draw and paint the first two parts, so nobody beat me up about not delivering the final episode.

Six months later, time was running out.

Michael Lynton (at that time President of Disney Publishing, and today the Chairman and CEO of Sony Pictures Entertainment) was pushing to see the script, so Marv nudged me to finish it.

And I was still stuck.

Then one Sunday morning I read David Mamet's *On Directing Film*, to which I've previously referred.

It was a revelation and immediately became one of the most important tools in my storytelling toolbox.

For the first time I understood how to tell a story with juxtaposed uninflected images, which we discussed earlier. To repeat, the basic principle involves understanding *exactly* which images are necessary, in order, to visually advance a scene or story.

I finished Mamet's book, picked up a notepad, and wrote, in order, a quickly jotted line of description for every image I absolutely *needed* to visually advance a bare-bones version of the story. It took about an hour. I did not include a single image more than was necessary, even though I had lots of ideas for additional scenes that would expand the story. If I had room, I could figure out which ones to add later.

Knowing that a *Disney Adventures* digest-sized page held up to four or five panels—and five was pushing it—I slashed hash marks between two, three, four, or five lines of text with each series of images between the breaks constituting a prospective page. In determining page breaks, I paid close attention to where scenes ended, where others began, and where page turns from right-hand pages made for dramatic story reveals at the beginning of the following spreads.

I then counted the number of pages in this stripped-down version of the story, anxiously praying I hadn't exceeded twenty-four pages. If I had, I'd need to rethink the story and cut something important.

I hit twenty-four pages on the nose, more a result of luck than intention, and did not have room anywhere to expand so much as a single image or scene.

I had invented, at least for myself, the writer's equivalent of *Plot Method* comic storytelling, where I committed to a succession of images that dynamically advanced the story, prior to narration or dialogue having been written.

With the images for the story complete, all I had to do was write the rest of it. Easier said than done.

Just as Stan Lee had to add balloons and narrative captions to make sense of Jack Kirby's and Steve Ditko's drawn pages, I had to add word balloons and narrative captions to my written visuals to pull my story together. Successfully linking very different panel images with balloons and captions was a challenge, but it worked.

I still lament the loss of scenes I could've expanded, but there was an unintended consequence from my switch in scripting techniques. The final part read like a speeding bullet, and it did not stop to smell so much as a single rose, just the way the climax to an adventure story is supposed to read.

Just like with creating comics, there's no one approach to writing a *Full Script* version of a script. As you tackle each page or scene in a story, if you keep in mind the entire range of possible writing approaches available, you'll have the best chance to write the most effective version of your *Full Script* story.

Let's consider which script style may fit best for a prospective collaborator or editor.

Begin by thinking of each script style as a different dialect.

You might be perfectly comfortable speaking *"Direct-it-on-paper Full*

Script," if the artists in your community are comfortable speaking *"Direct-it-on-paper Full Script,"* too.

But what happens when you have an opportunity to work with a really great artist who doesn't understand *"Direct-it-on-paper Full Script"*? He or she prefers *"I-like-the-freedom-to-interpret-how-I want-to Full Script."* Worse than not understanding *"Direct-it-on-paper Full Script,"* what if that script format offends her or him?

What happens when an editor wants you to speak to the artist in *"Plot-Method,"* and you can't figure out the action in your story until after you've written dialogue and/or narration?

If you understand the strengths and weaknesses of the different comic-script formats/styles/dialects, then you can make your choice of format based on what you need in order to produce the best possible work with the best possible collaborators, editors, and publishers.

We're going to discuss a range of dialects/styles in which a script can be created, so an artist, editor, and/or publisher will understand, in their language, what you wish to accomplish.

I am not promoting one scripting style over another, except to address where certain styles may better fit specific editorial or cultural needs. At the end of the day, it's all about the book, so this discussion is merely intended to offer potential tools for use.

There are two basic ways for a writer to approach the process of collaborating with an artist: the first is to write the script in a way that benefits the need of—or the writer's vision for—the story; the second is to tailor the script to the artist's strengths and/or around their weaknesses.

A hand thrusts above the sea of brows that have lowered to half-mast. "Yes?" I ask.

You ask, "Do artists work better from one scripting style over another?"

"Often," I reply.

"So is there a particular style that's better for all artists?"

"No," I respond. "Some artists thrive on strong visual direction, while others find it too confining. Maybe it's a result of personal artistic idiosyncrasies, prevalent comics-culture influences, and/or enough professional experience for artists to know what does and doesn't work best for them. Still, the results are the same: not all artists do their best work from the same scripting style."

"But what if writers don't know who the artists are going to be when they write their scripts?"

As I previously noted, sometimes—more often than not for independent creators—the script is what it needs to be, and it's up to the writer or editor to find an artist whose process or predilections fit best.

Other times the artist is on board before the script is written. Knowing an artist's strengths and preferences before writing the script gives a team the potential to build the best possible collaboration.

Also, even if there isn't yet an artist onboard, knowing different script formats allows writers to choose which format best suits the story and/or artists working in a restrictive publishing culture.

You ask, "What do you mean by 'working in a restrictive publishing culture?'"

Sometimes, the culture dictates the approach.

Marvel Comics used to stress scripting in the *Marvel Method*, which is now more commonly called the *Plot Method*.

It was Stan Lee's preferred way to write comics, which took great advantage of the storytelling skills of his collaborators, Jack Kirby, Steve Ditko, and others. He'd write a story synopsis—maybe tight and maybe loose—and artists drew the pages, putting in whatever visuals they wanted to advance the story, then he added balloons and captions to connect the story dots.

The upside to this approach is that it gives artists the freedom to create dynamic, exciting pages. The downside is that artists need to be great storytellers in tune with the goals, or the results are going to be nightmares to read, with too many badly paced expository balloons and captions.

My first issue of *Disney's Aladdin* for Marvel was written *Full Script*, with tight panel descriptions, narrative captions, and dialogue. The artist had difficulty dealing with the space taken up by the balloons and captions, so my editor, Hildy Mesnick, asked me to write my second issue *Plot Method*.

Disney's Aladdin was a humorous fantasy-adventure, and comedic timing was important for retaining the tone of the animated film. If I had simply handed in a *Plot Method* script to be drawn, there was no way the artist could have anticipated my pacing or gags, so I found a halfway measure that met Hildy's needs and kept my pacing. I wrote a *Full Script* version of the story without dialogue or captions, with each panel delineated and even some explanation about the nature of the dialogue or gags. The artist was no longer hampered by my dialogue or captions. Hildy sent me photocopies of the pencils, and I wrote the balloons and captions, keying them to the rough circles and boxes I drew on the photocopies. The result worked reasonably well.

I couldn't have made this adjustment if I hadn't known both script formats well enough to find a practical solution to the storytelling need.

Here's a more complicated example of adapting to the needs of a restrictive publishing culture.

Using Mr. Peabody's Wayback Machine, we're going to the mid- to late-'90s, some years before the comics publishing format known as graphic novels gained respectability in bookstores and libraries. *Maus* was still blazing the trail, and Neil Gaiman's *Sandman,* alongside manga, proved the medium could sell at bookstore cash registers.

I'd just met former Walden Books Marketing Senior Director and Longmeadow Press Publisher Ron Jaffe. He was (and still is) an advocate for the sequential art medium in traditional bookstores, and showed me Raymond Briggs's *The Snowman* as an example of what could be published for that market.

Published in 1978, *The Snowman* is a children's picture book classic that nobody in publishing or libraries called a "comic book," even though it was clearly sequential art. It's a compelling format, a full-color, thirty- two-page, oversized hardcover, using only panels (without word balloons or narration) to advance the story, just like Shaun Tan's more recent wordless comic masterpiece, *The Arrival.*

The Snowman puzzled me. Why didn't librarians consider it comics? Was it the over-sized picture-book dimensions? Was it the hardcover binding? Was it the story? Was it the drawing style? It's easy to see that it's a children's picture book, but why didn't librarians also consider it comics? It clearly used multiple panels of art on the page to advance the story, but they still never categorized it as part of the then-denigrated medium.

I gnawed on this bone for over a decade.

I approached this puzzle by asking and answering a series of questions.

Did hardcover binding turn a comic into a children's picture book, suddenly making it "not comics"? Clearly not.

If Batman was drawn the way we see the character in DC Comics, then published as an over-sized picture book, would it be a children's picture book for children aged 4-8? Clearly not.

What if Batman was drawn in a children's illustration style? This becomes an interesting question, because, while the drawing might be suitable to young kids, the content might not be suitable. At the time, there was a publishing program of Batman stories for young readers, with the character drawn in Bruce Timm's *Batman Adventures* animated style, which was more suitable to young readers than the traditional superhero comics drawing styles. Getting back to the question: would these be perceived as books with comics or animation characters, or would they be perceived as children's picture books? I think they would still be perceived as books based on licensed properties, perhaps for children, but with comics or animation characters. Nobody would call these upscale children's picture books, where every librarian and bookseller would call *The Snowman* an upscale children's picture book.

Pursuing the question further, what if the comics characters in children's picture books were from properties that already had the potential to skew towards younger readers, like *Calvin & Hobbes* or *Mutts*? I think the line starts to blur, but I think they still would be books with comic strip characters, rather than upscale children's picture books.

The blurring of the line is interesting, though.

The content is closer to a young reader's interest, and the drawing styles are more iconographic, which is better at attracting a young reader's eye.

I continued to ponder.

I searched for a clearly defined explanation, a formula, in which a children's picture book with *Mutts* in it would straddle the line between children's picture books and books for young readers, featuring comics characters.

I finally found a clue in Briggs's self-perception. He didn't consider himself a cartoonist or comic artist, even though he clearly worked in the form. He called himself an illustrator. Later, Shaun Tan expressed the same sentiment.

This is a distillation of the process I used to determine my answer to a question that nobody else was asking, to which I finally concluded:

As a property, *The Snowman* was original to the children's picture book publishing category. A short animated feature based on it came later;

Its story was aimed at young readers. You need to study the picture book category and culture to understand this further;

It was illustrated in a style more in line with children's illustration than mainstream comics. You need to study the picture book category and culture to understand this further, too;

The binding and dimensions clearly fit within the page length and publishing parameters of a children's picture book;

There were no word balloons. An amendment here for those thinking about *In the Night Kitchen* by Maurice Sendak, which owed a lot to Winsor McCay's *Little Nemo in Slumberland:* where there was lettering, the lettering should *not* use an obvious comic book or comic strip style; it should look more like calligraphy;

There were no clearly drawn panel borders, something observed much later by my future partner on *The Bramble,* Bruce Zick. Color, not line art, defined the panel borders;

Camera angle changes from panel to panel were limited, making the visual storytelling simpler and more accessible to the young reader who's not yet learned to read comics;

Changes in storytelling action from panel to panel were kept to a minimum, usually one, and no more than two, actions per panel, again to avoid confusing the young reader. And these actions didn't happen in conjunction with dynamic camera angle changes;

Conceived a nearly a decade into 21st Century, it would take a few years to find a publishing partner who shared this vision for what was possible.

It seemed odd there weren't more books like this being published. Then I noticed most creators of this kind of book were writer-artists. Upon further reflection, that made sense, because most children's picture book editors haven't edited sequential art and aren't intimately familiar with the unique nature of the medium.

Simply put, you can't direct well if you don't fully understand the medium you're directing. Children's picture book editors wouldn't know how to assign and direct comics writers and artists, with themselves at the center of the process, making sure everything is kept on track. This meant they were only likely to feel comfortable working with writer-artists who understood the children's picture book market well enough to create a suitable story, writer-artists who also had the chops to write and illustrate that story. It's not a common talent combination, which explained why there were so few wordless sequential art picture books being published as children's books.

With my Disney Publishing background, I understood the industry sensibilities for children's picture books, as well as what was required to produce a script from which an artist could draw. I also had access to several artist talent pools that could meet the qualitative demands required for high-end picture books, thus checking off all of the requisite boxes.

In short, I understood how to produce a lot of books in a publishing format that did not have a lot of creator competition. The creator in me loved that; the businessman in me saw Sutter's Mill in January 1848.

One question remained: was there a perceived need for this type of children's picture book?

There was only one way to get that answer.

Do it.

But first I had some publishing industry hoops to leap through. Flaming hoops, which ultimately involve the script format.

The children's picture book publishing culture leans heavily towards illustrators bringing to the process their own interpretation and vision of the story. Usually, the editor and/or art director chooses the artist to illustrate the book, and the writer takes a backseat to the editor/artist collaboration. How far back that backseat goes depends on the writer's pull with the editor and/or publisher.

But what do you do when the people in charge don't fully understand the process for creating this kind of unique book for their market?

This was my first flaming hoop: I needed to circumvent the culturally embedded process and get picture book editors to relinquish *direct* artistic oversight...to me.

Even today, I might or might not survive this hoop with prospective publishers, but I developed a plausible rationale for why I could: I was a book packager. Book packagers are already established in publishing as people who hire and work with teams of creators to produce books. I also had an established, flexible process for producing sequential art, which kept company editors and art directors involved at every stage of the process. The process allowed them to see what was being produced, review my thoughts, and approve the direction or offer notes for changes.

My second flaming hoop was more problematic and relevant to this chapter: most children's picture book editors do not know how to read a comics script.

My third flaming hoop stood right behind the second one: children's picture book artists need freedom to interpret the story.

Combining them, the apparent difficulty here is that a *Full Script* version of the story needs to, by necessity, indicate specific images to be drawn. So even if an editor understands a *Full Script* version of the story, the approach still undercuts the children's picture book culture that prefers an artist to make the visual interpretation.

When the book is a nearly wordless picture book, like *The Bramble*, the problem is compounded, because the visual progression *is* what advances the story.

This seemed like a great opportunity to write a *Plot Method* script. However, because this book was a mostly wordless picture book, a *Plot Method* script would lose my ability to pace the story sequences, something I thought was important for a successful editorial realization.

I couldn't resort to the full-script-without-balloons approach I employed with *Aladdin*, because there were very few word balloons in the story anyway. That script would have been, in essence, another alienating Full Script version of the story, which a children's picture book editor still might not have understood. Again, it's a different dialect than prose, which is what they're used to.

Tough as it seemed, there was a solution to this conundrum, a rather simple one actually: I developed a format that read like prose, allowed for an incredible amount of artistic interpretation, and set down my requisite panel-by-panel pacing. It left out camera direction, but clearly defined the content of the images that was needed to advance the story.

This simple solution didn't magically appear from out of the blue; it merged into my comics toolbox from another medium, film.

Early screenwriting included camera shots and movement, but with the rise of the director-as-auteur, the cultural rule of thumb in film shifted to "don't direct on paper," because it offended prospective directors who preferred to come up with visuals themselves. In the '90s, fledgling screenwriters weren't supposed to tell the director their ideas for shots or images. Inspire, yes; tell, no.

These were the same cultural issues I faced in children's picture book publishing.

During my failed '90s fling at trying to write feature film spec scripts, I picked up a screenwriting technique I liked quite a bit.

Established by writer-director Walter Hill (*The Long Riders, 48 Hours*) expanded by Shane Black (writer, *Lethal Weapon*; director, *Iron Man 3*) and adopted and imitated by countless others, characters, action, and images were Tommy-gunned onto the page in a series of short staccato beats, resulting in something akin to an extended haiku. Action was pronounced, images delineated; they were sometimes concrete and sometimes visceral.

I made one major adjustment to the style—more of a medium-related straightjacket, really—something that was not a cinematic concern but would make or break the sequential art storytelling: in my version, each paragraph needed to represent a panel on a page. This meant that, even though I was writing action, and sometimes several actions, each paragraph needed to have the *potential* for translation into a single frozen image that advanced the story. If I needed two panels then an action sequence needed to be two paragraphs. If a two-panel action sequence was described in a single sentence, the sentence needed to extend to two paragraphs with bridging ellipses.

As an example, here are two script pages from an early sequence in *The Bramble:*

A friendless loner, Cameron has tried to join a game of tag.

PAGE FIVE:

Smiling and enthusiastic again, Cameron swings back, missing as Scruffy easily evades the tag.

Cameron swipes at Lanky, who also evades the tag, while Lanky touches an index finger onto the top of Cameron's head and repeats: "You're it."

Cameron sweeps a hand at three boys, who easily escape the swipe in a move that's in concert and very nearly balletic. "You're it. You're it. You're it," they chant.

Then he slips, his foot flying up as though he'd stepped on a patch of icy rain.

As he lies on his back on the grass, dejected, not unlike Charlie Brown who just missed kicking a football, the group of older kids dance away from Cameron, arm in arm, chanting: "You're it. You're it. You're it."

PAGE SIX:

Then Cameron gets to his knees...

...and, now to his feet, turning a wistful eye...

...to the kids, who are back to playing their roughhouse version of tag.

He trudges toward the bramble, head down, depressed...

...reaches it...

...and sits down next to a ragged hole in the wall.

Not even Charlie Brown had it so bad.

* * *

A sea of hands waive frantically.

"Yes?" I ask.

You ask, "Are you saying that after everything you wrote about how comics *aren't* film, that your solution to the problem was to write comics *like* film?"

"Yes," I reply.

Know your tools and adapt accordingly.

My complaint about creators who write comics like film is that they don't take into account the potential ramifications of what they're doing.

I knew exactly what I was doing.

I was ceding the specific choice of camera direction and "frozen moments in time" to the artist, in exchange for a *Plot Method* script variation editors could understand and that would allow artists more visual interpretation. Most importantly, I was able to retain the panel pacing, and in such a way that I could critique whether or not the story sketches/layouts/thumbnails advanced the story.

To me, this was more than a fair tradeoff. It gave me a format where artists could play, but in a sandbox filled with a clearly defined story-progression.

You ask, "Looking at your script, what's an artist supposed to draw to convey that last line on page 6, "Not even Charlie Brown had it so bad"?

I answer, "That's the beauty of how this format fills the need for an artist to be able to interpret the script. The line sets Cameron's state of mind, but doesn't offer a clear image for how that state of mind can be interpreted. The simple solution is to show a longer shot of Cameron by the bramble, emphasizing his loneliness, with his head in his hands. But maybe holding the previous shot with just his head in his hands does the job. Either might be fine. What's important is that if the artist draws Cameron leaping into the air and shouting with joy, I can point to the line and ask, "Does this image reflect that idea?"

The determination has less to do with an image I suggested, and more to do with how the image corresponds to the storytelling need.

Those were the major flaming hoops I tackled with writing sequential art for the children's picture book culture, but other hoops appeared along the way.

There were age-related concerns that needed to be addressed, like keeping the visual storytelling simple for the very young, uninitiated comics reader, and it was easy to determine whether the thumbnails worked or didn't. Making this determination was never about what I would or would not have drawn; it was about whether the story was being communicated well to a young reader.

Because I am also an editor, designer, and book packager, and because I had a great working relationship with my editor, Andrew Karre, I was fortunate enough to be able to work directly with the artist, Bruce Zick. Bruce is an amazing talent, and working together made the results a true collaboration.

The Bramble (Carolrhoda Books, 2013) won the 2013 Moonbeam Gold Medal for picture books (ages 4-8).

Those were two examples of adjusting towards artists working in restrictive publishing cultures, but there are other reasons to make script-style adjustments.

Marv Wolfman wrote *A Man Called A•X* in a *Plot Method* hybrid, taking advantage of artist Shawn McManus's strong visual storytelling abilities.

Each comics page was written *Plot Method*, without panel delineation, but Marv added word balloons and captions in their proper reading order at the bottom of each intended page, leaving it to Shawn to design the page, determine the story flow, and place the word balloons and captions in their right-reading order.

This is a brilliant example of working with the best possible tools in a collaborative effort.

Let's dub it *Marv's Method*.

My suggestion to any writer following Marv's unique approach is to have the artist show rough layouts with the prospective balloon and caption placements. This way you'll know exactly how the artist intends the pages to look and read.

Let's examine some formatting for three potential scripted versions, using page 12 of **Silver-Hair & The Three Xairs** (collected in *Once Upon A Time Machine,* Dark Horse, 2012) as our story.

PLOT METHOD

Silver-hair wakes up in the alien bathroom, arrested by two glob-creature cops.

A glob-creature mother cries, because Silver-Hair drank her child.

The cops drag Silver-Hair out of the alien abode, and past her fallen basket, which has spilled the dead cute creatures she passed earlier in the story.

An angry mob of glob creatures, gathered outside the abode, would lynch her if they could.

There are eight trillion misunderstandings on the planet Xair.

This has been one of them.

* * *

FULL SCRIPT

<u>PAGE 12</u>

STORYTELLING NOTE: Our first pages moved Silver-Hair into and through woods pretty quickly, (neatly hiding her slaughter of innocent creatures), then we explored much shorter periods of time when she was in the alien abode, tried stuff out, seemingly learned from her mistakes, and tried stuff out again. All of this has been in preparation for page twelve, which, in five panels, concludes our story in chaos, revelation, and a sign-off narrative caption that redefines what we thought we were reading into something completely different, something that lends full weight to the first caption in the story, which began: "Once upon a crime..."

PANEL 1 (TOP TIER)

This is the same angle as panel 8 of the previous page, because, instead of being peacefully asleep, her eyes are now wide in alarm and panic, as off-panel voices show she has reason to be alarmed and panicked.

1 VOICE 1 OP: There it is!
2 SILVER-HAIR: (alien lettering) Huh?!
3 SILVER-HAIR: (connected to balloon above; alien lettering) What's going on?!

PANEL 2 (TOP TIER)

Two globular alien cops hold Silver-Hair by her arms; she is struggling, but obviously held so tight she won't be able to escape. We know they're cops by the badge-like things that are hung around their necks; they don't wear or need clothes, so everything they need hangs by cords or belts, even their stun guns. The first alien cop calls towards the ascending slope (which, yeah, will now be the descending slope, but we're not going to bother with going down it).

4 GLOB COP 1: It was in the cleansing chamber!

5 GLOB COP 2: These humans are disgusting creatures.

6 SILVER-HAIR: (alien lettering) Let me go, you butt-sucking Jell-O mutants!

PANEL 3 (WIDTH OF PAGE)

Below, in the large room: first we see two globular creatures holding the small empty bowl from which Silver-Hair drank. One of the two--let's call her Mom--is being comforted by the other, probably Dad. Mom points to Silver-Hair in melodramatic grief and exclamation. Design-wise, let's not give Mom breasts to designate her as female (and mammalian); as humans, they pretty much all look the same to us. The two glob cops practically carry Silver-Hair, still kicking and screaming, towards the open door.

7 MOTHER GLOB: Is that the thing that **drank** my child?!

8 GLOB COP 1: You have the right to remain silent...

9 SILVER-HAIR: (alien lettering) I'm a citizen of Earth, damn it!

PANEL 4 (WIDTH OF PAGE)

We're outside the alien abode, and this is probably the bigger panel on the page, and designed so the next one might work as an inset. We have a lot to see here.

First, on the left, we see Silver-Hair's overturned basket and the contents of several small, dead creatures that have spilled out: one is the creature that was peering at her in Image 2 of the collage spread, another is the fish-like creature that was leaping out of the water in the Image 4 of the collage spread, and yet another is the bird-like creature that was leaping out of the water in the Image 6 of the collage spread. If it makes sense without being too obvious, let's add to the toppled basket a couple other small alien woodland creatures she must have collected and killed. The point? This girl's been on a killing spree since the first page, and I think it's ironic that she's arrested and going to be incarcerated for the one killing that was likely an accident. Irony reins, and we'll likely play up this aspect in her bigger, future story. And yeah, I like planting this kind of stuff for readers to discover later when they reread a story.

The readers may or may not notice the overturned basket, because it's subtle and we really want them paying attention to the two glob cops dragging Silver-Hair out between them. She's stopped struggling, so that her feet now drag behind her, but she's still screaming bloody murder. Ahead of them, a gauntlet of outraged globular citizens demanding justice line both sides of the walkway, which leads to the road. Beyond them, on the road, an enclosed hover vehicle (with flashing lights on top, but let's not make it too much like a human police cruiser) is waiting for them. It has some kind of alien insignia on it, creating the impression that it's an official vehicle. A third glob cop waits by the open door.

10 GLOB COP 2: ...not that it'll do you any good.

11 SILVER-HAIR: (alien lettering) I know my intergalactic rights!

12 ANGRY GLOB 1: When's it going to stop?!

13 ANGRY GLOB 2: You humans have no respect for other life forms!

14 ANGRY GLOB 3: Blast them back where they came from!

PANEL 5 (POSSIBLE INSET OR CARVED FROM THE CORNER OF PANEL 4)

Angled down shot from the sky. To the left, we see the glob mob shouting up, but they're small and far away, so we can no longer hear (okay, read) what they're saying. They're what we're leaving. The upward-then-away sweep lines behind the hover cop-craft show that it has flown toward us, then away from us, and it is relatively small in the panel; we can't even necessarily see Silver-Hair in the craft, though the balloons tell us she hasn't stopped shouting bloody murder. I think we want to see here more of the world than the alien abode or the hover craft, because this is our going-away shot to end the story. We also need room for the balloons and the captions. Most importantly, though, we want to see them going away because we are going away, too; it's the end of the story.

15 SILVER-HAIR: (alien lettering) I want a lawyer!

16 SILVER-HAIR: (connected to balloon above; alien lettering) I want my mommy!!

17 CAPTION: There are eight trillion misunderstandings on the planet Xair.

18 CAPTION: This has been one of them.
19 TEXT: (floating or in a caption box) The End

*   *   *

MARV'S METHOD, A DETAILED PLOT METHOD WITH DIALOGUE AT THE BOTTOM OF THE PAGE

PAGE 12

STORYTELLING NOTE: Our first pages moved Silver-Hair into and through woods pretty quickly, (neatly hiding her slaughter of innocent creatures), then we explored much shorter periods of time when she was in the alien abode, tried stuff out, seemingly learned from her mistakes, and tried stuff out again. All of this has been in preparation for *page twelve,* which, in five panels, concludes our story in chaos, revelation, and a sign-off narrative caption that redefines what we thought we were reading into something completely different, something that lends full weight to the first caption in the story, which began: "Once upon a crime..."

PLOT

Silver-hair wakes up in the alien bathroom, arrested by two glob-creature cops.

A glob-creature mother cries, because Silver-Hair drank her child.

The cops drag Silver-Hair out of the alien abode, and past her fallen basket, which has spilled the dead cute creatures she passed earlier in the story.

An angry mob of glob creatures, gathered outside the abode, would lynch her if they could.

The glob cops cart Silver-Hair off in an alien cop-mobile to face the justice she may or may not deserve.

BALLOONS / CAPTIONS

1 GLOB COP 1: There it is!
2 SILVER-HAIR: (alien lettering) Huh?!
3 SILVER-HAIR: (connected to balloon above; alien lettering) What's going on?!
4 GLOB COP 1: It was in the cleansing chamber!

5 GLOB COP 2: These humans are disgusting creatures.

6 SILVER-HAIR: (alien lettering) Let me go, you butt-sucking Jell-O mutants!

7 MOTHER GLOB: Is that the thing that **drank** my child?!

8 GLOB COP 1: You have the right to remain silent...

9 SILVER-HAIR: (alien lettering) I'm a citizen of Earth, damn it!

10 GLOB COP 2: ...not that it'll do you any good.

11 SILVER-HAIR: (alien lettering) I know my intergalactic rights!

12 ANGRY GLOB 1: When's it going to stop?!

13 ANGRY GLOB 2: You humans have no respect for other life forms!

14 ANGRY GLOB 3: Blast them back where they came from!

15 SILVER-HAIR: (alien lettering) I want a lawyer!

16 SILVER-HAIR: (connected to balloon above; alien lettering) I want my mommy!!

17 CAPTION: There are eight trillion misunderstandings on the planet Xair.

18 CAPTION: This has been one of them.

19 TEXT: (floating or in a caption box) The End

*   *   *

Each approach has merit.

Each approach can result in something wonderful or something awful.

The *Full Script Method* gives the writer the greatest measure of control. *The Plot Method* gives the artist the greatest measure of control.

But choosing the correct scripting approach doesn't simply involve control.

It also involves capability and vision.

A good storytelling artist will do fine with the *Plot Method*, and will find a way convey the correct tone, whether it's exciting, dramatic, or funny, but the visuals will be different from how they are described in a *Full Script* version with camera angles. That's guaranteed.

Would I trust an in-his-prime Jack Kirby to dramatize my story, even if he'd stage it differently from me? Absolutely! In fact, I'd write the *Plot Method* script in such a way that Kirby would have room to play.

A good visual storyteller will do well with a *Full Script* version that's missing camera angles. But the visuals will be different from how they are described in a *Full Script* version with camera angles. That's also guaranteed.

A writer who needs an artist's conceptual and pacing contributions is more likely to consider *Plot Method, Marv's Method,* or a *Full Script* version without camera angles.

Would I trust Kyle Baker to dramatize any one of these versions, even if he'd stage it differently from how I envision it? Absolutely! At his best, Kyle is a visionary who'll take the ball and run with it, and the worst thing you can do to Kyle is tie his hands. He won't give you what you would've done; he'll do something different and arguably better.

Conversely, a writer with a finely tuned sense of timing and pacing, which needs to be realized, should produce a *Full Script* version with camera angles.

There's no right way, only different ways, where, for a range of potential circumstances, one scripting method might make more sense than others.

There is only what works or doesn't work.

If you can write well in each of these styles, you'll know which is best for you and your potential artist collaborators on any given project.

We'll be discussing collaboration in a later chapter, but for now, welcome to this chapter's exercise: write the same comics page in four different comics scripting styles.

1. *Plot Method.*

2. *Full Script Method,* but without any layout direction or use of camera position or angles.

3. *Full Script Method,* with camera angles and/or positions, writing the clearest image of the page layout, and each panel in it, that you can.

4. *Marv's Method,* a Plot Method page with dialogue at the bottom.

Here's the trick: from the perspective of the four different writing styles, each page must be exactly the same.

This means no direction in the *Plot Method* script can contradict any image in any of the other versions. No direction in the *"Full Script Method without camera direction"* can contradict any image in any of the other versions. No direction in the *"Full Script Method with camera angles"* can contradict any image in any of the other versions.

In theory—and only in theory—the same page could be drawn from each script.

In practice, though, each version is likely to be vastly different, because each version involves different and varying levels of contribution to the visual storytelling by writer and the artist.

And that's the point: understanding the potential the contribution well enough to determine the best scripting style for the story and the collaboration.

A hand flies above a Sea of Puzzlement.

"Yes?" I ask.

"If I put camera angles or specific description in the *'Full Script Method with camera angles'* version, doesn't that contradict the *Plot Method* and *'Full Script Method without camera angles'* versions?"

"How?" I prompt.

"Well, there's stuff in there that isn't in the other two versions," you answer.

"Stuff, yes," I explain, "but not necessarily stuff that *couldn't* be in the other two versions when drawn."

"*Couldn't* be,'" you mull.

"That's right," I clarify. "For instance, let's say your *Plot Method* version describes that a man's face reveals a wide range of expressions as he considers differently flavored scoops to add to an ice cream cone."

"Simple enough," you concede.

"But let's say the *'Full Script Method with camera angles'* version indicates the man has, in each of the panels, the same focused expression on his face as he considers his options."

"Well," you observe, "that's not the same."

"You're right," I agree, "it would be a contradiction. But what if the *'Full Script Method with camera angles'* version described each different expression the man has, as he considers his options, in each of the different panels?"

"That would be consistent with the *Plot Method* version," you conclude.

"Yes, it would be," I agree again, "and that's our goal, for each of the versions to be consistent."

Within the context of each scripting style, you need to successfully write the same page four times.

Now it's time to get to work.

Done already?

Did you take a day to review your scripts and make sure they fit the assignment parameters?

Good.

Who's first?

Stephanie raises her hand and shows us what she's got.

She says, "This is a one-page comic, a gag, magazine size, with lots of space for panels."

PLOT METHOD:

Sammy stands on the edge of a cliff and sees Lily standing on a big cloud above a ravine. He runs and jumps to join her, even though she tries to stop him. As he falls to his comedic doom through part of the cloud, the dissipation of the cloud reveals that Lily was really standing on the edge of a cliff on the other side of a ravine.

*   *   *

FULL SCRIPT METHOD WITHOUT CAMERA DIRECTION:

PANEL 1

Sammy stands at the edge of a cliff, waving across a ravine at Lilly, who's standing atop the middle of a big cloud, the other side of which is cropped by the border. For all we know, the other side of the cloud could be endless. Lilly waves back.

1 SAMMY: Hi, Lilly!
2 LILLY: Hi, Sammy!
PANEL 2
Sammy is stepping back from the edge of the cliff.
3 SAMMY: Just a sec!

PANEL 3

Lilly looks confused.

4 LILLY: Just a sec for what?

PANEL 4

Facing the direction of the cliff edge, Sammy's taken the position of a runner getting ready for a race.

NO DIALOGUE

PANEL 5

Lilly is puzzled.

5 LILLY: What are you doing?

PANEL 6

Poofing dust and speed lines behind Sammy show us that he has zoomed to an all-out sprint toward the edge of the cliff and the ravine.

6 SAMMY: I'm going to join you on that cloud!

PANEL 7

Lilly is totally panicked, holding out her arms for Sammy to stop.

7 LILLY: **_WAIT! STOP!_**

PANEL 8

Sammy leaps from the edge of the cliff, pulling a solo Thelma & Louise.

8 SAMMY: There's no stopping true love.

PANEL 9

Lilly can't look, her hands covering her eyes.

NO DIALOGUE

PANEL 10

Sammy's path shows us that he has fallen through the dissipating cloud toward his comedic doom. The still dissipating cloud reveals Lilly to be standing at the edge of another cliff, which was previously hidden. Lilly leans over the cliff, arms crossed, with an arched eyebrow and a snide expression (now that the shock is over).

9 SAMMY: **_AAAAIIIIIEEEEEE!_**
10 LILLY: There's no stopping true idiocy, either.

*   *   *

FULL SCRIPT METHOD WITH CAMERA DIRECTION:

PANEL 1 (TOP TIER; WIDTH OF PAGE)

A long enough shot so we can see, on the left, Sammy standing at the edge of a cliff, waiving at Lilly, who's standing on a cloud above a ravine. Lilly is standing atop the middle of a big cloud, the right side of which is cropped by the border. For all we know, the other side of the cloud could be endless (even though it's not). Lilly waves back.

1 SAMMY: Hi, Lilly!
2 LILLY: Hi, Sammy!

PANEL 2 (2ND TIER; ON THE LEFT)

Medium shot on Sammy, as Sammy is stepping back from the edge of the cliff.

3 SAMMY: Just a sec!

PANEL 3 (2ND TIER; ON THE MIDDLE LEFT)

Medium shot on Lilly, but not too close, because we're going to see her in a progression of shots that come increasingly close to her. We see all of her here, and the cloud she stands on, as she looks confused.

4 LILLY: Just a sec for what?

PANEL 4 (2ND TIER; ON THE MIDDLE RIGHT)

Another medium shot of Sammy, facing the direction of the cliff edge, and he's taken the position of a runner getting ready for a race.

NO DIALOGUE

PANEL 5 (2ND TIER; ON THE RIGHT)

Closer on Lily than the previous image we saw of her, and she's puzzled, raising a quizzical eyebrow.

5 LILLY: What are you doing?

PANEL 6 (3ND TIER; ON THE LEFT)

Poofing dust and speed lines behind Sammy show us that he has zoomed to an all-out sprint toward the edge of the cliff and the ravine.

6 SAMMY: I'm going to join you on that cloud!

PANEL 7 (3RD TIER; ON THE MIDDLE LEFT)

Closer on Lilly than the previous image we saw of her. Lilly is totally panicked, holding out her arms for Sammy to stop.

7 LILLY: ***WAIT! STOP!***

PANEL 8 (3RD TIER; ON THE MIDDLE RIGHT)

Closer still on Sammy, as he has just leaped from the edge of the cliff, pulling a solo Thelma & Louise.

8 SAMMY: There's no stopping true love.

PANEL 9 (3RD TIER; ON THE RIGHT)

Closest shot yet on Lilly, as she can't bear to look, the fingers of her hands interlaced and covering her eyes.

NO DIALOGUE

PANEL 10 (BOTTOM TIER; WIDTH OF PAGE)

In a longer shot, similar to the one in Panel 1, we see the path of Sammy's trajectory, as he has plummeted through the top of the dissipating cloud toward his comedic doom. To the right, the still dissipating cloud reveals Lilly to be standing at the edge of another cliff, which was previously hidden. Lilly leans over the cliff, arms crossed, with an arched eyebrow and a snide expression (now that the shock is over).

9 SAMMY: ***AAAAIIIIIEEEEEE!***

10 LILLY: There's no stopping true idiocy, either.

* * *

MARV'S METHOD:

PLOT

Sammy stands on the edge of a cliff and sees Lily standing on a big cloud above a ravine. He runs and jumps to join her, even though she tries to stop him. As he falls to his comedic doom through part of the cloud, the dissipation of the cloud reveals that Lily was really standing on the edge of a cliff on the other side of a ravine.

DIALOGUE

1 SAMMY: Hi, Lilly!

2 LILLY: Hi, Sammy!

3 SAMMY: Just a sec!

4 LILLY: Just a sec for what?

5 LILLY: What are you doing?

6 SAMMY: I'm going to join you on that cloud!

7 LILLY: **WAIT! STOP!**

8 SAMMY: There's no stopping true love.

9 SAMMY: **AAAAIIIIIEEEEEE!**

10 LILLY: There's no stopping true idiocy, either.

*   *   *

So how do we rate Stephanie's scripts? Does each version fit the parameters of the assignment?

A hand slowly rises from the sea of tentative expressions.

"Yes?"

The first person says, "I like the *Full Script Method* version without camera angles the best."

"Why is that?" I ask.

"It allows the artist the freedom to stage the gag, while focusing on what needs to be drawn."

Another hand rises.

"Yes?"

The second person says, "I like the version with camera angles better."

"Why is that?" I ask.

"Because I can clearly see how each panel is going to work, and it doesn't allow for misinterpretation by the artist. Even if the artist draws the story differently, it communicates the writer's intent better than the version without camera angles."

"But then the artist doesn't get to bring her own vision to the gag," the first person replies.

"And maybe that vision would've constrained the artist from making it better, or even ruined the gag," the second person says.

Another hand rises.

"Yes?"

A third person says, "I like the *Marv's Method* version best."

"Why is that?" I ask.

"Because the dialog clearly points the gag in a specific editorial direction, while still allowing the artist the freedom to stage the gag within the context of her style."

Another hand rises.

"Yes?"

A fourth person says, "I think everybody's ignoring the potential of the *Plot Method* version. I think this approach has the most interesting possibilities."

"Why is that?" I ask.

"Because the artist has so much more room to interpret the story that the results might be even better than what the writer originally envisioned. The results would be a true story collaboration, not just the artist drawing what the writer wanted."

I come back to my original question, "Does each version fit the parameters of the assignment?"

"Yes," everybody replies in unison.

Agreed.

Stephanie did an excellent job of presenting four versions of the same idea, and we have discussed the merits of each version.

A good visual storyteller with a sense of humor and/or drama will do well with the *Plot Method,* though the odds are the story will be completely different from the other versions. This version makes the artist a huge contributor to the actual story, not just an interpreter of what's been delineated.

A good visual storyteller with a sense of humor and/or drama will do well with the style that's missing camera angles. This version allows the artist to visually interpret a clearly written and delineated story.

A good artist lacking a sense of gag writing, or the kind of simultaneously humorous and dramatic pacing, could be helped best by the style with camera angles. The same is true for when a writer needs, for whatever reason, the story to be staged in a very specific way, like for instance a comedy writer with a finely tuned sense of timing and pacing.

Now, a writer who needs or wants the artist's conceptual and pacing contributions, yet has a clear idea of how the drama or humor unfolds, should consider *Marv's Method.* The dialogue keeps the artist focused on the editorial through-line, while the *Plot Method* aspect of the visuals allows the artist a free hand to create visuals that work best with it.

A hand rises in the back row.

"Yes?" I ask.

"You haven't told us about the *Thumbnail Method* yet?"

That's right. I was saving it for last because most writers won't be able to work with this approach to writing comics, but if you can, there are great advantages to take from its use.

The *Thumbnail Method* involves drawing a rough layout of a page, the panels on the page, the balloons inside the panels, and writing the words inside the balloons. There's no right or wrong way to create a *Thumbnail Method* comic script. It can be drawn as tightly or loosely as a creator wants. The creator can break down a page into panels, then sketch the visuals inside the panels, and add balloons and dialogue, or put balloons and dialogue inside empty panels, and then draw the visual around them. Or both.

More so than any other scripting method this is the clearest comic strip format, because anybody reading a *Thumbnail Method* script will know *exactly* how the comic will read, and only has to imagine how the artist's drawing style will embellish it.

This is a particularly effective way to write humor comics, because pacing and staging are integral to how a funny sequence works. Nothing can kill a gag quicker than poor staging, and it's harder to determine how well a humorous sequence is working with a full comics script.

When I worked for Creative Services/Publications at The Walt Disney Company, this is how we wrote comics in-house. We were all cartoonists who could write and draw. Our thumbnail scripts were sent to a South American studio to be drawn, a typed script of the dialogue was created from the thumbnails, the finished art was reduced to print size and copied, and then the copies of the art and script with dialogue were sent to Disney licensees around the world for translation and publication.

If you can draw or write into a layout, you then have full access to the sequential art toolbox, and process possibilities open up.

In the summer of 1979 at the San Diego Comic Con, fellow CAPS (Comic Art Professional Society) member Warren Greenwood introduced me to Dan O'Neill, the syndicated-cartoonist-turned-underground-comics-creator. Sometimes it's simply enough to meet one of our major influences, but then to call that person a friend and mentor is the kind of fantasy Ralphie daydreams about in *A Christmas Story.*

Dan O'Neill's *Odd Bodkins* was syndicated by Chronicle Features, and ran daily in my morning paper, the *San Francisco Chronicle,* from 1964 to 1970. O'Neill piloted the strip with all the subtlety of a Kamikaze, buzzing through the '60s with an insanely inspired mix of sociopolitical observation, philosophy, and commentary. In 1969, Glide Urban Center Publications published his oversized *Odd Bodkins* cartoon book/graphic novel, *Hear the Sound of My Feet Walking.. Drown the Sound of My Voice Talking...*

After the run of his strip, O'Neill instigated a cartoonist group called the Air Pirates. They worked together to produce *Air Pirate Funnies* (Hell Comics, 1971; "If you're looking for laughs, go to Hell"), *The Tortoise & the Hare* (Last Gasp Eco-Funnies, 1971), and others. The satirical use of certain copyrighted characters in the comics got the Air Pirates in hot water (boiling, actually) with The Walt Disney Company, and Disney's lawsuit in response got it in hot water (boiling, actually) with the Air Pirates, who formed the Mouse Liberation Front and took their satirical art show on the road for everyone to see. The results of this climatic confrontation took place with Disney winning in court and crying Uncle Walt about O'Neill continuing to draw the Mouse. Read Bob Levin's *The Pirates and the Mouse: Disney's War Against the Counterculture* (Fantagraphics Books, 2003) for the whole story.

While each of the Air Pirates produced their personal features for the comics, they also created stories in such a thoroughly original and collaborative manner—a revolutionary (pun intended) process—that it necessitated this preamble.

1982. Halloween in Nevada City, California.

Cheri, artist Jim Mitchell, and I drove up to visit Dan.

Somewhere between hanging out, driving around, and goofing off, Dan conducted an impromptu comics-writing workshop, demonstrating the process he and the Air Pirates used to produce so many pages so quickly, and with such wild creative energy and abandon. If I don't recall it exactly, though I think I do, the following gives a close approximation for how the process worked.

AIR PIRATES PROCESS:

Divide a sheet of paper into nine panels.

Using the *Thumbnail Method* to creating comics (rough-drawing the images, and writing directly into the balloons or narrative boxes), **Cartoonist #1** creates something in panel one, anything he/she wants.

Cartoonist #2 creates something *completely different* in panel three, perhaps a change of location, protagonist, or antagonist, but it needs to *not* have much to do with panel one.

Cartoonist #3 creates something in panel two, somehow bridging panels one and three.

Cartoonist #4 creates something *completely different* in panel five, perhaps a change of location, protagonist, or antagonist, but it needs to *not* have much to do with panel three.

Cartoonist #1 creates something in panel four, somehow bridging panels three and five.

Cartoonist #2 creates something *completely different* in panel seven, perhaps a change of location, protagonist, or antagonist, but it needs to *not* have much to do with panel five.

Cartoonist #3 creates something in panel six, somehow bridging panels five and seven.

Cartoonist #4 creates something *completely different* in panel nine, ending the page, perhaps a change of location, protagonist, or antagonist, and perhaps a cliffhanger for the page turn, but it needs to *not* have much to do with panel seven.

Cartoonist #1 creates something in panel eight, somehow bridging panels seven and nine.

If panel nine isn't the conclusion to the story, **Cartoonist #2** creates something in the first panel of the next page that either connects to panel nine from the previous page *or* is completely different. Either way, it sets up a repeat of the process noted above for this page.

The thumbnail script is now complete, created through a collaborative process in which no one collaborator had a clue about where it was going or what the story (if any) was about.

You can alternate this method with any number of cartoonists/ creators, or practice it as a solo exercise.

Its improvisational process allows for a wildly dynamic page, and frees up the imagination to work beyond a linear beginning-to-end storytelling process.

The downside to this process is that there isn't a theme or plot to rein in the creative chaos.

The upside is that the results are wildly fun and unpredictable. It is a great exercise for leaping out of a story sandbox and into the deep end of the pool of imagination. Whatever this process may lack in story or structure, it makes up for in spontaneity and creativity.

Sometime later in the next millennium, I used a variation of this process to write *BirdCatDog* (Graphic Universe, 2014), illustrated by

Meritxell Bosch, as well as our other books in the *Three-Story Books* series.

Each page contains a nine-panel grid. If you read only the top tier from the first page to the last, you get one perspective. If you read only the middle tier from the first page to the last, you get another perspective. If you read only the bottom tier from the first page to the last, you get yet another perspective. But if you read the pages from top to bottom, just as you would "normally," you'll see how the three stories blend to tell the whole story.

I wrote the script inside boxes on the nine-panel grid, a variation on the *Thumbnail Method*, to ensure the pages worked. In the case of *BirdCatDog*, I wrote up and down and back and forth in panels through the book, sometimes advancing the cat or the bird or the dog story for two or three pages, then came back to mix in the other characters, while also advancing their stories.

BirdCatDog (Graphic Universe, 2014) was a 2015 Eisner Award nominee for Best Publication for Early Readers (up to age 7). It won the 2015 Moonbeam Spirit Award Gold Medal for Imagination, was selected by *Kirkus Reviews* as one of the best children's books of 2014, and was in their top ten for "Middle Grade Readers of 2014 Who Like Quirky." It also received a glowing review from the prestigious children's publication, *The Horn Book,* and was included on the 2016 Little Mavericks Graphic Novel list by the Texas Library Association. The first in the *Three-Story Books* series, it was followed by *FishFishFish* and *SheHeWe* (Graphic Universe, Spring and Fall 2015, respectively).

The Air Pirates's process helps you learn to free-associate. How you bend it to your imagination and will is up to you.

So once again, there's no right way to write or create comics. There are only different ways, where, for any number of infinite reasons, one way or a combination of ways might make more sense than others.

If you write well in each version, you'll know which script style or combination of styles is best for you and your prospective artist-collaborator on any given project.

Chapter 12

The Reality Pill: Assessing Project & Collaborator Needs & Goals (before making a decision)

Before considering everything that follows, remember this: if it works, it works.

If you're happy, your collaborators are happy, and the project came out as you intended, that's all that matters.

If you and your collaborator(s) have a special relationship and simpatico understandings of what each of you needs to do and how you'll get compensated for what you need to do, as well as how you'll communicate through the process, then nothing that follows will improve that relationship, and you should take great joy in having that special relationship.

Most creators don't have that special relationship, even though they begin projects believing they do or might gain them through osmosis.

If you are this creator, this chapter is for you.

Let's call it The Reality Pill.

No relationships begin perfectly, and few rise to achieve that lofty nearly unattainable status.

As with new love that needs time, patience, and work to fully blossom into true love, creators need to build on that first enthusiasm prospective collaborators have for working together on a project.

It can be simple; it can be complicated.

I once worked for a guy whose operating philosophy was: "I want everything, so don't ask me to prioritize." There wasn't any give and take in that relationship, or at least not give on his part, but at least it was clear, if psychotically so.

Some writers want the artist to draw everything they indicate, and if the result doesn't work, they believe it's the artist's fault, not theirs.

They want everything and *don't* want to prioritize, or *can't*.

The creator who won't prioritize can (and likely will) continue to do whatever he or she does. In a largely collaborative medium this creator needs to be very good, persuasive, or wealthy to embrace this perspective and still succeed, depending on the definition of "success."

Let's presume a creator's heart and mind are in the right place.

A hand rises above a sea of perplexed expressions.

"Yes?" I ask.

"What's the *right* place?" you ask.

Great question. For this discussion, the right place would be for creators wanting to get the best work from their prospective collaborators to achieve an intended vision.

A hand bobs above the sea of lowered brows.

"Yes?" I ask.

"Does that mean the *wrong* place would be for creators to *not* want to get the best work from their prospective collaborators?"

In essence, though often accidentally, yes.

"What's 'the best' mean?" you ask.

"For this discussion, skipping personal and professional politics, which can get messy and further complicate the overarching point, 'the best' is what will help make the comic the best possible interpretation of the original vision."

I ignore the sea of angrily waving hands to continue my point.

Collaboration is a process.

It begins in numerous ways, prior to, during, or after the script is written.

It continues with some variation of *"Show 'n' Tell."* This paradigm presumes the writer initiates the story, but if the artist initiates the story, then swap the following writer and artist's roles to maintain the dynamic.

The writer and/or editor shows the artist something, the artist shows something back to the writer and/or editor, and the writer and/or editor responds with thoughts, notes, questions, and/or direction. Then the artist responds to the thoughts, notes, questions, and/or direction with thoughts, revisions, and/or new art or new pages, and the cycle repeats in some variation until somebody ends the cycle.

How the cycle begins, continues, and ends is at the heart of what we're discussing.

The goal: to end the cycle with a book that reflects an intended vision.

The first of two things to avoid: ending the cycle with somebody leaving in the middle of the process, thus beginning the cycle again with the search for a new collaborator or ending the project.

The next thing to avoid: ending the cycle with a book that does not reflect the intended vision.

We're going to work on avoiding both these things, and in so doing strive to achieve the goal.

By this point, we've studied many facets of writing with intention and unintentional miscommunication. We've learned what can go wrong, as well as what can go well, on both sides of the collaborative fence. And we've examined the root causes, free from the kind of judgment that tears relationships down instead of building them up.

To establish a successful collaborative process, each party needs to first understand the other's professional and personal needs and goals.

Until now, we've primarily determined what's important to you while setting aside what's important to your collaborator. Now we rectify this and acknowledge that a collaborative relationship, regardless of which of you is the driving force or gets more money for the time spent, requires a commitment of two or more parties.

A commitment is not based on how much harder somebody works than somebody else, or who's the creative force; it's an acceptance of the deal, a yes instead of a no, "I'm in" instead of "I'm not in."

The commitment can be complete or qualified.

If it's the latter, then each party needs to agree to the qualifications or there are rocky seas ahead that could capsize the project.

If it's the former, each collaborator still needs to understand *why* the other collaborators made their commitment.

Failure to do this can be the beginning of the end before it begins. It's why, more often than not, working relationships flounder and projects fail to live up to expectations. Understanding this is a huge baby step—let's call it the "adult step"—toward insuring a successful collaborative relationship.

The components of what made each party conclude "I'm in" or "I'm not in" are at the heart of determining a successful collaborative relationship. They are many, varied, and rarely carry equal weight.

The components divide into seven parts: project potential and requirements; personal assessment and requirements; collaborator assessment and requirements; and following your bliss versus your Spidey sense. Translation: What can it be, and what would it take to be it? What do I bring to the party, and what do I need to bring it? With whom would I be working, and what does he, she, or they need to commit? And how do I feel about it all?

PROJECT POTENTIAL

There are two basic project potential goals, creative and commercial.

For each, there is no simple way to separate the objective from the subjective determinations; nearly everybody thinks they're more objective than they are about their work.

However, with effort, you can separate the realistic from the delusional determinations.

PROJECT POTENTIAL CREATIVE GOALS

Setting creative goals is complicated. It requires breaking down portions of the "I want to do it" factor into any number of specific variables.

This project will be fun.

This project will be my first finished comic or graphic novel.

This project will help me grow as a creator, writer, and/or artist.

This project will redefine the superhero genre.

This project will tell my life's story.

This project will...what?

What do you want it do?

What do you want it to achieve?

What do you want to learn or achieve?

Know what you want. Be specific and practical.

"I want it to be the best comic ever published" is vague and (probably) unachievable.

"I want to write a children's sequential art picture book with only a few word balloons that introduces the first part of Joseph Campbell's *Hero's Journey* to very young kids" is specific and achievable. (This was my goal for *The Bramble*, Carolrhoda Books, 2013.) Nobody starts with a goal written like that; it gestates from the concept and competes for your attention with other prospective projects and their goals until it rises to the top of your consideration to become the next proposal or project you want to create.

Sometimes you might work on something just to see what it can be. That's fine. Know it, embrace it, and then everything creatively achieved after that is gravy.

Or set your sights high, aiming for the stars and perhaps only hitting the moon. Maybe your book isn't the *Citizen Kane* of comics but still introduces a unique and compelling story structure.

Maybe good is good enough.

Maybe very good is enough.

Maybe it isn't.

These are your goals.

Set them, strive to achieve them, and be satisfied or not satisfied with the result. It's up to you.

PROJECT POTENTIAL COMMERCIAL GOALS

Setting commercial goals requires creators to be realistic, have market savvy, understand their current place in consumer consciousness, and—here comes the tough part—with all other components in place, assess likely results.

I want this project to get published, and I don't care if it makes money or not.

I want this project to help make me a living.

I want this project to make me a fortune.

I want this project to establish me as a professional.

I want this project to get me noticed by Marvel or DC.

I want this project to help me build my brand.

I want this project to extend my brand.

I want this project to...what?

What do you want it do?

What do you want it to achieve?

How does it help your career?

Know what you want. Be specific and practical.

Nobody can realistically expect comics like *Teenage Mutant Ninja Turtles* and *The Walking Dead* to evolve into money trees, and that's the tricky part of setting commercial goals.

Goals can be met, not met, exceeded.

But don't count on "exceeded." That's unanticipated icing, even if it should be contractually planned for between collaborators.

A hand slowly rises in the back to get attention.

"Yes?" I ask.

"What do you mean about icing that needs to be contractually planned for?"

Without derailing the bigger train from the more important track, it means you need to plan for success.

I have an example in a situation that may seem similar to the lawsuit by Tony Moore, the first artist of *The Walking Dead*, but it is only similar on the surface because I am not privy to those contractual specifics and what anybody agreed to.

When Barbara Randall Kesel and I first discussed financial creator participation for The Pack, we made a philosophical determination. We believed that the first published book in a series established the intellectual property, and that the writer and the artist(s) for that book were The Creators. The Creators would get a creator's portion of all future proceeds whether they worked on future titles in the series or not. We also believed that writers and artists should get proceeds for the books they worked on, and those payments were a different piece of the pie than the creator portions. In short, payments and royalties for each book would go to The Creators as well as the writers and artists on specific books.

To specify, if the first book in a series *Bob Reigns In Hell* was written by Joe Schmoe and drawn by Marsha Moosha, then they are The Creators. For that first book's fabulous success they got a creator's portion of the advance as well as payment for making the book. Then the royalties came in, and they got their creator's portions and their separate book-specific portions. Then they retired and moved to Tahiti.

The second book in the series, *Bob Takes Over Heaven*, was written by Brenda Brash and drawn by Clark Park. Joe Schmoe and Marsha Moosha still get their creator portions of the advance and the royalties, but Brenda Brash and Clark Park get their portions of the book payments, too.

Bob Reigns In Hell is then turned into a hit HBO series. Joe Schmoe and Marsha Moosha get their creator portions of the payments, as well as their portions of the payments for having written and drawn the source material.

When the second season adapts *Bob Takes Over Heaven*, Joe Schmoe and Marsha Moosha still get their creator portions of the payments, and Brenda Brash and Clark Park get their portions of the payments for having written and drawn the source material.

Contractually planning for success establishes relationships and clears up any misunderstandings. It also becomes the foundation on which disputes are resolved.

A hand rises from the back row.

"Yes?"

You ask, "Isn't figuring out the deal putting the cart before the horse? Can't you figure out the splits when there's a deal and you know what you're splitting?"

"I'm not sure there's a worse time to figure out the deal," I reply. "Remuneration is on the table and everybody's trying to figure out how much of it they'll need to pay the rent or buy their kitties Kibbles."

"But what if the creators are friends? Surely that makes a difference."

A difference? Absolutely. That can make it worse. If one friend wants more than another friend thinks the first friend should have then the friendship can become compromised by negotiation. That may also be true when the negotiation takes place at the conception of the project, but at least at that point it's hypothetical, and there's less chance that somebody will feel their arm is being twisted off behind their back.

You raise your hand and ask, "Does the agreement need to be in writing, like a contract?"

Great question to which I offer an ambiguous answer, "It depends, and at some point you are likely to regret which way you went."

Not everybody can afford a lawyer to draft a contract between creators, but sometimes you can't afford not to.

If you're not comfortable working without a written agreement, don't.

If you're comfortable working with a handshake agreement, do.

With a friend, I'm okay with handshakes. With a friend of a friend, I'm often still okay working with handshakes. That doesn't mean you should or shouldn't.

However you come to an agreement, the point is that not everybody agrees on what is and isn't fair, and it's better to determine that before the work is started.

Here's an example where I didn't take my own advice.

Artist collaborator Scott Roberts and I contributed a story, *Silver-Hair & The Three Xairs*, to the 2012 Dark Horse anthology, *Once Upon A Time Machine*.

The anthology was initiated by writer Chris Stevens on the Digital Webbing forum, proposed much like a Mickey & Judy production: "Hey, let's put on a show in the barn!"

Each story needed to be a science fiction or fantasy spin on a classic children's story.

I was asked to submit a pitch, which I did.

The submissions were all posted on the site, and it was fascinating to see the stories and the responses to them from other creators. Did anybody ask about or offer the nature of the deal? Nope. It was a group effort, something fun where I thought a group of creators would contribute and participate equally, *"I thought"* being my first and biggest mistake.

My story was chosen as one of many, so I asked Scott Roberts (*Patty Cake, Rugrats, Prince Valiant*) to draw and color the twelve-page story, and we agreed to share equally. Scott Brown lettered for future considerations.

Between ourselves we had a deal.

However I didn't make a deal for contributing to the anthology; I *assumed* a deal.

Other creators were better about making their needs known.

Some only worked for payment.

Some stories needed color and lettering that had to be paid for, and Chris went out of pocket for much of this.

The project languished for quite a while, but Chris joined up with a packaging associate, and they got the book set up at Dark Horse Comics.

Then came the deal.

For our contribution they offered a single contributor copy, one book for Scott Roberts, Scott Brown, and me to share. We got to keep the copyright with only limited reprint restrictions.

Simply put and without hesitation, I refused the deal.

We negotiated, and in the interest of fair play, it was their book, their deal with Dark Horse, and their choice about whether to share royalties, if any.

Their position: anthologies don't make royalties so there won't be anything to share anyway.

My position: if there isn't anything to share then why not offer a creator portion of the royalties?

Their position: nobody else has complained, and everybody but you is thrilled by the prospect of being published.

My position: my goals are my goals, I won't compare them to anybody else's, and I won't contribute our story for a single copy of the book.

Their position: they upped the number of creator copies.

I took the deal to Scott Roberts.

I told Scott my feelings about the deal. Scott worked hard to draw and color the story, and I told him that I could go either way. I told him that I had future plans for the Silver-Hair character, and there could be an advantage in getting the story published. I was also okay with telling them where they could put their deal.

In short, I was okay with "yes" or "no."

I told Scott I would back his decision.

Scott said that since we'd already done the work he'd like to see the story published, so I accepted the negotiated deal. We got more copies of the book to share between the three of us.

I don't regret taking the deal; it was our choice to accept or not accept it.

I regret the process, and that I didn't follow common business sense and clarify the deal from the beginning.

Had I forced the deal before offering pitches and doing the work would Chris have said to every prospective contributor, "I own the book, and I'll give each of you a single contributor's copy"?

Maybe and maybe not.

If so, would everybody have accepted the deal Chris ultimately offered if the publishing opportunity wasn't already in place?

Maybe and maybe not.

If we'd forced clarification of the deal, maybe arguments over it would've spoiled the mood, and the anthology never would have happened.

Or maybe Chris would have offered creators profit participation, even if there never ended up being any profit to share.

We'll never know, because nobody, myself included, forced early clarification of the deal.

Coming back to the greater point, we make deals to plan for success, as well as for when we don't agree.

And if we don't make deals at the beginning, it can be harder to get what we want at the end.

PROJECT REQUIREMENTS
TO FULFILL CREATIVE AND COMMERCIAL GOALS

What pieces need to be in place for a project to achieve its goals?

We're going to review a few wide-ranging goals, and then determine corresponding needs.

They are: 1) finish a comic and don't care if it's published; 2) finish a comic and get it published somewhere, even if it's on a blog; 3) produce a comic that showcases you as a professional quality indie creator; 4) produce a comic that showcases you as a professional quality creator who can work with licensed characters; 5) produce a graphic novel that establishes you as a professional quality comics-lit creator; 6) produce a body of work that showcases you as a professional quality creator who could work with Marvel and DC characters.

These are just a sampling of goals, and they certainly aren't intended to have more or less value than any other goals.

Remember, the point is for *you* to set *your* goal, and whether it's to under- or over-achieve that's up to you and only to you.

My goal is for you to make an honest goal appraisal and practical recognition of what is and isn't required to achieve that goal.

If your goal is to simply see your story published, don't beat yourself up if it's not the *Citizen Kane* of comics. Conversely, if you're going to beat yourself up for *not* producing the *Citizen Kane* of comics then you need to raise your goal appropriately so you're beating yourself up for the right reason.

It is never easy looking into a mirror and describing what you see, but that's what's required. Delusion gets you nowhere except the psychiatric ward.

So let's begin.

If your goal is to finish a comic (creative) and you don't care if it's published or not (commercial), then what do you need to accomplish this goal?

1) A script;
2) An artist or artists who'll draw, perhaps color, and letter.

It's a starting place. There's nothing here that requires the work to meet a professional standard, and that's fine, because finishing the comic was the goal, not publishing it. If the work meets a professional standard, then you've exceeded your goal.

If your goal is to finish a comic (creative) and get it published, even if it's only self-published on your online blog (commercial), then your needs don't change much, as long as you have a self-publishing outlet.

1) A script;
2) An artist or artists who'll draw, perhaps color, and letter;
3) A self-publishing outlet.

Since self-publishing and distribution via a blog don't require outside editorial evaluation, there's nothing in these goals that requires the work to meet a professional standard. If the work meets a professional standard and/or somebody else publishes it, then you've exceeded your goal.

If your goal is to produce a comic (creative) that will become a showcase for you as a professional-quality indie creator (commercial), then your goals expand to include your talent and skill.

1) A script that meets a high minimum professional quality standard (set by professional indie creators);

2) An artist or artists who'll draw, perhaps color, and letter to a high minimum professional quality standard (set by professional indie creators);

3) A prospective readership, via online or print.

See how much the needs changed because your goal is now for this comic to be a professional showcase? Poor storytelling, drawing, and lettering can bring down the quality of a good script, so everybody involved needs to reach a high minimum standard.

What does this need potentially portend? It means not offering the project to any artist who is willing to work on the book, even if the artists you want to work with aren't interested. See how the goal draws a line in the sand about what you will and won't do to get it drawn? More about this later, but for now, if the right artists won't draw your comic, there needs to be a frank appraisal about how well you wrote the script.

There are additional factors to consider, which (again) we'll address later, but the mirror is often the best place to begin asking questions.

If your goal is to produce a comic (creative) that will become a showcase for you to write characters created by somebody other than yourself, like, for example, *The Phantom* or *The Green Hornet* (commercial), then your needs shift dramatically?

1) A script that meets a high minimum professional quality standard (set by publishers of licensed characters), that shows you can write effectively for the kind of licensed character(s) you want to write. To be clear, showing you can write Uncle Scrooge won't help you get a job writing The Phantom.

2) An artist or artists who'll draw, perhaps color, and letter to a high

minimum professional quality standard (set by publishers of licensed characters).

Your needs change quite a bit, because now your goal is showcasing your talent. Poor storytelling, drawing, and lettering bring down the quality of a good script, so everybody involved needs to be within an appropriate range of styles and reach a high minimum standard. To be clear, working with a Disney-style artist might not help you get a job writing The Phantom. Conversely, working with an adventure-style artist might not help you get a job writing Uncle Scrooge.

If your goal is to tell the story about a guy who lost his virginity and can't find it (creative), as well as to get it published by a graphic novel publisher and establish yourself as a comics-lit creator (commercial), the needs multiply and change profoundly. Now the quality of the finished work needs to meet a high minimum standard to get a prospective publisher's attention.

But it's not just about the quality of the work; it's also now about the execution of the writing and art. The styles need to fit somewhere in a range that's perceived by a publisher as "graphic novel" and not "superhero comic book." Translation: if it reads and looks like a monthly Spider-Man, Superman, or Batman, then First Second Books, Pantheon, Top Shelf, Drawn & Quarterly, Abrams ComicArts, and Fantagraphics aren't likely to be interested.

Presuming the concept and script meet the perceived needs, what happens if the prospective artist is primarily influenced by the work of Jack Kirby? As much fun as that approach might be, what graphic novel publisher would publish this version of the book? Probably none. But what if the artist's Jack Kirby-influenced style had a retro feel that gave the story a satirical spin on a quest by a guy in search of his lost virginity? It could work. And what if the artist was Bruce Timm, a brand-name comics creator with a readership that *would* buy this book even if printed on toilet paper? Maybe a graphic novel publisher *would* publish this version of the book.

Any assessment becomes incredibly subjective, and every "rule" can have any number of exceptions to it. A successful exception usually involves a unique vision and exceptional execution.

Our mission is to create a coldblooded determination about what's required to achieve your goal, while still keeping it broad enough to allow for a unique vision, a catalyst to help give the story its soul.

1) A uniquely compelling and/or commercially compelling concept, one that is fits inside the broadest possible range of prospective publishers' current publishing plans;

2) A script that meets a high minimum professional quality standard (set by industry publishers);

3) An artist or artists who'll draw, perhaps color, and letter to a high minimum professional quality standard (set by industry publishers).

The bar just got set really high. There are a lot of moving parts that affect whether or not your work rises to it. It's important to remember this exercise isn't math; it's about making determinations about what you need to do to achieve your goals, from creating the concept and writing the script to finding an artist who help the project achieve its goals.

If your goal is to produce a body of work that shows editors you can write superheroes (creative) for Marvel and DC (commercial), then your needs change quite a bit. So does any clear path to success.

What are the odds that creating some of the best crime graphic novels ever produced is going to coincide with Marvel's EIC wanting to bring in new talent? It worked out well for Brian Michael Bendis, but is that a course somebody can successfully chart? Probably not.

Does that mean the safest course is to create a new superhero universe? Not necessarily.

Does producing a brilliant body of comics work in any genre create potential steppingstones that allow you to have conversations about doing something different? Maybe, maybe not. It depends.

There is no safe or obvious course, because there are too many variables in play, including current editorial biases and trends, which cannot be predicted on an annual, quarterly, monthly, weekly, or daily basis.

To achieve this goal, you need:

1) Scripts with professional consistency that demonstrate a high quality understanding of concept, character, story, drama, action, and dialogue;

2) Artists who'll draw, color, and letter to a high minimum professional quality standard (set by industry publishers). This is critical, because most editors will read your sample comics but not your sample scripts, so you want your finished work to look as professional as possible;

3) Enough luck to be writing the right kind of comics at the right time for Marvel and DC comics editors to think you can fit into their current and/or future plans;

4) Access to Marvel and DC editors, unless they come knocking on your door.

Even if you don't achieve this goal of getting hired by Marvel or DC, the results of your work can pay off in different ways, like, for example, helping to establish your brand as a comics creator.

Shoot for the moon, and if you miss, land among the stars.

Success often comes in ways we don't expect, so be open to new opportunities.

And don't let any of these considerations derail you from following your bliss. The purpose of this exercise is to determine your bliss and do everything afterwards to help make it happen.

PERSONAL ASSESSMENT

Are you the right person with the right skill set at the right stage of your career to achieve your next goal?

Most people will answer, "What's the harm in trying?" or "(imagine the expletive) YES!"

That's fair, normal, expected, and also not the point, unless "(imagine the expletive) YES!" matches up with your creative and commercial project needs.

If your goal as a writer is to get Marvel and/or DC Comics to hire you, then having established your level of craft well enough to a prospective editor to consider you for an assignment is important for meeting that goal. How many writers got their first writing gig for Marvel or DC? Okay, yeah, there's that guy who roomed with an editor who just got promoted and didn't know better, but besides that? If you found somebody, congratulations and you've found the other exception to the rule.

That's the point.

There's no harm in trying, but this exercise is about setting realistic goals.

Now, what if you're an artist with a goal toward getting Marvel and/or DC Comics to hire you?

We're in trickier territory here, because an eye-popping portfolio that shows the requisite chops supersedes a lot of normal barriers. But "requisite chops" is the damning qualifier, because a Marvel and/or DC Comics editor has to imagine your work matching his or her needs. Even then, you could be the Michelangelo of comics and some Marvel and DC editors still won't hire you if you haven't already proven you can do the work on a timely, professional, and consistent basis.

Tackling a less-rigid goal, let's say you want a trade book publisher like First Second to publish your graphic novel. Do you need to have produced a body of work showing what you can do? Not necessarily, with "need to" being the damning qualifier. While having established your brand and developed a fan base brings real value to a publisher's decision, presuming access to your prospective publisher and that concept and execution meet a high requisite standard, you could be a complete unknown and still get your work published.

Personal dynamics and networking also come into play, along with any number of miscellaneous factors. While this isn't rocket science, it is odds-based assessment, meaning that it's okay to shoot for the moon regardless of odds, as long as you're practical about where you might land among the stars.

We're going to match up a series of personal assessments with previously noted creative and commercial project requirements, then determine whether the matches work.

Sam is an unpublished prose writer and unproduced screenwriter who hasn't written a comic story, but loves the sequential art medium, and is just now teaching himself to write comics. He has not yet completed a script for his graphic novel and has never collaborated with an artist. He spends time on several forums, soaking up tips about making comics.

Lily has written several online and anthology comics in collaboration with near-professional artists in a wide range of genres. She has strong skill sets for character, structure, dialogue, and story, and has built a solid professional network with indie creators.

Hercules has written a lot of superhero and adventure comics that have been self-published and posted online, collaborating with artists who are also trying to break into the business. He's sent samples to a wide range of comics industry editors, few of whom have responded, and those who did were not encouraging. He's had a few meetings with editors at local conventions, but none were interested in his creator-owned projects, and he's yet to receive any assignment work.

Stephanie recently graduated from SVA (School of Visual Arts), and writes as well as draws. Her drawing style is quirky, humorous, and accessible. Her writing is warm and personal, and she excels at bringing real characters with real problems to life. She's working on a graphic novel, and consistently posting a short number of pages each week. Her blog is building a devoted following.

Puck is Mr. Energy, talks a great game, is a proficient comics writer for a guy who just started out a few years ago, pals around with Marvel and DC assistant comics editors at conventions, is up to date on and passionate about superhero continuity, has written a few one-shots for comics featuring licensed characters, and he's teaming with a several up-and-coming artists on a number of creator-owned projects.

Considering each of these creators, let's now examine what they hope to accomplish on their next projects.

As a reminder the prospective projects are: 1) finish a comic and don't care if it's published; 2) finish a comic and get it published somewhere, even if it's on a blog; 3) produce a comic that showcases you as a professional quality indie creator; 4) produce a comic that showcases you as a professional quality creator who can work with licensed characters; 5) produce a graphic novel that establishes you as a professional quality comics-lit creator; 6) produce a body of work that showcases you as a professional quality creator who could work with Marvel and DC characters.

Sam wants to produce a body of work that showcases him as a professional quality creator who could work with Marvel and DC characters.

How realistic is this?

It's a fine long-term goal, but is Sam's first comic going to contribute to this body or work or is it more likely to be an exercise? Probably the latter, whether he likes it or not.

Goals one and two are more realistic for Sam/anybody who has not yet written a comic, unless they're a successful screenwriter or novelist dabbling in the form, in which case they're likely to get significant help from an editor.

What if Sam insists on producing the first comic as part of his body of work that showcases him as a professional quality creator who could work with Marvel and DC characters?

Well, then Sam needs to find a collaborator whose work is of a professional quality, preferably one who'll work with Sam to smooth out the beginner's mistakes in the script and make sure the comic reads well.

Without the money to hire that artist, what are the odds that Sam's maiden comics efforts are going to draw a professional quality comics artist into working for free on his project?

Well, if Sam's initial grasp of the form, story, and storytelling are brilliant, then he has a chance, especially if he's as good a schmoozer as Puck, but that's not in his bio, so odds are long.

This doesn't mean Sam shouldn't try to achieve his initial goal, but it would be wasteful for him to invest his time and energy on the first comic and quit if it doesn't help him achieve his goals. If his next effort and the one after that don't help him produce comics that help him build his body of work that showcases him as a professional quality creator who could work with Marvel and DC characters, then at which point does Sam give up? How much failure for how many years is too much? There might be a reason Sam is an unpublished prose writer and unproduced screenwriter; maybe he gives up too soon. Maybe he hasn't defined the steps in the ladder well enough to gage incremental progress, steps that could satisfy him personally and professionally, and ultimately lead to achieving his goal.

This is the value of setting realistic and achievable goals.

Had Sam simply set his goal at finishing a comic and not caring if it's published, or finishing a comic and getting it published somewhere, even if it's on a blog, then his goal would have been more achievable, and he would have then an opportunity to build on that success and develop as a comics creator.

Lily wants to finish a comic and get it published somewhere, even if it's on a blog.

Is this a realistic goal?

Absolutely. Goals don't need to be hard. If Lily wants to experiment out of the limelight of professional publication that sounds like a lot of fun, and if she exceeds her creative and commercial goals she has every reason to be satisfied.

Hercules wants to produce a comic that showcases himself as a professional quality creator who can work with licensed characters.

He's not giving up. Hercules has a passion for working with characters already in the culture, and he wants to make his mark.

He's written a lot of samples to show what he can do, but editors haven't responded well enough to hire him.

What can he do on his next comic to help change that?

There are a lot of moving parts in the answer to this question, with no way to distinguish which of them is most pronounced. Also, one of those moving parts can jam up the others, so let's examine the parts and see how they affect the whole.

Before examining his past work and determining what needs to be accomplished, let's ask Hercules to look into a mirror.

If Hercules is an asshole, inadvertent or intentional, he's going to have to be pretty talented and proficient for an editor to overlook that trait. Let's assume Hercules is a nice enough guy.

If Hercules is socially awkward and shy, that can make for some pretty tough meetings, but it can be worked around. You don't need to be pals with your prospective editor, (though it helps), but well-written email correspondence can be enough to get and keep an editor's attention, if you have the right material and editor. Let's assume Hercules is okay in meetings or on the phone and speaks professionally well enough to not cause concern.

As a footnote to this part of the discussion and in answer to your obvious question: yes, it's very hard to get editors' attention, to get them to return emails, to get them to consider your work, to get any kind of feedback at all, but this part of the discussion is about you, not them. If your work is universally praised, then you have a chance to reach an editor and make a good impression.

A hand rises in the back row.

"Yes?" I ask.

"But if my work is universally praised, then I've already done the work well enough to get an editor to pay attention to me."

"That's right," I answer.

"But how do I get to the point where my work is universally praised?"

Great question. The answer is what we're discussing: you set a series of short-term, achievable, escalating goals, each one a rung on a ladder.

For example, if you've frequently written the best short comics in anthologies, reviews and reader reaction will reflect that, and this becomes future ammo for introducing yourself to editors. Your progression is about identifying and creating rungs on a ladder, and if you're fortunate enough to skip a few rungs on your climb toward your goal, that's a good thing.

Still, it's better to be prepared to climb them than to think you'll skip them.

Back to Hercules, who probably thinks we've forgotten about him.

Noting that there are no off-putting personal issues, let's examine Hercules's past work and process.

Hercules is largely based on a writer with whom I briefly corresponded, but he's also an amalgam of a writer-type whose work does not rise to his or her level of confidence, a writer-type that does not respond well to constructive criticism directed at his or her samples. That's a problem because it's awfully hard to work with people who are convinced they've done great work, when they haven't.

A hand rises in the back row.

"Yes?" I ask.

"What if Hercules has done great work, and you're wrong?" you ask.

"Well," I begin, "there's the rub. The answer depends on how much I clarify what is or isn't working, and why. It also depends on how well Hercules can step back and assess his work objectively."

There's no simple answer to this question, but there is a short answer, one you've heard before: make sure your work reflects your intention. If the criticism reflects what you intended, then you know the reader simply didn't like what you intended. If the criticism reflects a perception different from your intention, then it's wise to figure out where the work fell short.

Ultimately, the real answer comes back to goals.

If it's Hercules's goal to do whatever he wants to, then that's fine. His work is his responsibility, not mine or anybody else's.

But Hercules wants to write licensed-character comics. These are comics an editor has the responsibility to produce, comics that are based on properties somebody else owns, and it is usually the editor's job to clarify the vision for the comic, and for the creator to embrace that vision. So Hercules responding to every critique or note with argument and obstructionism is a response that does not bode well for him to achieve his goal.

A hand rises in the back row.

"Yes?" I ask.

"But wouldn't Hercules act differently if he was paid to write a comic?"

"Maybe," I reply. "And maybe not."

Maybe it's only his insecurities that cause him to react defensively and personally to notes given to his samples, instead of recognizing that the editor from whom he's trying to get work has a responsibility to guide the licensed-character comic in a specific direction.

Or maybe he never had a saddle placed on him, and bucked for everything he was worth.

Moving on, and presuming Hercules at some point learns to respond well to constructive criticism and notes, what can he do next to produce a comic that showcases himself as a professional quality creator who can work with licensed characters?

He needs to produce a story that is near enough in tone to the kind of story he wants to write for a publisher.

He needs to write a script sample that shows a clear understanding of sequential art.

He needs to write a script that can be handed to any editor and artist for a clear understanding of how the story and characters unfold.

He needs to find an artist whose quality of work is of a professional caliber.

A tentative hand rises in back.

"Yes?" I ask.

"If Hercules is trying to find work as a writer, why is it important that the artist's work is professional?"

"Great question," I reply. "It's because most comics editors won't take the time to read a script sample, but they might browse through a finished comic to see if they like it."

I ignore hands waving like wheat on a field, and continue.

If the drawn comic doesn't look good or read well, then Hercules is not likely to capture an editor's attention. That's why the execution needs to meet a minimum professional standard.

And if an editor likes Hercules's comic and wants to assess his level of craft, he might ask to see the original script.

Or instead the editor might give Hercules an assignment.

At this point, Hercules accomplished his goal of producing a comic that showcases himself as a professional quality creator who can work with licensed characters.

What's his next goal?

Perhaps it's to sell a pitch for a licensed character comic.

It would seem Hercules is near accomplishing this next goal...well, nearer perhaps, but not near.

Getting a chance to pitch is different than selling the pitch, just as getting a comics job is different than finishing the comics job.

If Hercules has properly prepared, then he will produce a professional quality script that the editor can hand to an artist.

If Hercules has properly prepared and the editor has notes, then he will be able to address those notes.

If Hercules has properly prepared, he will be able to take advantage of this opportunity, sell his pitch, write his first professional comic with licensed characters, and consider his options for the next rung on his ladder.

Stephanie wants to produce a comic that will showcase her as a professional-quality indie creator.

Reviewing Stephanie's short bio, she's already doing the work that will help her accomplish her goal.

She attends comics conventions, meets other creators, is personable, dedicated, and diligent.

A graphic novel is a huge time commitment, but her dedication to it, as well as the quality of the work produced, may be her best calling cards.

Could Stephanie contribute to anthologies? Sure.

Could spreading herself too thin take away from her self-imposed schedule for finishing her graphic novel? Sure.

Stephanie is the comics world's version of an "author," somebody with a clear vision for what she wants to do.

If Stephanie weren't already so accomplished, I'd suggest small indie projects to help her develop her skills and level of craft, but she's a natural cartoonist with a vision and the ability to deliver on that vision.

Stephanie should be trying to meet as many editors as possible, not only to get their assessment of her work, but also to gain insight into her best options.

Her online graphic novel is compelling and deserves publication, so her next challenge is finding an editor who recognizes her abilities and offers her an assignment or embraces her graphic novel for print publication...or both.

As a side note, I met the real Stephanie over a decade ago, when she was just starting out. I immediately offered to find a project for her to work on, and she declined because she had a vision for what she really wanted to do.

She is now a successful graphic novel creator.

Knowing what you want, knowing how to get it, and having the ability to produce it, alongside the dedication to stick with it, is a formula for success.

Puck wants to produce a body of work that showcases himself as a professional quality creator who could work with Marvel and DC characters.

Like Stephanie, Puck is well on his way to accomplishing his goal, but, unlike Stephanie, there's one glaring concern: if Puck pals around with editors at Marvel and DC, why haven't they already given him an assignment?

I've seen Pucks come and go.

Most of their work is "okay," but not special.

They have a working knowledge of the current superhero universe mythologies, and excel at probing their complications.

But when it comes to creating compelling stories that rise above the standard tropes, they fall flat.

Right now, Puck's work is competent, and he's hooking up with artists that will soon get the attention of Marvel and DC editors. If Puck stays on his current path, he can ride their coattails and accomplish enough of his goal to get a few tryout stories for Marvel and DC.

And then, like the Pucks before him, Puck will probably disappear from the public view because nobody noticed or cared enough about his work.

On the other hand, he might get lucky and land a job as an editor, and perhaps that's where his strengths ultimately lie.

But let's say Puck really prefers to be a creator.

Let's say Puck views the next rung in the ladder, the one that's above getting professional consideration by Marvel and DC, involves becoming their next Flavor of the Month/Big Thing/Star.

If Puck wants to be different from the previous Pucks, if he wants to succeed where other Pucks failed, then he's got to do a better job of putting his work where his mouth is.

There's no denying that his ability to schmooze is a great superpower, but it only gets you so far.

If Puck really wants to be an impactful comics creator, he's got to concentrate on making his work better, not just acceptable; he has to find ways for his work to rise above the rest. This particular Puck needs to look long and hard in the mirror and evaluate his own work with the same energy and vitriol with which he assesses the work of others.

He has to be his own toughest critic.

Since simply *wanting* to be better isn't enough, Puck needs to strive to be better, which requires study, work, and diligence.

He needs to not settle for the first good idea until he's determined that it's the best idea among a number of good ideas.

He needs to understand and utilize the full sequential art toolbox in order to make the best use of the medium.

Puck is at a crossroads, where he can coast downhill on what he's already accomplished, or he can recognize that turn likely involves a dead end to his writing career and take the other longer, steeper, harder, and potentially more satisfying road to his preferred destination.

PERSONAL REQUIREMENTS

What do you need?

This is different from "what do you want?" We all know you want universal praise, critical acknowledgment, financial success, and probably some awards to validate your efforts and decorate your walls, but what do you really *need*?

There are two types of needs, what you need to do the work and what you need in the rest of your life. Hopefully the two are compatible, but they're often not.

The first is simple. You will have any number of needs to do the work, but let's discuss two common examples.

Do you need to be paid a living wage for working on the book or do you simply need it published to help start building your brand as a creator?

A hand rises in back.

"Yes?" I ask.

"How do I know really know what I need?" you ask.

"Simple," I respond. "Suppose you determine you need to be paid a living wage. Then a really great artist says she'd love to work on your book. Her idea is that you should finish a couple issues so you can set it up at Image. Now, if you're okay with that, did you really *need* to be paid a living wage for writing the book?"

"No," you reply.

Let's try another one.

"Suppose you determine you need to own the project, because it's your brainchild. You're okay with an artist getting page rate and royalties, but you need to own and control the project. Then a really great artist says he'd love to work on your book, but he needs to share ownership in the project because he's been screwed too many times by people who took advantage of him. Now, if, in order to get this artist to work on the project, you're okay with sharing copyright, did you really *need* to own the project?"

"No," you reply.

So maybe your initial stance is a starting point, one that you're willing to adjust depending on the situation.

Do you see how getting to the heart of the question specifies the need, even when it's complicated?

Test your perceived need to see if it's really what you need.

We all tend to fool ourselves, but it's better if we don't let that make us fools *of* ourselves.

The personal need is more complicated.

Do you need that extra hour of sleep, the hour you could otherwise use to write or draw before going to work?

Do you need to spend time with your family and friends instead of working on your comic?

A dedicated creator needs to be aware of the tradeoffs for her or his time.

Life sucks your time away, regardless of how you use it, so use it with intention.

Is playing a videogame more important than writing or drawing the next page of your comic?

If the answer is, "yes, at that moment," that's okay, because you're consciously considering the tradeoff. Maybe you recognize and respond to the time you need to recharge your creative batteries, and hopefully you're not *pretending* to need that time when you really don't. (That's you fooling you.)

Conversely, if you've set aside outside responsibilities in favor of writing or drawing your comic, and haven't planned for it with those counting on you, then your personal life is a potential train wreck that could derail everything.

It's hard work to maintain the balance between what you need to work on the comic and what you need to maintain a stable personal life.

When committing to any project you need to know what you need for yourself and in tradeoff to write or draw your story.

Money, rights, time, and relationships are just four likely variables,

variables that need to be noted, juggled, and accounted for.

Whatever your needs may be, consider their tradeoffs, and share them with those you care about. You *need* your friends and loved ones working with you, not against you.

PARTNER/COLLABORATOR ASSESSMENT

Just as you made a personal assessment, consider whether or not your prospective collaborator has the chops to help you meet your goals for the project.

A hand sprouts in back among the sea of blank expressions.

"Yes?" I ask.

"I hear the term 'chops' a lot."

"Yes," I reply.

"It seems to be a shorthand for the 'ability to do the work,'"

"Yes," I agree.

"The term is conclusive, but how to I arrive at that determination?"

Great question.

To assess artists and writers as prospective collaborators, consider three variables: the quality of the work, the appropriateness of the style for the project, the ability to deliver on schedule.

If a writer or artist's best work is not good enough for the job, the writer or artist might not have the chops.

If a writer or artist's range of styles does not overlap the range of styles that are appropriate for the job, the writer or artist might not have the chops.

If the writer or artist does not have the ability to do the work within the necessary timeframe, the writer or artist might not have the chops.

You ask, "What do you mean by the 'necessary timeframe'?"

Maybe the artist is too slow to meet the deadline. But if there's no deadline, then it doesn't matter how slow the artist works.

This is why your goals need to be clear and accurate. If you don't know what you really need from the finished comic, then how can you know what you need in a prospective collaborator?

Goals dictate needs.

If your goal as a writer is simply to team up with an artist to do something fun, that's fine. With no qualitative or timeline goals, a ten year-old has the chops to do this.

If your goal as a writer is to publish a comic that will get comic book or graphic novel editors interested your work, then the artist needs the chops to produce a professional looking book.

If your goal as a writer is to publish a four-issue miniseries that needs to be finished in six months, and which will, upon publication, serve as your calling card to comic book editors, then the artist needs the chops to produce a professional looking book on time.

If you don't find the right collaborator with the chops to fit your needs, then your odds of meeting your goals diminish.

PARTNER/COLLABORATOR ASSESSMENT AND REQUIREMENTS

Taking a new tack on the previous discussion, a hand rises from the back row.

"Yes?" I ask.

"What if the artist has the ability to do the work within the necessary timeframe, but doesn't have the time?"

That is another great question, and this is why we're dividing the prospective collaborator assessments from the requirements.

The artist might very well have the chops to do the work within the necessary timeframe, but he or she might not get from the project what he or she wants or needs to do the work.

"Can you give me an example?" you ask.

"Sure, and let's go to the extreme to drive the point home. Let's say you have a brilliant crime noir comic script that's ready to be drawn. What happens if you ask Frank Miller to work on it for free?"

There's a deathly silence from the front row to the back, the point driven home.

Once you determine your prospective collaborator is right for the job, consider whether their needs line up with them working on your project.

What does your prospective collaborator want, money, fame, and/or the freedom to play?

Is a prospective collaborator likely to get what he or she wants from working on the project?

If so, that's great; if not, that's not so great.

What does your prospective collaborator need, a talent showcase, to simply work on a fun comic, to make a little extra money, to make a living?

It is risky to work with a prospective collaborator who needs more than the finished project can realistically deliver. When he or she suddenly realizes the need is unattainable, or a better opportunity comes along, he or she will jump ship. This is virtually guaranteed, and it is hard to blame anybody for this, even after making a commitment to the comic, because the potential results were set unreasonably high.

If you really want this prospective collaborator, and the prospective collaborator really wants to work on your comic, then it is better to acknowledge the project will likely not help them achieve all their needs, and that if something comes along in the interim it'll be okay for them to leave the project. With this arrangement agreed to, it's more likely the collaborator will come back to finish what he or she started, providing that fits your needs.

This is how you build bridges and keep them standing.

FOLLOWING YOUR BLISS VERSUS YOUR SPIDEY SENSE

Even though we're discussing extraordinary efforts to break down assessments, wants, and needs into definable components, this isn't math.

To repeat, *this isn't math.*

This discussion is about making checklists that help you figure out what to do when faced with questions that don't have obvious answers.

The tendency is to follow your gut.

Most people do it.

Most people can't explain their gut, and that's fine.

You love it and want to do it, or hate it and don't want do it. Simple.

We're parsing that which isn't simple.

At some point, you fall in love with a project, fall out of love with a project, or never like it at all. These are those indefinable matters of the heart, which we're going to add to the discussion and attempt to define, or at least identify well enough so you'll recognize them for what they are.

For most creators, following your bliss or trusting your Spidey sense in making a decision probably outweighs all the other mitigating factors.

A hand rises in the back.

"Yes?" I ask.

"If this one will likely count more than the others, why are we considering the others? Isn't it just easier to do it or not do it based on whether we want to or not?"

Great question.

In truth, the "I want to" and "I don't want to" factors likely already involve some of the other determinations. We're bringing them forward to make them definable so that you can interpret what was previously instinctive.

There's a lot of gray area in making a determination about whether a prospective collaborator is the right person to work with, and sometimes your gut instincts tell you to give the prospective collaborators a chance to prove themselves.

That's fine.

It's okay to take risks, as long as you understand and accept them.

Then, if things don't go the way you hoped, you won't second-guess your initial determination; you'll know you took a chance and lost, which is better than wondering why you lost.

And if the work and the relationship go the way you hoped they would, you can embrace your instincts and working process.

Choosing a collaborator is like picking an agent. If you post an online query for an artist to draw your comic, don't say yes to them, just because they said yes to you.

Be discriminating and realistic.

Chapter 13

Options of Ownership
and Work-Made-For-Hire

Welcome to the most controversial topic in the history of comics.

In its most combative form, the question: *should somebody else own a comic and/or characters you created?*

The counterpunch: *should you own a comic with somebody else's characters or properties?*

Two extremely loaded questions, which are struck like blows from Superman and The Hulk.

But this isn't that battle for superhero supremacy; it's a complicated question with a lot of moving parts, conflicting emotions, business goals, and ideologies.

Some creators build barriers to discussion: *I won't do work-for-hire comics.*

Some creators pursue the discussion with a moral argument: *I want what's fair, and a publisher doesn't have the right to own what I make.*

Some used to work on comics owned by others, felt burned when the properties became successful as a whole or partial result of their efforts, and have sworn off work-made-for-hire comics.

Some are pragmatic: *I need to earn a living.*

Some are romantic: *I want to write for characters I love, even though somebody else owns them and will own what I write.*

Some will sell their creation because the people producing the comic say they need to own it to pursue mutually beneficial opportunities, such as publishing, film, TV, licensing.

Some will do anything to get published, and sell their creation for that opportunity.

Others work on comics owned by others and comics they own themselves, depending on the circumstances.

These are all fair determinations.

So how do you figure out what's right for you?

Understand the moving parts, conflicting emotions, business goals, and ideologies, and you'll be able to make your own determination.

A quick twentieth century tour in the Wayback Machine adds context to the contemporary conflict.

At the dawn of the American comic strip, comics helped sell newspapers. Legal precedence had not yet been established, and a couple notable cartoonists hopped back and forth between publishers with their creations to get the best possible deal. This was great for the cartoonists, but jumping ship to get better deals upset the newspaper publishers where it hurt most: the wallet.

After some of the early 20th century legal dust settled, cartoonists worked on staff, were paid a wage, and newspapers owned the comics.

Newspapers spawned newspaper syndicates, which distributed comics, news, and columns to other newspapers for a price.

As the business evolved, cartoonists were freelancers, and syndicates signed them to contracts to distribute their comic strips. Even though cartoonists were no longer employees, syndicates were not going to let cartoonists jump ship and take their creations with them, so the syndicates insisted on owning the comics.

A hand rises from the back row.

"Yes?" I ask.

"Why did the cartoonists tolerate it?" you ask.

"Two reasons," I answer. "First, early comic strip creators were well paid for their successes. Comic strips became mass-market cultural icons. Cartoonists became stars.

"More importantly, the Golden Rule applied. The syndicates had the gold, and they made the rules."

There was no viable financial or creative alternative. If you wanted to be a comic-strip cartoonist, the newspapers and syndicates owned your work.

As comic books evolved from collected comic strip collections, this practice continued.

The Golden Rule applied.

A few creators, like Will Eisner, managed to retain ownership of their properties, but in the worlds of newspaper syndication and comic book publishing, work-made-for-hire was the rule, not the exception.

The book publishing culture was different. Cartoonists like Dr. Seuss and Crockett Johnson owned their work, and thrived. For decades, book publishing was the panacea to comics creators wanting to own their work, but comics in books were still an Ugly Duckling, and there was not yet enough consistent financial success in this category for publishers to hatch more than the occasional egg.

Decades passed, comic book stores opened, underground comics defined a generation, mainstream comics expanded into the direct market, newspaper syndicates increasingly relented to the contractual demands of strip cartoonists, new independent comic book publishers were founded and flourished as a direct result of creators owning their work, collected editions sold into bookstores and proved the market, manga brought a new generation of readers flocking to bookstores, graphic novel publishing became the fastest growing trade book publishing category, and the end result has been a seismic shift towards comics creators owning their work in independent comics and trade book publishing.

He who *makes* the gold makes the rules.

But work-made-for-hire still exists and is the only option when working with certain publishers in certain situations.

Drawing a conceptual line to separate two extremes, a creator who develops a wholly original work has numerous opportunities to own the published work and a creator who works on a property derived from something owned by somebody else has few opportunities to own the published work.

Now, what could entice somebody to work on a property derived from something owned by somebody else?

Money and/or opportunity.

"What kind of opportunity?" you ask.

To an infinite number of degrees, it's the opportunity to work on something you like, get published, and/or establish or add to your professional reputation.

What could entice a creator who develops a wholly original work to let somebody own the published work?

Again, money and/or opportunity.

"What kind of opportunity?" you ask.

"The same as before."

"So I have to figure out what I want," you reply.

"And what you need," I add.

If you're going to work on somebody else's property, how much do you love it and how much financial compensation do you need?

A hand rises in back.

"Yes?" I ask.

"What about royalties?" you ask.

"What about royalties?" I reply.

"If you own the published project, don't you get royalties?"

Great question.

Payment traditionally breaks down into three parts: Advances for work not yet done, which often follows the signing of a contract; payment for work completed, which is either paid out when pages or portions of the work are complete, e.g. the script, all the sketches, some or all the pencils, inks, and/or color, and/or delivery of the final approved electronic files; royalties, which are a split of the contractually agreed to profits.

A hand rises in the back row.

"Yes?" I ask.

"Your phrasing 'split of the contractually agreed to profits' feels...um...parsed."

"It is," I reply.

Without devolving into all the myriad contractual possibilities, royalties are generally considered to be a percentage (or percentages, depending on escalators) from one of these three categories: the gross, the adjusted gross, or the net.

The gross is how much money was made at a retail level. A filmmaker or actor, for example, might receive a percentage of the gross profits of a film. So if an actor gets 5% of the gross, and the film makes $100,000,000 at the box office, then the actor gets $5,000,000. If the contract stipulates that this 5% of the gross is on top of the $10,000,000 fee paid in advance to the actor for performing, her total is $15,000,000. If the contract stipulates that the production company or studio must first recuperate the $10,000,000 fee paid in advance to the actor from the percentage of gross profits, then the actor will not get anything from the gross profits until the film earns another $100,000,000, from which 5% will earn another $5,000,000.

The adjusted gross is generally considered to be the amount of money received by the publisher, after the retailer and distributor take their portions. For example, from all the sales of a book, whether the sales are retail or discounted, let's say booksellers get 30%, the distributor gets 40%, and the publisher gets 30%. So if a creator gets 20% of the adjusted gross, and a publisher brings in a total of $20,000, regardless of expenses and costs, then the creator gets $4,000. If the creator was paid an advance or page-rate total of $5,000, and the contract stipulates that the publisher must first recuperate advances paid to the creator, then the publisher will not owe anything to the creator until after the book has made another $5,000 adjusted gross, 20% of which is $1,000.

The net is generally considered to be the amount of money the project makes for the publisher *after* contractually defined expenses are deducted. Defining these contract expenses is complicated and variable, historically the subject of much negotiation. For example, the infamous "Hollywood net" includes deductions for studio salaries and overhead, as well as film distribution, even where the studio is doing its own distribution. Carving away these huge amounts of money from the potential profit compounds the impossibility for even the most successful films to ever reach a Hollywood net profit.

Returning to a less draconian publishing net, a creator might get 10% of the net, with potential deductions from the adjusted gross including the cost of printing and expenses tied directly to the cost of making and promoting the book. In this scenario, if a publisher brings in a total of $30,000, and expenses and advances totaled $10,000, then the net profit is $20,000. The 10% net royalty from this is $2,000.

If the creator was paid an advance or page-rate total of $5,000, and the contract stipulates that the publisher must first recuperate advances paid to the creator, then the publisher will not owe anything to the creator until after the book has made another $30,000 net, 10% of which is $3,000.

A royalty can have escalators, which are increases in royalty percentages when dollar or unit sales hit specified targets. For example, a creator could get 10% of the net for the first 20,000 units sold, 12% for the next 20,000 units sold, and 15% for units sold after that point.

These are simple scenarios, solely intended to introduce publishing mathematics concepts, meaning you can expect more complication in a publishing agreement.

However your deal is structured, ask yourself the following question:

based on realistic sales expectations, how much can I expect to make on the front and back ends of the deal?

If you don't know the market and history of sales by your publisher and in your publishing category, it's time to do your research. There's no easy way around this. It's one thing to be disappointed by sales that didn't reach expectations; it's another thing to be disappointed because your expectations were unrealistic.

A hand rises in back.

"Yes?" I ask.

"So I get royalties if I own the property, but I don't get royalties if I don't own the property, right?"

"Wrong."

Royalties are often confused as being part and parcel with ownership; they're not.

Ownership is one thing, and payment, of which royalties can be part, is separate.

You can write and/or draw a comic that is work-made-for-hire and still get royalties, if the contract covers it and sales meet the minimum contractually required standard. DC Comics established a deal along these lines decades ago.

Conversely, you can write and/or draw a comic that is creator-owned and not see a cent from its publication.

To prove the point, I contributed a story to the *Once Upon A Time Machine* anthology (Dark Horse, 2012). As co-creators, Scott Roberts and I retained copyright and received comp copies in exchange for the use of the work, but there was no profit sharing or royalties between the packagers of the book and the creators of the stories.

So, with a wide range of qualifications for considerations of desire, ownership, and payment, how do you cut through the chaff to make a personal determination about what is right for you?

Ask yourself tough, comprehensive questions.

If you're going to work on your own property, how much do you love it and how much financial compensation do you need? If the offer is "a flat fee of nothing to not very much," then your determination for whether you'll do the work should be based on why you need to see the project published or produced. Do you have the time? What do you get out of it? How does working on it help your career? Is there reasonable and achievable backend compensation?

If the offer to work on somebody else's property is "a flat fee of nothing to not very much," then your determination for whether you'll do the work should be based on why you need to see the project published or produced. In this case, what do you get out of it? How does working on it help your career? Do you have the time? Are you thinking about saying "yes" because nobody else invited you to the party? Is there reasonable and achievable backend compensation? Will the project still have been worth working on if the person who owns it makes one dollar and you don't get an extra cent? If you're answer is "yes," will the project still have been worth working on if the person who owns it makes a million dollars and you don't get an extra cent? If you're answer is "no," look for the dividing line between what's okay and not okay.

If the offer of payment from somebody who wants to own a project you initiated is "a flat fee of nothing to not very much," then your determination for whether you'll do the work should be based on how much and why, in all the possibilities described above, you need to see the project published or produced.

If the offer of payment from somebody who wants to own your property is "a flat fee of nothing to not very much, and royalties for sales in publishing and/or film," then your determination for whether you'll do the work should be based on how much and why, in all the possibilities described above, you need to see the project published or produced *and* how much you believe those royalties will happen.

If the offer of payment from somebody who wants to own your property is "a page rate that will feed and house you for the duration of the work," then your determination for whether you'll do the work should be based on how much and why, in all the possibilities described above, you need to see the project published or produced *and* how much you need the money that will feed and house you during the duration of the work.

Be a pragmatist. Consider the tradeoffs. Make the choices that are important to you and that will help you achieve your goals.

A hand is rises in the back row.

"Yes?"

"What do I do if I don't like the deal but really want to work on the book?" you ask. "Isn't there some middle ground that can be worked out?"

"Sometimes yes, and sometimes no," I reply.

Marvel Comics is not going to let you own the Spider-Man comic you write.

DC Comics might pay you royalties if sales justify it.

Dark Horse Comics might or might not insist on controlling the film rights.

An anthology might or might not offer something more than comp copies.

An independent comics publisher might or might not negotiate the split of the net profits.

Sometimes you can negotiate and sometimes you can't.

But when the final version of the deal is sitting in front of you, the trick to setting the line between what you will or won't accept is figuring out the difference between what you *want* and what you *need*, in all the possibilities described above.

You may not have the power to force the deal you want or need, but he who does the work *decides* what he will or won't do.

CHAPTER 14

CREATING AND SELLING YOUR PITCH
PART 1

This begins a three-chapter series on various ways you can improve your hitting percentage with editors.

This is *not* going to be about self-promotion, which is always useful, or how to network successfully within the industry, which may be one of the most valuable tools a beginning professional can learn, or how to pitch verbally, which is an art form in itself.

This is about writing and selling your pitch with the written word.

I won't cover all aspects of what it takes to sell your pitch, but I will address the ones I find most frequently lacking from the thousands of pitches I've read over the years.

Baiting the Hook

If you could choose, would you rather your pitch be compelling or boring?

Yeah, that's what I thought. Here's a way for you to achieve the former and avoid the latter.

Some years ago, I was part of a writer's group with Marv Wolfman, Craig Miller, and several others. Each of us was writing a screenplay, mine being that most commercial of ventures, a cross-genre Western-mystery-action story...but enough about that naive period of my life.

Marv and Craig were working together, and one night they tested some pitches for a TV show. As Marv will gladly admit, the first pitch was not going well...which had nothing to do with whether or not the story was compelling. The pitch just seemed to drone on and on, and it was awfully hard to care about what was going on in the story.

One member of our group interrupted the pitch halfway through, and said, "Hold it."

He stuck a thick pretzel stick between his lips as though it were a cigar, puffed out his stomach to affect as pompous a demeanor as possible, and said, "Pretend I'm a producer. Tell me why I should give a shit about your story."

After Marv kept Craig from throttling the guy who was happily munching the pretzel stick, he asked for a moment to collect his thoughts.

It was an interesting couple of minutes, each of us sitting in Craig's living room, waiting, exchanging glances, watching the gears turn in Marv's head, gears just like the ones that ground up and spit out Chaplin in *Modern Times*, only here, we were watching Marv conceive a different approach to pitching stories.

Hesitant at first, searching for the right language, Marv began again. He said, "This is a story about (character name here) falling in love with a woman who's doomed to die."

"Oooooooooo," the rest of us said. (If you knew the character's name and the series you'd have said, "Ooooooooo," too).

We wanted to know more.

And that was the point. Marv created an opening that would drive the rest of the pitch—the same pitch we'd heard before that had bored us into thinking a hammer bashed against our heads to end the misery might be better—and this time around, we were all leaning forward, mesmerized by the story, eagerly anticipating its next moment.

He'd figured out something that isn't taught in classes or books: in order to successfully pitch a concept, you have to give away the good part at the beginning...even if the good part doesn't happen till the end of the story.

This is different from how we've learned to dramatize stories, where we tantalize the readers and save the good part for the end. (Okay, you're probably asking, "What do you mean by, 'give away the good part?'")

Here's an example: This is the story about a psychiatrist who works with a boy who claims to see ghosts, only for the psychiatrist to discover that's *he's* one of the ghosts the boy sees.

See, I gave away the good part. (For those of you who aren't familiar with the story, never mind.)

Why does this type of pitch work? Why, after hearing the good part, do we want to hear more, even when we know the big reveal at the end? The answer to this is the secret of a successful pitch: editors/film producers/friends/whomever want to know why they're listening to the story you have to tell. They *need* to know ahead of time where to focus as the story unfolds. That's very tough to do without knowing what the story is about or where it's going.

In other words, you have to bait the hook in your story well enough so that your listeners or readers will bite into it. Once they've bitten, you can take whatever time is necessary to reel them in.

I'm going to show you how to prepare a worm for your hook.

First, there are many types of worms.

Sometimes it's something as simple as the pitch that sold the movie, *Twins*, which was, more or less, "What if Danny DeVito and Arnold Schwarzenegger were twins?" "What ifs" can be very compelling, but it's rare to come up with one and sell it, so that's not a worm we're going to discuss further.

The high-concept "(movie title) meets (movie title)" can also be effective, and sometimes, when you hear it, the pitch may even evoke a story, but not often.

Let's take *Independence Day* meets *Darby O'Gill and the Little People* as an example.

After conquering the Earth and plundering it for its mineral resources, aliens attempt to capture pots of gold from the leprechauns. This triggers a call to arms by the Wee Folk, who team up with humans and use magic to overcome the scientific superiority of the aliens.

Now, I'm not sure any of you could imagine that briefly outlined story from my "(movie title) meets (movie title)" example, (maybe you thought it was "magic" versus "science fiction"), and that's part of the problem with this kind of hook. The story isn't immediately clear, and all you can hope to evoke from this kind of pitch is the genre and tone. The other difficulty with this type of hook is that it's hard to come up with one that's immediately compelling. If it's your superpower to effectively come up with these then more power to you, but that's not going to be true for most creators. More often than not I read something like *Silence of the Lambs* meets *X-Files*, which tells us nothing.

For this reason, this is also not the worm we're going to choose to bait the hook.

Another worm that's especially tough to use as bait is the "perfect title." An example of this is *Cowboys & Aliens.* This title immediately evokes the tone and cross-genres of the film, doesn't need to say more, and it immediately makes people smile. They get it. That said, I think these kind of ideas come from what Brian Augustyn refers to as "the blue," meaning they appear out of the blue from moments of inspiration you hope will occur but can't count on.

One type of pitch I think you should avoid, though some editors profess to like it, is the cliffhanger pitch. This one is supposed suck a reader into the height of a story's drama, then it teases about where it may or may not be going. The intention is to get the editor to call the writer and exclaim, "What happens next?!"

This pitch goes something like this: This is the story about a girl who likes a boy, and they fall in love and get married. At first they have problems, then they come back together. But does their newfound happiness last when he finds out she's pregnant with another man's child?

I find this kind of pitch the most annoying, because it wastes my time. How can I determine whether I'm interested in buying a story when I don't know how it ends? This is the pitch that treats the editor like a reader—offering the dust jacket version of the story and hoping the editor will plunk down the money to buy it. It's like throwing empty peanut shells at the monkeys in the zoo.

But I want my peanut—*dammit!*—and I can be pretty frustrated when I don't get one.

I say hit the editor right between the eyes with your best shot. Tell him the good part, the reason he should give a shit about your story.

Here's how to bait your hook, based on the paradigm developed from Marv's epiphany:

"This is the story about a _____ who _____, only for _____ to discover _____."

The key to making this paradigm work is remembering that the second part of the sentence *must* be thematically linked to the first part of the sentence, *must* be about the protagonist, and *must* identify the core problem and resolution—acts one and three—of your story.

The strength of this paradigm is that it gives you something around which you can build the spine of a story. In turn, it helps determine what unfolding plot complications do or don't fit with it, so there are residual benefits.

The weakness of this paradigm is that you have to know what your story is *inherently* about, and you'd be surprised how few writers know, beyond the unfolding of their plots, what their stories are *inherently* about.

Here's an intentionally poor hook that fits into this paradigm: "This is the story about a girl who really likes a boy, only for the boy to discover that he likes playing with toys."

Even with the commonality of what they each "like," the two halves aren't *really* connected.

Also, it's not told from one character's point of view, so the hook falls apart on several levels.

We don't know which one we're supposed to root for.

Still, in its present structure, the hook can be improved. For example: "This is the story about a girl who really likes a boy, only for the boy to discover that he would *prefer* to play with toys."

Now, this introduces conflicting forces, but still doesn't tell us which of them is the protagonist.

Here's the pitch straightened out: "This is the story about a girl who really likes a boy, only for her to discover he's too young for her."

In this version, she's the protagonist.

Or: "This is the story about a boy who likes playing with a girl, only for him to discover he'd *prefer* to play with toys."

In this version, he's the protagonist.

Here's another example of a pitch that works: "This is the story about a man who tries to buy everything in the world, only for him to discover that he can't buy back his lost childhood."

Yep, this is arguably the greatest film ever made, *Citizen Kane*, conceived as a single sentence. For those who don't know the film directed by Orson Welles, trust me, there's a lot more to the story (and its telling), but this concept is at its heart.

Any story can be conceived in this manner, that is, any story that holds together.

Practice it on stories, books, and films you've seen. It's better starting with stories created by others.

I'm going to repeat that: *it's better starting with stories created by others!*

You are too close to your own stories to be objective at first. It is tougher cutting the story chaff from the good stuff grain.

I have read the tortured efforts of creators trying to fit everything, including the kitchen sink, into this paradigm, because they can't identify the good part and cut the rest.

"But it's *all* good!" they cry.

Simply put, it's better to learn the paradigm first, then apply it to your own story.

"What if my story or series is about a team of characters, where there's no single protagonist?" you ask. "If I focus on just one of them, doesn't that misrepresent my story?"

"Great question!" I note.

If your story or series is about a team, treat the team like a single protagonist. Surely there is some bond holding them together, and that needs to be key to your hook as well.

For example: "These are the stories about a group of political operatives in the West Wing of the White House, who strive to achieve their principled goals for the country, only for them to discover that governing often requires them to compromise their principles.

See how much of *The West Wing* was left out, but how much was clarified?

The trick to writing a hook for a story or a series is that you have to ignore most of the characters, settings, and plot machinations, and cut right to the heart of the story as it affects your protagonist or team.

To accomplish this, you must repeat the following mantra: just tell the good part.

You don't have to tell the whole story in one sentence. That's what the rest of the pitch is intended to do.

CHAPTER 15

CREATING AND SELLING YOUR PITCH
PART 2

Welcome to the second piece of the pitching pie-that's-not-in-the-sky.

"But I'm still working on the first piece," you sputter, spraying crumbs.

"That's fine," I reply, my transparent face-shield in place, "but once you've set the hook you've got to start reeling in the fish...er, editor, and that's where this comes in handy."

"So this is about writing the actual pitch?"

"That's right," I confirm.

This second chapter shows how to conceive and write your complete story in an abbreviated form that reflects the tone of the finished work, thus allowing editors to more quickly and effectively grasp your intention.

Have you noticed that when you show your pitches to editors/producers/friends/relatives they can't see the potential for what you envisioned?

Remember having to explain the nature of that potential?

Remember promising them that the finished story will fulfill that potential?

Remember that look of patronizing encouragement or doubt?

Remember feeling (to quote Butch Cassidy) "you have vision and the rest of the world wears bifocals"?

Pitches are roadmaps for where you're going with your stories. They are also the promises of things to come.

This chapter is about not saving your good writing till later; it's about writing the most compelling pitch you possibly can. For that you need to...

Sell, Don't Tell

All writing is selling.

All of it.

Every last word.

Whether you realize it or not, through the process of writing and communicating, you're selling ideas. And you're selling yourself as the purveyor of those ideas.

If you're a technical writer, you're selling accuracy or process.

If you're a nonfiction writer, you're selling an interpretation of facts.

If you're a columnist, you're selling a perspective, just as I'm doing now.

If you write fiction, whether the medium is comics, film, prose, or plays, you're selling your vision of what's happening to characters that don't exist in places you may have never been to. You're selling readers on any number of things: that a character is a sweetheart or a monster, that he or she is motivated to behave or change in a particular way, that an image or setting looks or smells or feels a specific way. And you're selling us the idea that these things all mesh together.

You're selling us on your vision of an ordering of events that never happened, and you want us to become completely immersed in the story and its world.

So, should the initial selling of your vision begin by showing the finished manuscript?

Obviously, it shouldn't, unless you have a publisher who's already going to buy it.

Selling—or, if the word "selling" somehow offends you, *getting the reader to embrace your fiction*—needs to begin at the earliest possible moment you're trying to get somebody to read or listen to your broad-strokes overview, with a goal toward getting them to ask for more.

That's the purpose of a pitch, for somebody to want to read the longer version of the story you're pitching.

Writers pour their hearts and minds into writing pitches, and I don't question their effort. However, when a publisher's guidelines request a one-paragraph, one-page, or two-page synopsis, most writers' pitches read like a laundry list of events with over-long paragraphs, run-on sentences, smaller fonts, crowded margins, and twenty-pounds of story stuffed into a two-ounce story bag.

You ask, "Don't you think a pitch should tell what happens?"

Yes...and no.

Your pitch is a roadmap, a really small one, and when you force every street onto it they're so tiny and crowded together that the important ones don't look different from the smaller ones, and the reader is likely to make a wrong turn and get lost. It's like needing directions and getting a map without labels. A proper broad-strokes roadmap should simply indicate the important streets and turns to get the reader to their destination.

It's exactly like the directions you'd give to a pal to get to your house. Would you list all the streets he's going to pass? Of course not. You're more likely to say, "Stay on Elm for two miles till you reach Main Street, which has a light, then turn right."

When pitches are presented as packed-together sequencing of events, editors have to cull through them to find the emotional arcs of your story, and they've got a better-than-even chance of missing the diamonds you planted at the heart of your story.

So what are you selling, a sequencing of events or your story?

The complete sequencing of events for your story is important, but not at the pitch stage. At this stage you'd be surprised how little, beyond the concept and the arc of the story, is important.

The art to writing a pitch is remembering that your primary goal is to sell the reader on why characters are doing what they're doing, and evolving the story in an organic and compelling manner. Like the unnecessary streets on your directions to a pal, too many details in a pitch obscure larger concerns, and readers get lost.

You may think that charming nuances add depth to your pitch and help sell it, but this is rarely the case. An abundance of detail throws off the perceived balance of what is and isn't important about your story.

For example, imagine you're in a room that's completely empty of furniture. There are five huge diamonds lying at different locations on the floor, with the overhead light refracting off each of them. They're not too hard to see, right? These signify the important parts of your story, the aspects that determine its uniqueness and arc.

Now imagine you're in the same room, and the room is three-inches deep in rubies, emeralds, sapphires, and opals, along with those same five diamonds. How easily do you think you can find those diamonds now?

Yep, pretty difficult, and there's a good chance that two, three, or four diamonds could be missed.

When you over-pack your pitch with unnecessary plotting and details, this is what readers have to sort through to discern what's special, to determine whether they want to read more.

Why make it difficult? Why put in stuff that gets in the way?

What are you selling?

Here is an example from the beginning of a story that represents the kind of plot-stuffing I've seen in pitches and treatments, all because the writer couldn't bear to leave out events he or she was certain would help it sell.

Version #1 of the beginning of a story: "Harry is fired from his job. He's been fired a lot. He's depressed. He trudges out of his office and down a long hall, with everybody witnessing the failure they all knew was coming. He takes the elevator to the ground floor, steps out of the elevator, through the expansive lobby, and onto the street. He cries out for mercy from a cruel universe, and gets hit by bird droppings. He buys a gun from a street-corner crook and drives home. When he sits down, he tears his pants on a chair spring, but he's so depressed he doesn't even care. What's one more rip in his life, a life that's now over? He puts the gun to his head, pulls the trigger, and is sprayed with water. The gun is a water pistol."

Version #2 of the beginning of a story: "As losers go, Harry is the champ. Fired after only twenty minutes at his new job, he cries out for mercy from a cruel universe and a bird poops on his head. Defeated, he buys a gun on his way home, puts it to his head, pulls the trigger, and is drenched by a squirt of water."

The first version is filled with a lot of unnecessary detail, has some nice moments, but it's a longish set-up, with each element carrying the same story weight. Until Harry tried committing suicide with a water pistol, there was little in the writing to suggest this was supposed to be funny, and the water-pistol reveal isn't written well enough to work as a punch line. The lack of consistent and representational tone shows serious misjudgment, as there's no reason for an editor to believe this writer could write a comedy.

I can't tell you how many times I've heard a writer say, "But I'm really a good writer. Just wait and see."

Don't save the good writing till later. If you can write comedy, horror, superheroes, whatever, the tone of your writing in the pitch should convey this. If it doesn't, editors can't discern how well you write.

The first version tells the story.

The second sells the story. It sets the tone, using language that sells it as a comedy, and it sells the writer as the person who can deliver on the promise of the pitch.

Sell; don't tell.

Write your pitch so that the reader will have the appropriate emotional response, and you're halfway home.

Now, let's take you the rest of the way.

The second version may have been better at evoking the tone of the story, but is that enough? It's probably fine for a treatment, but it's not good enough for a pitch. You want to grab readers by the throat and not let them have a chance to wiggle free.

This is where we discuss the idea that less is more.

Version #3 of the beginning of a story: "Harry is a nowhere man who's floundered in life and failed at everything he's tried, even suicide."

Version #2 may or may not be amusing...but *Version #3* is written in broad-strokes and immediately propels us into the character and his dilemma.

Let's continue the story about poor Harry: "Harry packs everything he has of value into his bag. It's a small bag. He stands in the doorway to his bedroom, which he's kept spotless for nobody besides his goldfish to notice—but goldfish don't notice much, do they? He sighs. Then he walks down the hallway one last time, sighing continuously. Finally, he stands in the open front doorway to his house and closes it with an even bigger sigh. He sighs on the way to his car, and is interrupted only by his neighbor's dog, as it manages to catch him and tear the other leg of his pants as a going-away present. Once safely inside his car, Harry turns the key in the ignition, and hears the clicking of a battery that's nearly expired. More sighing. Harry opens his bag, takes out the Crest-encrusted toothbrush, slips it into his shirt pocket, and walks away from his bag, his car, his house, and his life. He's going to walk the sidewalks of suburbia, like Caine, in search of new failures."

Back to the broad-strokes *Version #3*, which carries us from the inciting incident to Harry's plan: "Harry is a nowhere man who's floundered in life and failed at everything he's tried, even suicide. So he leaves behind every trophy of his failure, determined to walk the sidewalks of suburbia like Caine in search of new failures."

Conceptually, there's nothing missing from the broad-strokes *Version #3*, so the editor/producer/relative/friend can immediately tell what's important about the story.

They immediately spot your diamonds on the floor.

The expanded version may be fine for a more detailed outline, which comes later in the process of story development, but when you're trying to sell somebody on what's compelling about your story, shorter will always be better.

Less is more.

Thus far, what you've read about *Harry Walks Like Caine* is only the premise and inciting incident.

When this needs to be a one-page or two-page pitch, you'll have plenty of space to tell us the rest of the story about Harry walking the sidewalks of suburbia like Caine.

If you use the *Version #2* style of writing for a two-page pitch, you'll quickly run out of real estate and end up with several options.

You rush the middle and ending, and the focus of the pitch is out of balance, weighted to the front.

You run five pages long, and trim out words and phrases, rather than rethinking the pitch with broader strokes, and the pitch feels chopped up.

You reduce the text from a readable 12 pt. type to a tiny 7 pt. type, extend margins, combine paragraphs, and hope the editor doesn't notice. I kid you not; this happens. And editors notice.

This is what happens when you try to cram your entire plot into too little space.

"Well, sure," you say, arms crossed and feeling defensive, "You wrote the premise, which is the easy part. Try doing that for the rest of the story!"

Okay.

Here's the entire second act (which is approximately half the story): Not once in 237 attempts, has Harry Who Walks Like Caine successfully stopped the serial pie-thrower (known as the Crazed Clown) from splattering pie-company executives. However, at the scene of the last splattering at Acme Pies, he discovers a meringue-spotted driver's license that reveals the true identity of the Crazed Clown. The name on the license is his. Armed with this knowledge, Harry is determined to stop himself, and it's going to be a battle to the death!

The trick to conceiving your story in broad strokes is remembering the purpose of each of your acts. For the sake of convenience, I'm going to only deal with the three-act structure:

Act One: *Problem.*
Act Two: *Complication.*
Act Three: *Solution.*

Leave out the detail and you'll be fine. Write even one line that involves a character actually completing an action then you're already taking your pitch into the red zone of over-complication.

Write in arcs, not in events, and you'll clearly convey the elements that drive your story.

This applies to defining your characters, too.

You have a pretty good idea about Harry's nature, right?

You don't really need to know more about him, do you?

No, you don't, not for the pitch.

Save Harry's upbringing in a circus sideshow till later.

Robert McKee taught me this aspect of character motivation: nobody does more than they think they need to do to get what they want.

Translation: *to get what they want, most people do as much as they think is necessary, and no more.*

When I worked at DC Comics in the mid-'90s, I was Group Editor of Creative Services, and I saw all the pitches that were being distributed for executive approval.

One pitch, written by a famous writer I won't identify, read something like this: "In this series, I'm going to keep doing what I did in the (insert character name here) mini-series." That was the entire pitch, and it sold.

Why?

Could it be that the DC Comics editorial staff knew exactly what it would be getting from this famous writer? Absolutely.

There needs to be a body of work before an editor or producer can have this degree of confidence about what they're going to get.

If you're writing a pitch, never presume that the person reading it is going to give you the same benefit of the doubt about anything.

It's your job to instill a sense of confidence, and to do that you have to sell them on your story...and yourself.

CHAPTER 16

CREATING AND SELLING YOUR PITCH
PART 3

Now we come to the Ugly Duckling, the subject that nobody talks about, the one left standing in the corner of the party with whom nobody wants to dance.

In short, this is the common sense chapter that says, "Don't put your hand in the fire. It'll hurt."

Then you say, "I would never put my hand in the fire," as your burnt hair curls and skin sizzles.

Here's a truth I've discovered since first writing the earliest version of this chapter: *we all put our hands in the fire.*

We all become so enamored with what we create that we're just sure everybody else will love it if they'd only give it a chance.

Let's repeat part of that last sentence, "...if *they'd* only give it a chance."

See whose responsibility it will be when the story's rejected? Not yours, *theirs.*

So let's reveal the ugly truth: every rejection is your responsibility.

Editors need to be made comfortable, and no matter what pains in your ass they may be, they hold the keys that allow you to enter the kingdom.

They are not all geniuses or morons, all good or bad, all wise or careless. They're each different. They each have different strengths and weaknesses, preferences about what they do and don't like, whom they do and don't like, and when they do and don't like stuff. Editors don't have to be fair or reasonable, and they don't have to be good at what they do.

In the face of this, you simply need to determine whether you can or will work with them, and you have to be as professional as possible when making this determination, because they can inform industry associates about your behavior...and will.

This is a minefield, and the more you're aware of it the less it will hurt each time you die.

Each time you die.

Welcome to the videogame of life, where you learn everything possible from the last time you died so you might not die the next time.

I've died many times, and will continue to do so.

So will you.

But that's what we have to do to make stories come to life.

The previous two chapters were about tailoring your pitch so that somebody will become enamored with your story and want to see it developed further.

Let's presume your pitch communicates *exactly* what your story is about, in content, character, and tone, that it is beautifully written and at a comfortable length, that it hooks the reader at the beginning and reels him in like a trout. This constitutes as perfect pitch as you can hope to have created for your story.

So you submit your perfect pitch, and somebody says, "No, thanks."

How could this happen?

Where did you fail?

Did you fail?

Yes, and no.

You failed to sell the pitch, yes.

But if the pitch perfectly communicates the story you hope to write (or have written), then you've *succeeded* in getting that person to determine whether or not your story will suit his or her needs.

In short, he or she *knows* he or she doesn't want it, no matter how well the finished piece will be executed, and that's the silver lining of this cloudburst that momentarily doused your dream.

This is your first step toward...

Learning Where To Play In the Sandbox

Imagine all the types of stories that have been (or will ever be) written as existing in a gigantic metaphysical sandbox.

What Marvel wants is in one corner, not too far from what the DC

Universe is looking for. Vertigo is somewhere over on the other side. Image, Dark Horse, NBM, IDW, Fantagraphics, Drawn & Quarterly, and all the rest—no offense intended for any omissions—have their spots staked out, too.

When somebody says, "No, thanks," he or she is also saying, "You're not playing in our part of the sandbox."

We've already established that the pitch is well-written, so "no, thanks" will more likely mean one or more of the following:

"We don't publish stories in that genre."

"We can't sell your story."

"We have something—or many things—like your story, and we don't need (or can't sell) another one."

"We can't embrace your story."

"We don't know you."

"We only work with published writers/creators who've established themselves in the marketplace, critically or commercially."

Each of these explanations is fair. Each is a signpost in the sandbox that helps determine what you will or won't be submitting to them in the future. Some signposts read, "stop," "wrong turn," or show you the detour route, (an example of one would be for you to establish yourself as a creator before coming back).

All of these are shorthand for "we don't like it" or "we can't sell it."

The problem is that most editors don't have the time to post any of these signs in the sandbox for creators to read, so you're forced to guess what might've gone wrong, which can be very frustrating.

If you want to minimize your speculation about which of the signposts refers to you or your submission, then you have to eliminate the obvious possibilities.

You have to target the right material for the right publisher.

How many of you just said, "Well, duh"?

Yeah, that's what I would've said a few decades ago, but that was before I learned that it's as important to become familiar with the culture of a publisher as with what they publish.

You may have the coolest idea for Batman in the world, one that could spin the franchise on its head and send it leaping in its most profitable direction in years, but DC Comics is careful about whom they'll let play with their toys.

Let's say you've never worked with DC Comics before, but you've written some well-received books by other publishers, nothing measuring a 7.0 on the Richter scale, but material that was respected enough to give you a shot.

In your pitch, you reveal that Bruce has a twin brother who was kidnapped at birth. Through a sequence of events—probably something involving a deathbed confession by the nurse who stole the child and raised him as her own—Robert Cain, a local thug in the organized crime community, discovers that he is really David Wayne Jr., the elder twin of Bruce Wayne, and Cain becomes obsessed about the brother who stole his birthright, and sets out to claim his inheritance.

That might be an interesting premise, but nobody's going to let you write that story as anything other than an Elseworlds.

In TV Land, this is what's called a staff-written show, in other words, something they'd only let you write if you worked on staff or closely with the staff. This story changes the Batman mythology in a significant way, and only people in power—whether they're editors or writers of influence who may or may not be Frank Miller—make these changes.

Over twenty years ago—ancient history in comic book industry terms—when I was Group Editor of Creative Services at DC Comics, I was responsible for the Submissions Department.

I remember culling through proposal after proposal, reached one by an unknown writer, and laughed.
It was terrific, as was his next one and the next. Great stuff. Inspired. I showed them to Dean Motter, who worked in my department, and he loved them, too. Dean then spent the next week showing them to editors, and nobody wanted to see more. Nobody.

Why?

Because this writer was unpublished, and he hadn't earned enough stripes to get the editors' attention and be able to play with the DC Comics toys.

It's not my intention to criticize the DC Comics editorial staff for not pursuing these pitches. My goal is for you, as a creator, to realize that companies have different barometers for whom they will and won't hire, and it is incumbent on you to determine the nature of these barometers.

If it is your goal to write for DC Comics or Marvel, then you should realize it's nearly impossible to do so without a body of work behind you, unless you work within the company or have somehow established a relationship with an editor who's willing to stick his or her neck out on your behalf. Failing these options, your next rung on the ladder is to find somebody who's more interested in publishing your story than in your publishing history.

So, if you're charting your career path towards DC or Marvel, what kind of stories should you be writing?

Well, you could try publishing a brilliant body of work in crime fiction comics, like Brian Michael Bendis, and hope that a top editor will be inspired to extend his search for new voices beyond the superhero/heroic fantasy genre.

But is that the exception or the rule? Let me tell you a bedtime story that's certain to cause sleepless nights.

Once upon a time, the writer of an independently published comic once submitted his superhero book as a writing sample to a top editor. The editor said, "I really enjoyed it, but we don't do comedy."

The late Peter Ledger once told me about a conversation Richard Hescox (a talented painter and mutual friend) had with an advertising agency art director. The art director skimmed through Richard's portfolio like he was at the dentist's office flipping through an *Entertainment Weekly*. Suddenly he stopped, peering closely at a page with new discrimination. He looked up from the illustration of a Halloween pumpkin, and said, "You can paint pumpkins. I have a project that requires somebody who can paint pumpkins." Richard got the assignment, knowing full well that wouldn't have been the case if he hadn't already had in hand a completed illustration of what the art director was looking for.

Peter and his then-wife, Christy Marx, named this the *"Pumpkin Syndrome."*

Keep this story in mind when creating a body of material or stories for specific locations in the sandbox. I'm not suggesting you write for anybody other than yourself. You simply can't control who's sitting on the other side of a desk, and even where your writing is spot on you may only be able to assess the results of an editorial encounter with: "inspired thinker" or *"Pumpkin Syndrome."*

As obvious as this reads, when you're in a position to create something for the publisher of your choice, you should familiarize yourself with the material they publish, and the culture in which it's produced.

For DC or Marvel, it's incumbent on you to understand their respective character universes and not try to affect core mythological changes, like the one about Bruce Wayne's evil twin, until after you've earned a measure of trust and been given a green light to do so.

"Yeah, yeah," you say, "That's DC and Marvel. What about the others."

Where you're not concerned with fitting into an established mythology you still have to fit into an established sensibility and publishing history.

You should anticipate that a proposed series about topless, large-breasted, she-male demons that seduce their victims to death is not going to play too well at Top Shelf.

You'd think this was obvious, but I've seen hundreds of pitches that weren't anywhere close to what I said I was looking for. More so, I've seen pitches that were exactly what I said I was *not* looking for.

Why would somebody send me something that is exactly what I said I did not want to see?

Because creators will send anything to anybody in the hope that somebody will embrace their vision. I sympathize with this, but when you send in material that's completely inappropriate to the publisher's professed needs, the quality of your pitch becomes less relevant, you greatly reduce the chance of setting up anything, and your judgment comes into play.

Red Skelton did a weekly skit on his '50s/'60s TV show about a mean little kid. The kid often encountered situations that were too tempting for him to ignore, even though he knew he would be punished for what he contemplated. At the moment of decision toward the end of each skit, he inevitably grinned—it was a wide, toothy, devilish smirk—and said, "If I dood it, I get a whippin'—I dood it anyway."

And then he dood—er, did it.

So...

...if you dood it...

...if you send your pitch to people who've stated they're looking for something different from what you're sending, or if they don't have a history of producing that type of material, that's fine.

Go for it.

Dood it.

But if the pitch is rejected, it's equally important to know that it's because you weren't playing in the right part of the sandbox.

From here, there are two options.

Keep doing whatever it is your doing, and that's fine. Ultimately, you may become a self-publisher, and there are numerous success stories in this area and with crowd-funding.

Or see if you can't find someplace closer in the sandbox to where the publisher is playing, someplace that allows for your areas of interest to overlap their areas of interest. There's a history of success here, too.

Ultimately, what matters is that you're creating stories that land exactly where you want them to in the sandbox.

And if somebody happens to be there to pick them up, all the better.

CHAPTER 17

COMICS EDITORS ARE LIKE
A BOX OF CHOCOLATES

Let's start by nailing the shoe on the other hoof.

How many comics creators are *great* comics creators?

No hands go up.

That's right, only a small percentage of comics creators are great comics creators.

Should we judge the ideal contribution of comics creators to the finished book by the work of the good ones or the bad ones?

No hands go up.

Yeah, it was a rhetorical question, and the answer is obvious.

Now, when discussing editors, do you typically discuss the potential for their ideal contribution or how they're just frustrated creators who don't understand what you do?

I'll answer this one: too often it's the latter and not the former. Why do you think that is?

A hand slowly inches above a sea of perplexed expressions.

"Yes?" I ask.

"I think we tend to complain about somebody telling us what to do," you respond honestly.

"Do you get a sense how an editor's direction helps your book get better?" I query.

"Not yet," you reply. I note the forward thrust of your clenched jaw.

"Do you think a good editor should help make your book the best possible version of your vision?" I ask, setting you up.

"Absolutely!" you exclaim, not seeing the set-up.

"Then shouldn't a discussion about the potential for editorial oversight be based on editors who do their jobs well, instead of editors who don't do their jobs well?" I ask, bringing the topic full circle.

"Um..." you respond, realizing you're trapped. "For a discussion about the *potential* contribution of an editor, yes," you admit, with legitimate qualification.

That's right, there are a lot of bad comics editors, and I could name names, tell stories, and not stop for about a week.

But there are also a lot of good comics editors, and their contribution to your work could go a long way towards helping you become a better comics creator.

In 2006, during a program at Comic-con International, a panel of editors unanimously agreed: a good editor helps creators fulfill a specific vision, whether it's the creator's, editor's, or publisher's vision.

That still holds true.

But there's more to it, a lot more, because creators aren't mind readers.

Comics editors need to possess a high level of craft, or they don't know what they're talking about.

Comics editors need to be able to schedule, or they don't know how a book is really progressing, and they'll panic only after it's too late to still produce good work.

Comics editors need to be flexible to the potential for talent to produce their best possible work, and that requires an understanding of the strengths and weaknesses of the entire sequential art toolbox and all the available processes. If editors don't know the range of possibilities for how creators work, then they don't know how to play to their strengths.

Comics editors need to be able to communicate.

Comics editors need to be able to identify or clarify aesthetic and commercial goals, so everybody understands and works toward a mutual objective.

To clarify, where the comics editor needs to embrace a creator's vision, the editor first needs to be able to define that vision, get the creator to agree to it, thereby creating a standard by which he or she can evaluate the work.

On the other hand, where the comics editor needs to convey a company vision, he or she still needs to be able to define that vision, get the creator to understand it, thereby creating a standard by which he or she can evaluate the work.

What's the point, the reason, the advantage in this?

It sidesteps the issue of editors making changes simply because that's what they want to do.

Yes, there are too many editors who make changes simply because they can or because they've done a poor job of explaining to the creators what needs to be accomplished, but we're not discussing these editors; we're discussing the "good" editors, the people with the ability to direct all aspects of the writing and art toward unified visions that have been communicated and agreed to by all the concerned parties.

Besides that it helps everybody work together and get along, this job requirement serves a practical purpose: comics editors need to be able to identify where work derails, and offer available options to get it back on track.

Visionary consensus also gives editors a valuable tool: the ability to point to something in the completed script, layout, pencils, inks, and/or color and say, "That's not what we agreed to."

Suddenly the discussion isn't about what the editor wants versus what the creator wants. It's about getting it right; it's about fulfilling the vision.

Comics editors need to be facilitators, not dictators, even when they have the final say.

Just like creators, comics editors have wide-ranging strengths, and not all these strengths are the same.

Some comics editors are great because they have a great Rolodex of talent, talent who, when left alone, will do what's required with minimal supervision.

Some comics editors are great because they have a fresh vision for tired material, and can find and direct creators to work to that vision.

Some comics editors are great because they can identify new talent, and help them reach their potential.

There are so many different ways comics editors excel, and fall short.

Yes, some comics editors are just looking for a stepping stone to their own writing career.

Yes, some comics editors think their job is akin to a film director, the auteur—*I'm looking at you, Hitchcock!*—who says, "Jump," and expect creators to ask, "How high?"

Yes, some comics editors are control freaks who expect you to read their minds.

Yes, some comics editors are glorified traffic managers who keep track of schedules, and survive by doing the bidding of their higher-ups.

Yes, some comics editors don't know enough about what they're doing, and will consistently hang talent out to dry for their own incompetency.

Comics editors are like a box of chocolates; you never know what you're gonna get.

So what can a comics creator do about this?

Well, we're already doing it. We're pegging strengths and weaknesses so you'll know 'em when you see 'em.

Rather than shying away from editors on general principles or because you don't like to be told what to do, consider interviewing your potential editors, asking them about their process, what they love about comics and working with creators.

Find out how well they fit with you.

But here's what's important, what's *really* important: *be careful.*

Don't let them know you're interviewing and evaluating them, even though you are.

Don't challenge their beliefs. Probe them to discover their nature, and keep your observations about them to yourself.

This is not sneaky, phony, or deceitful. This is what you should do at any professional meeting or interview to learn what you need to. It's also where you get to present yourself as who you are and what you believe, within the context of your goal for the meeting.

This is the way to figure out how and if you want to work with an editor, while the editor is likely trying to figure out how and if they want to work with you.

Sometimes you won't have a choice, and you're stuck with what falls from the candy box. Still, if you've done your scouting well, you'll know what flavor you've got, and you'll have the best possible chance to make the most of the relationship.

A hand goes up.

"Yes?" I ask.

"How can we make the most of a relationship with the worst kind of editor?" you ask.

"Good question. The answer is that even bad editors need to get their books finished, as well produced and on time as they've allowed the book to be. Bad editors report to somebody, too, and the more you can help them get their books out the more they're going to appreciate (as well as they can) your contribution.

"When you *know* an editor is a poor communicator or scheduler much of this responsibility falls on your shoulders, whether it's fair or not."

"Because I'm going to get blamed for the screw-ups anyway?" you guess.

"That's right," I answer. "You need to work defensively, communicate as well as you can, give editors the best opportunities to have their say, and recognize that no matter how hard you try, the blame for whatever goes wrong can still come down on your head.

"But it won't be because you didn't see it coming, and you'll be as prepared for it as professionally possible."

A hand goes up.

"Yes?" I ask.

"Do we have to work with an editor?" you ask.

"Nope. You can self-publish in print or online, or you can find a publisher that doesn't oversee the production of your work. Otherwise, yes, you're going to work with an editor."

Your hand drifts down, as though sinking beneath the waves of hope.

With this in mind, let's nail the shoe on the other hoof again and discuss a story that will help you prepare for what lies ahead.

I could tell numerous stories about writers who stepped up, responded with enthusiasm, learned what they needed to, and delivered great work. These stories are inspiring, but they don't show the missteps as clearly. They also don't show how misinterpretation and miscommunication can derail a potential relationship.

A few years back, a fairly new comics writer with a number of self-published comic books to his credit wrote me for assignment work. To clarify: he wasn't looking for me to help publish his work; he wanted me to assign him a comic to write.

I offered to review a comics script sample, something representative of his very best work at the highest level of craft, and specified I did not want to see any back-and-forth ballooning, also called crosstalk, inside panels. To clarify, crosstalk occurs when a character speaks at least once before and after another character speaks in a single panel. For example, if Character 1 speaks first, then Character 2 speaks, and Character 1 speaks again, that's crosstalk.

Crosstalk in comics is my personal and professional bug-a-boo, partly because most inexperienced writers don't understand how much it slows down reading, but it doesn't usually work well, because most inexperienced writers don't consider the layout—who's on the left, who's on the right—for it to work well, or even conceive enough space for it in panel descriptions. This leaves the visual storytelling problem solving to artists, which may or not get solved well, and is why we too-often end up with cluttered, badly laid out panels that read awkwardly. Unless you're Brian Michael Bendis, the Master of Crosstalk Inside Panels, you're better off reducing the number of panels in different ways than jamming them with dialogue.

A hand rises in back.

"Yes?" I ask.

"But isn't it the artist's job, to figure out how to stage back-and-forth ballooning?" you ask.

At one level, yes, but if the comics panel description can't be drawn and ballooned as written, due to poor or conflicting direction, then the artist has to figure out what from the description to keep in and what to throw out. That shouldn't be an artist's job.

"Can you give me an example of what won't work well?" you ask.

Sure.

DESCRIPTION: Hold the shot of the previous panel, with George on the right. He's just been shot in the stomach, holds it with one hand—we see blood seeping through his shirt. He holds a gun in his other hand, aimed at Mary, but he's not firing it. Mary's on the left side of the panel, shooting at George again, her three newly fired shots are whizzing by him.

GEORGE: I can't believe you shot me.

MARY: I can't believe you didn't die.

SFX: (Lily's gun firing) BLAM! BLAM AGAIN! BLAM ONCE MORE!

GEORGE: That's because your cooking gave me a cast iron stomach!

MARY: Well then eat *this!*

SFX: (Lily's gun firing) BLAM REDUX!

You might (or might not) be entertained by this exchange, but the panel would be a nightmare to draw and balloon. George's first balloon would have to be on the left, probably at the top, with a pointer to the right. But then Lily's first balloon needs to be below or to the right, with a pointer going to her on the left. Since it's not good to have pointers cross each other, placing the balloon to the right of George's likely won't work, so her balloon probably needs to be below his. There goes some vertical space. Then we need to read the three shots from her gun, which would be on the left side of the panel. Then we need to read George's balloon after the shots, with the pointer aimed at him on the right. So his balloon needs to be below the shots or to their right, which means it probably needs to be lower in the panel. Then we read her balloon below or to the right of his, with the pointer going to the left. And then, the icing on the cake, we need to finish with another sound effect of her gun firing, and it has to be clear it from her gun, not his.

This is an impossible panel to draw and balloon well, and probably needs to be two or three panels to work well.

A script should offer clear images in panels that can be drawn and ballooned; it shouldn't present a series of nearly impossible hoops that an artist has to jump through just to get the direction half right.

The terrible truth is that most writers aren't Brian Bendis, who is a master of the back-and-forth ballooning. Bendis understands layout, balloon placement, how to overlap balloons so readers know where to start and what to read next, the use of pointers, and exactly how readers will perceive what he intends them to perceive.

So this writer sent me his script, hoping I'll get beyond page two, really like his story, and hire him. We all want that.

But two pages were enough to assess his level of craft.

The writing was sloppy, with vague panel descriptions and no sense of the world, staging, character descriptions, expressions, or clothing. And it was filled with the back-and-forth ballooning I had so specifically noted I did not want to see.

Did I leave it there? Did I write back, "Thanks, but no thanks?"

I did not.

I wrote a critique. My notes for the first two pages of his script were extensive, with a goal towards showing him how to write with intention. My goal was also to determine how well he responded to notes, to see what he would be like to work with.

The writer responded that he was sorry I didn't read the whole story, even though I'd told him my goal was only look at a couple of pages to determine the level of craft. He said that most of his comics were collaborations with an artist who had no problem interpreting and drawing from his scripts, and that the character descriptions weren't an issue, because he and the artist worked these out separately from the script.

And he said he hadn't understood what I meant by not wanting to see back-and-forth ballooning, which is why it was in the script.

To conclude the story of this short-lived relationship, the writer did not offer to make changes or show another script that reflected the level of craft I required.

Imagine now that you're the editor in my situation: a writer comes to you, wanting an assignment. He gives you a writing sample that contains exactly what you asked not to see. You spend time from your day to help him, give him extensive notes, and then he argues about the validity of your response, says he didn't understand your initial direction, but says so after you reviewed his work, instead of before when there was an opportunity to get assignment clarification.

Do you hire this writer?

Probably not.

Why not?

Doesn't everybody deserve a second chance?

I tend to think so, but people also have to be ready for it.

This writer clearly was interested in finding an editor who would embrace what he was already doing, and that's okay. I was clearly not that editor.

More importantly and practically, this writer had focused experience working directly with an artist who understood him. He clearly didn't understand or want to embrace a process in which he submitted the script to an editor, who would then be the one to work with an artist, an artist who probably wouldn't understand how to interpret his script. In short, the writer didn't know how to write a script that was self-explanatory, that read with intention.

Further, what does this writer's response say about his ability to understand and take direction? Would his response give you any degree of confidence in trusting that he would deliver what you needed? Add to this a probable deadline. What happens if the work is delivered on time but isn't what's needed?

Who's on the hot seat, sitting next to the writer who failed in the assignment?

That's right, the editor who hired him.

Where did this hookup go wrong?

Let's go back to the writer's goal and process for achieving that goal.

He wanted assignment work. Check.

At some point during the process he located an editor he thought might have assignment work for him. Check.

He contacted the editor to get assignment work. Check.

The editor agreed to read a writing sample. That was more than most editors would do, so he was ahead of the game.

The editor gave notes, which he didn't like. Bingo.

Should he have offered to send a revised or different sample that reflected the notes?

If so, then the last stage is where the relationship derailed, and the writer needed to work harder on his level of craft and to be flexible to the needs of the editor for whom he wanted to work.

But what if the writer didn't want to change to fit the needs of an editor who might never have hired him?

If so, then the relationship derailed at a much earlier stage, perhaps in his selection of an editor.

If so, then how many editors are out there who will work with a new talent and give assignment work without criticism or direction that has to be addressed? Take my word for it: none.

Then perhaps the process derailed when the writer decided to look for assignment work. Bingo. The writer didn't get the editor he wanted because he came in with an unreasonably focused goal that didn't fit his skill set or temperament.

While it's difficult for individuals to assess their own level of craft, it's another thing entirely to show willingness and make an effort to work with others.

A hand rises in the back row.

"Yes?" I ask.

"Presuming a creator's level of craft is good enough, is there anything wrong with wanting to get assignment work to do things the way you want to do them, to find an editor who'll embrace you for who you are, instead of trying to change you into somebody you're not?"

Great question.

For some creators, yes, and other creators, no.

If a creator's work and working process is already a known quantity, and if that's what an editor needs for a job, then it makes perfect sense for an editor to hire that creator. In fact, that's why I tend to work with creators with whom I've already worked.

But if a creator's level of craft and working process are not known quantities, then the creator needs to prove him or herself. Proving yourself can be done in two ways: build a body of successful work that makes editors want to hire you for what you already do well; or develop the talents of a chameleon and adapt to the needs of the editor who's considering you for a job.

This is where this writer went wrong; he wanted to be embraced for what he'd already done, without having set a high enough standard of quality. Again, that's not his fault, because most people don't know how to look into a mirror and assess what they see. However, when his standard was challenged, he showed zero interest in improving, and that's what knocked him out of the game.

A poor level of craft and an inflexible attitude toward improving makes anybody a poor fit for becoming any type of assignment creator.

So where editors are like a box of chocolates, creators are like a box of chocolates, too.

The first step towards creating a successful working relationship with a prospective editor is figuring out the flavor you want to be, then delivering on that flavor to the best of your abilities.

And remember, everything is a learning experience.

Today's failure can evolve into tomorrow's success.

Chapter 18

Comics Into Film:
A Cautionary Tale

Why has the Hollywood continued to pay attention to such comics and graphic novels as *The Walking Dead*, *Persepolis*, *30 Days of Night*, *V For Vendetta*, *Wanted*, *Whiteout*, *Sin City*, *300*, *V For Vendetta*, *A History of Violence*, *American Splendor*, *Ghost World*, and *Road To Perdition*, when they don't have any costumed characters with unique abilities or a penchant for fighting crime? None of these fit the public perception of a "comic book movie," so why did Hollywood choose to adapt them into films?

Let's start by demolishing some stereotypes that usually end up with newspaper, magazine, and television writers putting "pow" and "bam" into reviews.

If you asked most non-comics fans to name some films and TV shows that were adapted from comic books, they might mention *Avengers*, *Superman*, *Batman*, *X-Men*, *Spider-Man*, *Iron Man*, *Thor*, *Daredevil*, *Hulk*, and any number of sequels and live-action and animated superhero TV series based on Marvel and DC Comics characters.

These people might also guess *The Matrix*, *Darkman*, *Robocop*, *Star Wars*, and, of course, none of these was adapted from a comic.

What is it about this last group of films that reinforce a stereotypical expectation of comics? Each is in the superhero/heroic fantasy genre and involves good-versus-evil storytelling, and for decades the general public has confused this genre with the comics medium, and treated the two synonymously.

A "comic book movie" is now understood to be a film that's simpleminded and filled with action, but this pejorative doesn't accurately define the content of a comic book, nor is Hollywood's tendency toward simple storytelling the reason they've pounced on the comic book industry for editorial source material.

If it were true, why would they continue to make such films and shows as *American Splendor, Ghost World, Road To Perdition, From Hell, Blade, Bulletproof Monk, Judge Dredd, Jeremiah, The Crow, Josie and the Pussycats, The Mask, The Rocketeer, Swamp Thing, Sabrina the Teenage Witch, Teenage Mutant Ninja Turtles, League of Extraordinary Gentlemen,* and *Hellboy?*

There are several reasons, some fairly obvious, some not so obvious at all.

First, let's tackle the obvious ones.

Comics and film share the trait of being visual storytelling media, so it's easier for production and studio executives to *see* how comics stories unfold.

Comics make an easy-to-read sales tool, and, since Hollywood executives have notoriously short amounts of time to read, comics make a convenient alternative to a 300-page novel.

Now let's move on to the reasons that are not so obvious and may provide additional insight into Hollywood's decision-making process.

It's important to understand that making movies is a numbers game, for studios, production companies, and creators. To clarify, this means that there is a weeding-out process that begins with whatever gets submitted, and ends with whatever gets released. Everything else gets weeded out for one reason or another. So if you're a production company looking for a studio to "green light" a project, you put as many properties as you can handle into the pipeline, thereby increasing your odds for getting something released.

Yes, people win the lottery with one ticket, but the odds are better with ten tickets.

And double-yes, it's important for a production company to have passion for the properties they control, but getting something made is still a numbers game.

Let's explore those properties that *don't* get made "for one reason or another."

When the studios had writers, actors, and directors (and everybody else) under contract, there were no legal issues about who controlled what.

They controlled it all, and could do whatever they wanted with it, and did.

With the collapse of the studio contract system, that all changed, and decades later, with the rise of the Hollywood package deal, it changed even more.

The package deal works like this:

Someone—could be an actor, director, writer, or producer—has a concept, treatment, or script that they like. Their goal is now to put together the right combination of talent to get this property set up at a studio. This combination of talent, along with whatever they decide they want to do, is *"the package."*

Each person attached to the property have likely contributed their own two cents worth about what form the story should take, and each owns a piece of that pie.

There's one thing about this pie, though. It can be divided, but it can't be separated. Nobody can take their twenty percent of the pie and go home without ruining the other eighty percent.

And I mean ruining it for good.

Literally, that's how the pie crumbles.

Getting a film set up, in the best of circumstances, is a complicated business, which is why you often read how long it takes for some films to get made, sometimes years.

And often they never get set up at all, all too often, in fact.

That's the big downside to the Hollywood package system. Too much time, effort, and energy goes down the drain.

The upside is that participants get a much bigger slice of that pie than they ever would have in the studio system.

Now let's move on to comics, why they're perceived as bankable, and what advantage they may have over a bunch of movie stars, screenwriters, directors, and producers sitting around and figuring out what kind of package they can put together.

Let's say you're a producer, and you control the rights to a comic. You still have to put a package together for the studios, and everybody still gets their same two cents worth about how the film should be developed, and it could still take the same number of months or years to find a studio that's interested in bankrolling this particular package, but if the deal falls apart and the pie crumbles around it, there's still one piece of the pie remaining.

The comic.

With the comic in hand, you, the producer can begin again, making certain that any new participants in the package are only familiar with the comic, and not any incarnation of the comic that was ever developed.

Controlling an original intellectual property, such as a comic, is like having disaster insurance for unforeseen events, and don't we all want that?

Now that we've established why the comics medium makes an attractive sales tool, what concerns might a studio have about a comic that it's interested in acquiring?

Basically, there's always a concern about how well a story can be adapted from one medium to another. Story structure paradigms in comics and movies/TV are different, storytelling tools are different, and the manner in which they're perceived by the two audiences/markets—reading vs. watching—is different.

It's true for novels, and it's true for comics.

Any translation can lose the power of the original piece, and there's no way to determine how well something's going to come out until it's been attempted.

This is the major reason so many films based on comics properties or novels end up so crappy. Because of their costs, movies and TV are two media you can't easily afford to rethink all your decisions and go back to the keyboard to start over.

So if a studio is concerned about how well the adaptation from one medium to the other is going to be handled, and you don't already control a property as popular as Spider-Man, then what kind of comics property is Hollywood more likely to be interested in?

Properties are divided into four basic categories:

- *Concept-driven*
- *Execution-driven*
- *Character-driven*
- *Market-driven*

The potential for the success of your property is driven by at least one of these. Some exceptional properties will have elements from two or more of these categories, but most new concepts will only have one or two.

Concept-driven. This idea, on concept, is immediately compelling or evokes a similar response from numerous people, and it can usually be stated in a few words or with a title.

For example: "This is a story about a psychiatrist who works with a boy who claims to see ghosts, only for the psychiatrist to discover that *he's* one of the ghosts the boy sees." Another example, where the title *is* the concept: *Cowboys & Aliens.* With each of these, a film executive "gets it," so, even if the initial attempt to flesh it out doesn't meet expectations, people aren't likely to lose faith in the initial cool concept, though the screenwriter of a "failed" effort is likely to be looking for different film script work.

Execution-driven. This is the antithesis of the concept-driven project. The success of execution-driven projects is based solely by how well familiar, complex, or esoteric material is handled. Examples of this are *American Splendor, Ghost World,* and *Road To Perdition.* It takes vision and the right combination of talent to shepherd an execution-driven project into becoming a successful adaptation.

Character-driven. These are properties created around a character or group of characters, where the interaction between the characters in the environment produces a wide range of potential for stories, as opposed to one quintessential story. Because of the periodical nature of their titles, most superheroes fall into this category, as do *Judge Dredd, Jeremiah, The Crow, Josie and the Pussycats, The Rocketeer, Swamp Thing, Sabrina the Teenage Witch, Teenage Mutant Ninja Turtles,* and *Hellboy.* Since Hollywood's needs are for a quintessential story about one protagonist or group of protagonists— at least for a pilot or first film—that means the tough part of adapting one of these properties into a film is *finding* that quintessential story. And if it can't be found, then it has to be created, which usually involves altering the origin, so the first act of the adaptation melds better with the second and third acts. The best example of a solution to this problem was making the Joker the man who killed Bruce Wayne's parents in *Batman.* The problem with altering origin stories is that too much change can alienate the original fan base. The reason most character-driven properties get adapted into films or TV shows is that they *also* fall into the next category.

Market-driven. These properties were successfully produced in other media, and have carved out a place in the popular culture.

Comics such as *Superman, Batman, Wonder Woman, Spider-Man,* and *The Hulk* were already established in the public consciousness before they were adapted into TV shows and films. From a marketing perspective, this makes them no different than *Charlie's Angels, Harry Potter,* or *The Lord of the*

Rings, all of which got made because of their previous track records and penetration into the culture. This helped studio executives anchor their decisions to give the filmmakers hundreds of millions of dollars to make their films.

You need a bigger hook than a character with extraordinary powers or a fantasy epic with elves and fairies to get Hollywood's attention. Likely, either of these would need to have strong/unique concept-driven elements to be considered for adaptation into the film medium. The same holds true for adaptations of books. Check how many of the great fantasy and sf novels *still* haven't been adapted into film, and aren't likely to be in the near future.

Why not? Because, if they're not mired in some form of development hell, they're likely execution-driven properties that require the right combination of talent to successfully pull off the adaptation.

Superhero, sf, and fantasy stories get adapted into film because of their unique story hooks or their previous successes in other media, not simply because of their genres.

In fact, the conceptual elements of inside-the-box/traditional superheroes, sf, and fantasy that largely appeal to its fans don't necessarily appeal to a mainstream audience, and this begs the question: how are the comic-book-shop comics readers and movie audience similar?

Essentially, they're *not.* The former is a niche-market reader, and the latter is a mainstream audience.

This doesn't mean some successful niche-market properties can't be successful with a mainstream audience, but material specifically tailored to the comics reader doesn't generally translate well.

Reasons for this are complicated, but essentially, the comics-industry interest in continuity, as well as in some pretty wild cross-genre mixing—*X-Files* meets *The Lord of the Rings* and *Buffy the Vampire Slayer*—often make the properties inaccessible to an audience that can only have so much information thrown at it in two hours of running time.

If you're wondering how to straddle the editorial line between what makes sense as a film and what will appeal to the traditional comics reader, you don't.

If—and that's a big if—you decide to write a comic that will have an opportunity to be adapted into a film, then you *must* produce a story that will appeal to the film market. Its potential appeal to the comics market *must* remain secondary.

If you *can* appeal to both markets, that's swell, but never set out to serve two masters, or you'll be everybody's wishbone.

Here's a complication: any number of comics could be created and successfully adapted into films, but most of them are in genres that don't have a strong, commercial foothold in the comics specialty shop market. This means, for the foreseeable future, the comic book publishers that pay page rates are not likely to be interested in publishing these stories.

In contrast, other, smaller comics publishers are looking to increase profitability by gaining control of the film and TV licensing rights of the books they publish, so they can broker the properties to production companies and studios. For this reason, they've become more flexible about what they're interested in publishing.

Here's another potential complication: should a publisher publish your book, with the intended goal of also brokering the rights to Hollywood, then you now have a partner for the duration of the contract, and what you have in writing between you defines the nature of who controls what. There are a wide variety of contracts and publishing options out there, and you should consult with other creators and a lawyer to determine which deal best fits your needs.

When a production company or studio wants to acquire the rights to your comic, it's important to know how you *really* need to be involved in the adaptation.

You might try to attach yourself as the screenwriter, but studios—not production companies, *studios*—are reluctant to let *any* creators adapt their own work. If the adaptation fails, the project loses momentum, you get fired, somebody else gets hired, and this is the beginning of the production spiral that leads to the infamous development hell. However, if you're a screenwriter with legitimate credits and a proven track record in film, they're more likely to let you adapt your own work.

With film industry experience (or even without it, though this is a much slippery road), you might also try to attach yourself as a producer. This may be one of the few ways to shepherd an adaptation without being the screenwriter and/or director.

The downside to creators trying to attach themselves in these ways is that a studio would have to want the property pretty badly to go this far for a creator, and you're more likely to blow the deal by demanding producer credit than not.

Some creators insist on creative control from beginning to end, because they don't want to have happen to their baby what they saw happen to *(INSERT NAME OF REVILED COMICS-TO-FILM MOVIE HERE)*. These people should never even *think* about having their work adapted for film until they write something that ends up as big as the Harry Potter books. This level of creator control in film or TV only comes with enormous proven financial success.

Some creators simply want to be kept in the loop.

Some don't care; just give 'em the check.

Some see this as the first rung in the ladder of their Hollywood writing career.

Why is it important to figure this out ahead of time, before giving up the rights?

It would be nice if *American Splendor, Road To Perdition,* and *Ghost World* were typical examples of faithful adaptations, but they're not.

More typical are the adaptations of *League of Extraordinary Gentlemen, Daredevil,* and *From Hell,* where the finished films appear to be the result of filmmakers choosing only one or two of the colors from a bag of M&Ms (the bag representing the original stories) and throwing away the rest. Commercially, some of the most successful adaptations have been radical reinterpretations of the properties, *The Mask* being a prime example.

So, if you don't like how the adaptation is proceeding, can't you just put on the brakes and say, "Hey, wait, guys—this isn't what I had in mind. I take it back."

Um...no. There are no take-backs with movie studios. Too much time, energy, money, and momentum is at stake.

When a studio exercises an option and purchases the rights to your comic, it will be purchasing all rights, specified by the contract, and that's the nature of the film business.

If you don't like it, then it's not a business for you to consider (and think how much time, energy, and aggravation I just *saved* you).

As previously noted, unless you have extraordinary power, you will almost certainly have to give up all licensing rights to your comic when it's sold to a major studio.

"But—but—but—" you stutter. "Can't I continue publishing stories about my character?"

This is why I wrote that it's important to know what you want, before giving up any rights.

Sure, you can continue publishing, if you get it in the contract, and this isn't really that much of an obstacle.

Sure, you can write the first draft of the screenplay, if you get it in the contract.

And sure, you can get the director to salute you every morning when you walk on the set, if you get it in the contract.

Whether you *can* get what you want in writing is a different issue, and don't get your hopes too high on these last two points.

However, if it's *really* important to you, get it in writing, get *everything* that's important to you in writing.

The key is: know what you want, know what you need, know the difference between the two, and also understand what is *reasonable*, so you won't wonder what happened if it doesn't work out.

So, how do you know what's reasonable?

There are a lot of creators out there who will give you advice based on their own experiences. You should listen to their advice, and take into account what's important to them. No doubt, what's important to you, as you read this, will change when you become more aware of the wide range of available options.

If you don't have legal representation, you can ask other creators for referrals to their lawyers, and you should find out more than their names and numbers. Find out the nature of their experience, especially whether they specialize in the entertainment industry or not. Find out their rates. Find out how well they explain things. If you've spent months and years developing a property then you should spend some money to protect that investment of time.

What does any of this mean to you, a creator, who's interested in having your comic book adapted into film?

Well, it depends where your priorities lie, and I recommend knowing up front whether film-and-comics are the tail-and-the-dog, or visa versa.

In other words, to you, which wags which?

Know the answer to this, and you'll know how to apply any of what I've described above.

Chapter 19

Adapting To the Cinematic Sandbox

Every writer has his or her own process for determining how to best adapt material from one medium—whether it's comics, prose, or TV—into film.

Your interest here could be as a creator whose work is being adapted, you could also be the writer looking to adapt somebody else's work, or you might just be interested in watching the train wreck that may or may not take place. Regardless of which it is, it's important to understand the process in which you're participating or observing.

In adapting a property from one medium into film, some rip the heart out of the original piece and do whatever they want to do, simply because they can. There are a lot of these people in Hollywood. I'm not just ragging on writers, because directors and producers often do the same thing to screenplays, but when they're doing it to screenplays that are from writers who just eviscerated somebody else's work...well, on these days, I believe in karma.

Other writers try to adhere slavishly to the source material, or as many aspects of the material as possible, as was evident in the first two Harry Potter film adaptations. In this process, the results usually don't take best advantage of the visual storytelling possibilities of the film medium, but they do manage to not offend the fan base. They may bore them to death, but they don't offend them.

The above examples are two extremes, and sometimes these extremes produce vibrant cinematic results, but this isn't a discussion about being so lucky or talented that you can escape the pitfalls.

Those are the extremes; now let's discuss the two middles.

The first one is a process for figuring out how to consider what to keep and what to toss. It's not new, in that many screenwriters have practiced and written about it before, William Goldman in *Adventures in the Screen Trade* being the most prominent example, but this approach is embedded at the core of most successful adaptations.

The key to a successful adaptation is getting to the heart of the story, isolating what it's really about—not what it *could* be about, but what it *is* about, concept-wise or thematically—as opposed to how it tracks in terms of plot or in its sequence of events.

The first step to discovering what's at the heart of a story is by simply looking at where it begins and where it ends. Then you look at the bridge between the two, examine the journey, and ask yourself, "What's the moral of the story?"

Yep, it's that simple. When you figure out the moral to the story, which can also be called the "moral argument," "theme," or "controlling idea"—the statement that the story makes about one or more things the writer wants to convince you are or aren't true—then you've got a spine around which to wrap your adaptation.

My favorite example to prove this point is how one of my favorite writers, David Mamet, adapted an early draft of Thomas Harris' book, *Hannibal*. For the uninitiated, this book was the follow-up to *Silence of the Lambs*, which, in turn, followed *Red Dragon*.

Excesses and wanderings aside, I liked the book. By the time I'd reached the climax, I'd already figured out that it was the thriller equivalent of *My Fair Lady*.

"Huh???" you say.

"Yep," I say. *My Fair Lady* is about a woman who is refined and defined by a man with whom she ultimately comes to a separate-but-equal understanding. *Hannibal* is about a woman who's being pulled in several different directions by a number of men, each of them wanting to refine and define who she'll be as a person. Hannibal wins, and they ultimately come to a separate-but-equal understanding.

At their hearts, the two stories much different.

Whether it was by direction from the producers or director Ridley Scott, the adaptation was re-imagined as a story of unrequited love by Hannibal for Starling. Nope, I'm not guessing; Scott says this on the DVD commentary, and it's the best clue as to why Jodie Foster chose not to reprise her role as Starling, as well as why the finished film is episodic and unfocused. There's so much in it that doesn't belong in a love story between Hannibal and Starling, and, even if the events *were* in the book, the results are unsatisfying.

If you accept that *Hannibal* is *My Fair Lady*, then the solution to the adaptation and Foster's possible participation should have been a simple fix.

My Fair Lady is a musical adaptation of the stage play, *Pygmalion*, by George Bernard Shaw. In this original incarnation of the story, Eliza Doolittle allows herself to be molded into a "lady" by Professor Henry Higgins. When Eliza realizes she's been taken for granted, she leaves the professor, just as she does in the scenes toward the end of *My Fair Lady*. But in the original play she *doesn't* return to him at the end, and the bullying professor gets his comeuppance.

Since Jodie Foster was reported to have hated what happened to her Starling character in the book, the people shepherding the film could have easily steered the adaptation in the direction of *Pygmalion*, where Starling is manipulated by a number of different and powerful men, but ultimately breaks free of all their influences and regains her footing as her own woman. Pretty compelling stuff, and Foster might have been onboard for that.

After this, the next step would have been to eliminate and/or refocus the rest of the novel's story that doesn't work to this end.

Sure, easier said than done, but in the end it would've been a lot less work than trying to turn *Hannibal* into a love story while smoothing out all the stuff that didn't fit, which is something they did not end up accomplishing anyway.

Conversely, *Silence of the Lambs*—a film that's often referred to as a horror film, and contains many truly horrific images and sequences—isn't structured like a horror film; it's a buddy movie.

Ted Tally, the screenwriter, recognizing that he couldn't condense the entire novel, established the relationship between Starling and Lecter—two characters with opposing goals who are forced to work together to achieve those goals—at the center of the story, and he only kept in whatever else was necessary to have each of the characters achieve his and her goals.

In this manner, he was able to refashion the novel into a screenplay, with considerably less story/plot than the original book contained and still have it work as a whole, making it a distant cousin of buddy pictures like *48 Hours* and *Die Hard With A Vengeance.*

Finding the heart of the story and staying true to it is the form of adaptation that snuggles up closely to our second example from above, the obsessively faithful adaptation, but one that doesn't forget its cinematic necessities. As a process, it's the one that worked for *The Lord of the Rings* and the third Harry Potter film, and has the best chance of breathing the cinematic life of the original material onto the screen.

That said, without the right thematic lynchpin, or any consistent thematic lynchpin, it's impossible to consistently determine what to keep and what to toss.

Two terrific examples of doing it well are the comics-to-film adaptations of *Road To Perdition* and *Ghost World.* Each latched onto the key emotional thrusts of the characters and the drama and brought the films to life with few core changes.

For those familiar with the graphic novel and the filmed version of *Road To Perdition,* one change of note was the ending.

At the conclusion of the book, the son, enraged, guns down his father's killer, gets his dying father to a confessional, then is revealed to have grown up to be a priest who's just completed his memoir about his father's life. We know that he will suffer a life of penance for his acts, even though he ultimately chose the road of peace.

At the conclusion of the film, the son can't bring himself to take the life of another, not even his father's killer, not even to save his own life, but his wounded father manages to kill the killer himself and is gratified to know, before dying, that his son has been freed from the cycle of violence that drove this story.

In the book, the act of penance and commitment to a life of peace is necessary; without it, we don't know whether or not the cycle of violence would be broken. In the film, it isn't necessary to show what happened to the boy because we know the cycle's already been broken. This is likely one of the contributing factors as to why Sam Mendes chose to excise this scene from the film; it became extraneous. The filmmakers stayed true to the thematic point of the novel that the cycle of violence *needed* to be broken, and that was enough.

Stepping back to the type of film that tries to adhere slavishly to the source material, the adaptation of James Ellroy's novel, *The Black Dahlia,* was a critical and financial disaster. The novel is the first in Ellroy's famous L.A.

Quartet (the third of which was adapted into the critically and financially successful *L.A. Confidential*), and the screenwriter, Josh Friedman—creator of the 2007 TV series, *The Sarah Connor Chronicles*—had no moral/thematic compass by which to drive his adaptation, or not a simple enough of one to hold all of the necessary elements in balance.

In *The Black Dahlia*, Friedman tried to hold onto too much of the novel's labyrinthine plot, which forced him to limit characters and motivation, and reduce the ending to a wincingly bad example of character-exposition-as-denouement. He packed fifty pounds of story into a five-pound bag, which reduces this particular form of adaptation to one simple problem and solution: When you've got too much story for the space or time that's required, use the heart/theme/moral argument of the story to cut away the chaff that doesn't fit.

And yes, per the *Hannibal* example, you still need to identify the right heart of the story.

Now, what about stories that are acquired by production companies and studios as nothing more than fodder for what they hope to accomplish?

"What??!!" You exclaim. *"Does this happen???!!!"*

"You bet," I respond.

Where there isn't the goal of bringing millions of faithful followers of the source material into the theaters to witness a cinematic reenactment of their favorite book, comic, or TV show, the production company or studio could very likely have acquired the original property because there was something unique about a facet of the concept or plot that they wanted to use in the creation of an entirely new animal/property.

For example, the first adaptation of Raymond Chandler's Philip Marlowe novel, *Farewell, My Lovely*, was for the 1942 film, *The Falcon Takes Over*. The Falcon was modeled after The Saint, each of which starred George Sanders, and which, like The Saint, was a long-running series of theatrical programmers. (For those of you under a hundred, theatrical programmers were short films from the '30s and '40s, often near an hour in length, used to fill out a theater's double-bill.)

A more recent example of taking what you need and leaving the rest is what the brilliant Charlie Kaufman did in his adaptation of Susan Orlean's *The Orchid Thief*. He wrote a film about himself having trouble adapting the book into a film, and it was directed by Spike Jonze under the title, *Adaptation*.

Some similar adaptations, which are more close to home for comics readers, include *Man of Steel, Batman Begins,* and the Spider-Man and X-Men franchises. There's an added difficulty in discussing these films, because the original properties are owned and controlled by corporations, but that only means more people are getting a vote; it doesn't change the dynamic. Even though the goal of these adaptations was to remain true to *certain* qualities of these name-brand characters, the companies and filmmakers recognized that the adaptations needed to cherry-pick from the properties what was perceived as salvageable, then build them from scratch in a new place that was outside the boundaries of comics continuity and company mythologies. Regardless of whether they were successful—though I believe they mostly were—this is how these adaptations were approached.

In this kind of adaptation, the trick is to figure out *what* and how *much* you need to salvage from the source material to build your new animal and keep it structurally sound, and then you should chuck the rest. Oh, and there's no reason to feel badly if you're the writer who's doing that, because the author of the source material knew or should've been made aware that this is what was going to happen when the production company or studio acquired his or her material. Authors certainly have the right to disagree with the creative choices/decisions that are made—Ursula K. LeGuin is more than entitled to do so for what was done to her first two Earthsea novels—but these are the chances creators take when they cede control.

This form of adaptation is a variation on the rip-the-heart-out example above, but when it's handled with the skill of a surgeon the heart is successfully transplanted into a new body that could never have come to life without the operation. To some it's a thing of beauty; to others it's Frankenstein's Monster.

We've covered the four primary types of adaptation:

1) Completely faithful, even to the point of obsession;
2) Faithful, but flexible to the cinematic medium;
3) The isolation of useful concept and plot material in the development of similar but separate properties;
4) Rewriting whatever you want to because you can.

So, what should you do if you're the screenwriter?

Sometimes, screenwriters are presented with obstacles in source material that makes successful adaptation a dicey proposition at best.

Sometimes the obstacles are creative; sometimes they're commercial.

If you're brought into a project, the goal of the adaptation will likely be made clear, or you should work to ascertain the goal.

If you're free to make the choice, you know the nature of the options. Okay, now let's switch horseshoes.

As the creator of a comics property, and where you're *not* one of the lucky ones who gets to write the film or TV adaptation of your own comic, you get to sit back and watch some version of the process I've just described above.

Knowing what you now know, you have several options:

1) Sign the contract, take the money, remind yourself that the comic still exists, no matter what anybody did in the adaptation of it to a film or TV show...and accept the idea what they're going to create is a completely different animal.

2) Sign the contract, take the money, and work to make yourself a constructive advisor on the adaptation that you all agree you're going to make...and understand that even as an advisor, your role will be limited.

3) Make certain that you get the vote you want in determining what will or won't be done with the adaptation (even though choosing to do this will very likely limit the number of people willing to work with you to some number just above zero). Don't count on being Frank Miller on the set of *Sin City*, though it's nice to dream, and some dreams do come true.

4) Don't let anybody adapt your material from what you originally created for whatever reasons you want. It's okay to be Bill Watterson not allowing *Calvin & Hobbes* to exist in any form outside the comics.

Whether you're the writer adapting somebody else's work or the creator whose work is being adapted, when you know what you want something to be, it'll be easier to help it be exactly what you want.

Now, imagine you've been transported to the world of *Indiana Jones and the Last Crusade,* and you're standing in front of a table that's covered with dozens of different cups. Any one of them could be the Holy Grail.

If you choose the right cup, the fruit of your efforts could live forever.

If you don't choose the right cup, your vision for the adaptation will die.

Choose wisely.

CHAPTER 20

YOUR PROFESSIONAL SELF-ASSESSMENT

Congratulations for getting through this course without too many blisters and scars, hopefully just enough to give you calluses and a taste of what it'll be like in the real world.

This last assignment is deceptively simple: without reviewing the book again, write down what you learned.

A hand goes up.

"Yes?" I ask.

"You used the word 'deceptive.'"

"I did," I reply.

"So where's the complicated part of this assignment?"

Objectivity. Objectivity is hard, perhaps the hardest part of looking in the mirror and noting what you see.

Anybody who believes this isn't hard hasn't tried to do it.

There are two points I've consistently pressed.

The first is to write or create with intention. Do that and there's a greater chance readers will perceive what you want them to perceive.

The second is breaking down circumstances, relationships, and aspects of the craft into component parts. We did this so you can examine, with less complication, each facet, and then understand and bend them into something that helps you achieve your goals.

I know many of you struggled with this and found it difficult to study the trees *then* the forest, so don't underestimate the difficulty.

So look back, again, without opening the book, and write down what was new, and make an assessment of how (if at all) it's affected your perception of the craft or business of sequential art.

Done?

Good.

Okay, now please review the chapters to see what you might have missed.

You should be amazed at how much you forgot to add to your list. That's because, as we progressed, you assimilated so many aspects of the craft that have become second nature.

Wax on...wax off.

This is what you've taken from this class, but, more importantly, it shows the advancement of your level of craft and a newer understanding of what it takes to be a professional.

Now you're on your own, released from the nest.

Happy hunting and good fortune!

CODA

BY SETH GODIN

After you've done your best work

And it's still not enough...

After you've written the best memo/blog post/novel/ screenplay you can possibly imagine writing, after you've contributed your pithiest insight or gone on your best blind date...

...and it still hasn't worked...

...you really have no choice but to do it again. To do your best work again, as impossible and unfair as that seems.

It compounds over time. Best work followed by best work followed by more best work is far more useful and generous than merely doing your best work once and insisting we understand you.

Appendix I

AN OPEN LETTER
To Film People
INTERESTED IN Coaxing Comics Creators
To Produce Film Ideas
As Comics/Graphic Novels

Dear writer, director, or producer (who wants to have a comic produced from your screenplay idea or script so that it will help you set the project up as a film or TV show):

You have a screenplay you want produced as a comic series or graphic novel.

You're looking for somebody to help realize that vision.

You're probably not funded, because hardly anybody who wants to do this is funded. But you're willing to share profits, probably on the graphic novel, because hardly anybody wants to attach comics creators to their profits from the film. The difficulty I (and anybody in comics) will point out is that independent comics are rarely profitable to anybody except a publisher, but often not then either.

Most (good) artists won't work without the prospect of page-rate pay, but most will create spec art to help get a project going...if the plan to publish and get paid for it isn't pie-in-the-sky and has a reasonable chance of success.

The problem is that only a few major comics publishers will pay a decent page rate, and the ones that do want to control rights. Smaller comics publishers don't have good budgets, and those of us working in the industry work to keep our pieces of the pie as large as possible so the prospective income can be viewed with something other than a microscope.

Crowd-funding is the current pot of gold, but success there is tied to a ton of variables, which includes having already created enough of a following that will fund the project. A tip about crowd-funding: proposals that require a lot of money have much more difficulty getting funded.

Here is the reality that undercuts all of this: most creators, myself included, have projects of our own we're already creating on spec, which we want to see published as comics.

So the trick (and it *is* a tough one) is to give a team reasons to work on *your* thing instead of *their* thing.

With no guarantee of payment or success, this is a really slippery slope to climb, even if you have the next *Avatar* and the next Jim Cameron attached (before anybody knows for sure they're the next *Avatar* and Jim Cameron).

If you've already spoken with a number of comics creators, much of what I've written is already familiar.

Here's the thing: we're not locking the door; we're showing you what the door looks like, and a viable, practical plan needs to be developed to function as a key to opening that door.

Most film people don't want to discuss the door; they want to discuss their cool projects.

I realize I haven't written one word about the importance of the quality of your story, writing, or your background in film or TV.

Are these important?

Absolutely.

But they're not the tricky part. Let's assume your story is terrific and would make a great film. Per above, that's not the tricky part.

Do you remember the end of *The Wolf of Wall Street*?

Sell us the pen.

If you haven't seen the film, the translation is: you need to show comics creators *why* they need your pen.

Best advice: if you can set it up as a film without the comic, do it. Then it's your pie.

If you can't and really need the comic, share the pie.

If you don't share the pie, every prospective contributor to the project will know you want to (or need to) sell the project based on their work, and that you're not willing to fully share in the success that they helped create.

This is just a friendly tip before you dip your big toe in the deep end of the pool.

If you need our contribution, don't be greedy.

We're willing to give you our time, but don't take our time for granted.

Sincerely,

LEE NORDLING

Lee Nordling

Appendix II

READING LIST / MORE HOMEWORK

Taking a page from my second chapter on pitching, there are so many gems (great books) sitting on the shelf, it's difficult to spot the diamonds among the emeralds, rubies, and sapphires, so let's just consider *my* diamonds, and I'll leave you to discover and share others for yourself.

Understanding Comics, Reinventing Comics, and *Making Comics* by Scott McCloud

Comics & Sequential Art and Graphic Storytelling by Will Eisner

Panel One Scripts by Top Comics Writers by Kurt Busiek, Neil Gaiman, Nat Gertler, Dwayne McDuffie, Trina Robbins, Greg Rucka, Jeff Smith, Kevin Smith, and Marv Wolfman

Panel Two: More Comic Book Scripts By Top Writers by Mike Baron, Otto Binder, Peter David, Mark Evanier, Scott McCloud, Bill Mumy & Miguel Ferrer, Sara Ryan, Gail Simone, Judd Winick, Lea Hernandez, Steve Leialoha, Chuck Austin, Steve Lieber, Mark Heike, and Pop Mhan

Words for Pictures: The Art and Business of Writing Comics and Graphic Novels by Brian Michael Bendis

Panel Discussions by Durwin S. Talon

Danny Fingeroth's Write Now! Magazine edited by Danny Fingeroth

On Directing Film by David Mamet

The Anatomy of Story: 22 Steps To Becoming A Master Storyteller by John Truby

Appendix III

Lee Nordling Bibliography

Nonfiction (writer)

Your Career in the Comics—a comprehensive overview and the definitive work on newspaper comic strip syndication, utilizing interviews with cartoonists, newspaper editors, and syndicate executives—Andrews & McMeel (1995)

Darwinism In Comics—an essay on ageism in comics, SilverBulletComicBooks.com (2001)

What It Takes To Sell Your Comic Strip: A Pop-quiz—published in conjunction with a Nordling career profile and interview by *Danny Fingeroth's Write Now! Magazine,* Two Morrows Publishing (Fall 2002)

What If…Bill Jemas—an essay on Marvel's leadership in comics, SilverBulletComicBooks.com (2003)

What It Takes To Sell Your Pitch—a three-part column, written for Marv Wolfman's column, *"What the…?"* SilverBulletComicBooks.com (2003)

Comics Into Film: A Cautionary Tale—*Danny Fingeroth's Write Now! Magazine,* Two Morrows Publishing (Spring 2004)

Mort Walker Conversations—full text of 1995 interview with Mort Walker, Mississippi University Press (2004)

Adapting To the Cinematic Sandbox—*Danny Fingeroth's Write Now! Magazine,* Two Morrows Publishing, (January 2007)

Children's Picture Books with Sequential Art (writer)

The Bramble—writer/designer—Carolrhoda Books/Lerner (Fall 2013). Art by Bruce Zick.
- Moonbeam Gold Medal for Picture Books (ages 4-8)

BirdCatDog (3-Story Books)—writer/editor/designer/packager—Graphic Universe (Fall 2014). Art by Meritxell Bosch.
- Best Children's Books of 2014 from *Kirkus Reviews*.
- Top 10 Middle-Grade Books of 2014 for Readers Who Like Quirky from *Kirkus Reviews*.
- 2015 Eisner nominee for Best Publication for Early Readers (up to age 7).
- 2015 Moonbeam Spirit Award gold medal for "Imagination."
- 2015 Unanimous selection committee member nominee for inaugural Little Marverick list, ages K-6.

FishFishFish (3-Story Books)—writer/editor/designer—Graphic Universe (Spring 2015). Art by Meritxell Bosch.
- 2015 inaugural nominee for Little Marverick list, for ages K-6.

SheHeWe (3-Story Books)—writer/editor/designer—Graphic Universe (Fall 2015). Art by Meritxell Bosch.
- 2016 Eisner nominee for Best Publication for Early Readers (up to age 8).

Andrew the Seeker (Game for Adventure)—writer/editor/designer/packager—Graphic Universe (to be published Spring 2017). Art by Scott Roberts.

Belinda the Unbeatable (Game for Adventure)—writer/editor/designer/packager—Graphic Universe (to be published Fall 2017). Art by Scott Roberts.

Chavo the Invisible (Game for Adventure)—writer/editor/designer/packager—Graphic Universe (to be published Spring 2018). Art by Scott Roberts.

Graphic Novels / Miniseries

Cowboys & Aliens—graphic novel editor—Platinum Studios (September 2006)

Blood Nation—miniseries editor, except re-coloring—Platinum Studios (February 2007)

Watchdogs—graphic novel editor—Platinum Studios (February 2007)

Unique—miniseries editor, script—Platinum Studios (March 2007)

Weapon, The—miniseries editor, script & layouts—Platinum Studios (June 2007)

Nightfall—graphic novel editor—Platinum Studios (July 2007)

Love Bytes—graphic novel editor—Platinum Studios (April 2007)

Big Amoeba, The—graphic novel editor—Platinum Studios (April 2008)

Super Larry—graphic novel editor—Platinum Studios (June 2008)

The Adventures of Tymm: Alien Circus, volumes 1, 2, 3—graphic novel series editor—Platinum Studios (2008).

Black Is For Beginnings—editor/packager—Flux/Lewellyn Publications (2009). Story by Laurie Stolarz. Script by Barbara Randall Kesel. Art and tones by Janina Janina Gorrissen

Comic Collections / Anthologies

Rugrats: It's A Jungle Gym Out There—compiled collection content, content editor, and writer of introduction, Andrews & McMeel (September 2004)

A Baby's Work Is Never Done: A Rugrats Comic Strip Collection—compiled collection content and content editor, Andrews & McMeel (September 2005)

Once Upon A Time Machine—anthology story, *Silver-Hair & The Three Xairs*—writer, Lee Nordling; art, Scott Roberts; lettering by Scott O. Brown—Dark Horse (2012)

He-Man and the Masters of the Universe Minicomic Collection—editor of misc. content from 1980s—Dark Horse Comics (November 2015).

Comic Stories (writer)

Aladdin—*The Return of Jafar*—adaptation of the Disney feature—*Disney Adventures* (June 1994)

Aladdin—*Aladdin's Quest*—original story based on the Disney feature—*Disney's Aladdin* #1, Marvel Comics (October 1994)

Aladdin—*The Sword of Aladdin*—original story, based on the Disney feature—*Disney's Aladdin* #3, Marvel Comics (December 1994)

Aladdin—*Greedy in Agrabah*—original story, based on the Disney feature, co-written with Bobbi JG Weiss—*Disney's Aladdin* #4, Marvel Comics (January 1995)

DuckTales—*The Magic Word*—original story, based on the TV series—Disney Publishing (1987)

Gargoyles—*Stone Cold*—original two-part story that was adapted into an animated cartoon episode of the show—*Disney Adventures* (December 1994/January 1995)

Goofy—*Goofy Alexander*—original story, co-written with Floyd Norman—*Goofy Adventures* #3, Disney Comics (August 1990)

Gummi Bears—*Tummi the Werebear*—original story, based on the TV series—Disney Publishing (1987)

Kite in the City—*Never Everlasting*—original story and series creation—*Off-Registration* (2013)

Mickey Mouse—*The Big Fall*—original story—*Mickey Mouse Adventures* #7, Disney Comics (December 1990); reprinted in *Walt Disney's Vacation Parade* #5, Gemstone Publishing (July 2008)

Mickey Mouse—*A Phantom Blot Bedtime Story*—original story—*Mickey Mouse Adventures* #8, Disney Comics (January 1991); reprinted in *Walt Disney's Vacation Parade* #5, Gemstone Publishing (July 2008)

Mickey Mouse—*Space Mickey and the Throgg Ray Wars*—original three-part, serialized graphic novel—*Disney Adventures* (July-September 1992)

Mighty Ducks—*Wipe Out!*—original story, based on the animated TV series—*Disney's Action Club* Volume 1 #5, Acclaim Comics (1997) (unpublished)

Quack Attack—*The Pulpster Prize*—original story, based on the TV series—*Disney Adventures* (unpublished)

Quack Attack—*Dr. Livingstork, I Presume*— original story, based on the TV series—*Disney Adventures* (unpublished)

Rugrats—*It*—original story, based on the TV series—*Rugrats Comic Adventures,* Volume 2 #5, *Rugrats Comic Adventures* (1999)

Rugrats—*Tommy's Game*—original story, based on the TV series—*Rugrats Comic Adventures,* Volume 2 #5, *Rugrats Comic Adventures* (1999)

Rugrats—*The Bed Zone*—original story, based on the TV series—*Rugrats Comic Adventures,* Volume 2 #6, *Rugrats Comic Adventures* (1999)

Timon & Pumbaa—*After Voux*— original story, based on the animated TV series—*Disney's Action Club,* Vol. 1 #3—Acclaim Comics (1997)

Comic Strips

Curtains—original comic strip; writer/artist—*Valley News, L.A. Funnies* (1983)

Donald Duck—Disney daily feature; staff writer—King Features Syndicate (1987-1988)

Gummi Bears, The—Disney daily feature; staff writer—King Features Syndicate (1987-1988)

Harry Tales—original comic strip; artist and co-writer with Cheriese J. Lane Nordling—*Fantasy Book Magazine* (1983)

Mickey Mouse—Disney daily feature; staff writer—King Features Syndicate (1987-1988)

Pink Panther—daily feature; editor—Universal Press Syndicate (2012) (not released)

Rugrats—Nickelodeon daily feature; editor & occasional writer—Creators Syndicate (1998-2003)

Scamp—Disney daily feature; staff writer—King Features Syndicate (1987-1988)

Sherman on the Mount—daily comic strip; ghost writer—Los Angeles Times Syndicate (1986)

Winnie the Pooh—Disney daily feature; staff writer—King Features Syndicate (1987-1988)

Children's Books

365 Ways to Say Good Night—art director—Dutton Juvenile / Penguin Publishing (April 1998)

Bad Ol' Puddy-tat (Wonderscope Books)—adaptation of Tweety & Sylvester cartoon shorts—Looney Tunes Books/Penguin USA (September 1997)

Caws and Effect—a hardcover adaptation of a *New Adventures of Winnie the Pooh* TV episode—Twin Books (May 1991)

Disney's Aladdin Movie Storybook—designer, using stills and concept art from animated film—A Golden Book/Western Publishing Co. (1992)

Disney's Aladdin—adaptation and design into prose-comics hybrid of the comic written by Bobbi JG Weiss, based on the Disney animated feature—Disney Junior Graphic Novel, Disney Comics (1992); reprinted in hardcover as Disney's Aladdin Annual, Fleetway Editions Ltd./Egmont House (1993)

Disney Giftwraps: Snow White and the Seven Dwarfs—giftwrap art; concept designer—Harry N Abrams (March 1993)

Fast and Furry-ous (Wonderscope Books)—adaptation of Road Runner & Wiley E. Coyote cartoon shorts—Looney Tunes Books/Penguin USA (September 1997)

Ghost of a Chance, A—a hardcover co-adaptation with Don Ferguson of a *Chip 'n' Dale Rescue Rangers* TV episode—Twin Books (August 1991)

Little Mermaid, The—a hardcover co-adaptation of the Disney feature film—Twin Books (1991)

"The Martians Are Coming! The Martians Are Coming!" (story/game book format)—Looney Tunes Books/Penguin USA (unpublished)

Mickey Mouse in Bing Bong—an original Mickey Mouse adventure—Twin Books (November 1990)

Mickey Mouse in Cactus Kid, The—an original Mickey Mouse adventure—Twin Books (November 1990)

Mickey Mouse in Phantom Blot, The—a hardcover adaptation of a Mickey Mouse adventure—Twin Books (November 1990)

Old Man and the Sea Duck, The—a hardcover adaptation of a *Disney's Tale Spin* TV episode—Twin Books (January 1992)

Prince and the Pauper, The—a hardcover adaptation of the Disney animated featurette starring Mickey Mouse—Twin Books (1989)

About the Author

Lee Nordling is an Eisner-nominated and award-winning writer, editor, designer, and creative director. He worked on staff at the Los Angeles Times Syndicate, Disney Publishing, DC Comics, Nickelodeon Magazine, and Platinum Studios. His book, *The Bramble*, won the 2013 Moonbeam Gold Medal for Picture Books (ages 4-8), and *BirdCatDog*, a 2015 Eisner Awards nominee, received the Moonbeam Spirit Award Gold Medal for "Imagination," and was chosen by *Kirkus Reviews* as one of the best children's books of the year. *SheHeWe*, the third book in his *Three-Story Books* series, was a 2016 Eisner Award nominee for Best Publication for Early Readers (up to age 8). Lee lives in Pennsylvania with his wife, Cheri, and numerous pets that earn their kibble by offering inspiration.

About Marv Wolfman

Marv Wolfman has created more characters that have gone on to television, animation, movies, and toys than any other comics creator since Stan Lee. They include: Blade the vampire hunter, Deathstroke, The New Teen Titans, Bullseye, The Black Cat, and hundreds more. Marv's mega-series, *Crisis On Infinite Earths*, is hailed as not only the first company-wide crossover epic, but after thirty years, still the best. Marv also writes novels, animation, videogame, and more.